THE
TRIALS
OF
WALTER OGROD

THE
TRIALS
OF
WALTER OGROD

THE SHOCKING MURDER,
SO-CALLED CONFESSIONS,
AND NOTORIOUS SNITCH THAT
SENT A MAN TO DEATH ROW

THOMAS LOWENSTEIN

CHICAGO
REVIEW
PRESS

Copyright © 2017 by Thomas Lowenstein
All rights reserved
Published by Chicago Review Press Incorporated
814 North Franklin Street
Chicago, Illinois 60610
ISBN 978-1-61373-801-6

Library of Congress Cataloging-in-Publication Data

Names: Lowenstein, Thomas (Thomas Kennedy), author.
Title: The trials of Walter Ogrod : the shocking murder, so-called
  confessions, and notorious snitch that sent a man to death row / Thomas
  Lowenstein.
Description: Chicago, Illinois : Chicago Review Press, [2017] | Includes
  bibliographical references and index.
Identifiers: LCCN 2016035571 (print) | LCCN 2016049188 (ebook) | ISBN
  9781613738016 (cloth : alk. paper) | ISBN 9781613738023 (pdf) | ISBN
  9781613738047 (epub) | ISBN 9781613738030 (Kindle)
Subjects: LCSH: Ogrod, Walter. | Death row inmates—United States—Case
  studies. | Murder investigation—United States—Case studies. | Trials
  (Murder)—United States—Case studies. | Judicial error—United
  States—Case studies.
Classification: LCC HV8701.O37 L69 2017 (print) | LCC HV8701.O37
  (ebook) | DDC 364.152/3092—dc23
LC record available at https://lccn.loc.gov/2016035571

Typesetting: Nord Compo

Printed in the United States of America
5 4 3 2 1

For my mother, and father, and Nick
And for SUF

If the devil does not exist, and man has therefore created him, he has created him in his own image and likeness.

—Fyodor Dostoyevsky, *The Brothers Karamazov*

There is a Latin expression, I never learned how to pronounce it: Falsis in uno, falsis in omnibus. . . . *"If a person testified falsely about one material fact, he testified falsely about everything."*

—Joseph Casey

CONTENTS

Part III: A Convoluted Thing

AUTHOR'S NOTE

MY ORIGINAL IDEA FOR THIS BOOK was to portray a death penalty case from all perspectives—the victim's family, the defendant, his family, the lawyers on both sides, the detectives who worked the case. I wanted to write about the death penalty when it "worked"—killer caught, tried, convicted—and even thought that, through my research, I might come to understand something essential about murderers. It was 2001 and I was working for Dr. Robert Coles, learning about social documentary writing, which I tried out in a couple of articles about criminal justice issues and politics for the *American Prospect* magazine, where I also worked as an editor of a policy website.

I wanted to try to understand murderers because my father, US Representative Allard (Al) Lowenstein, was murdered by a mentally ill gunman when I was ten, and though we knew who did it and why, for us, as for most family members of murder victims, there is no "why" that makes sense. You are crushed, sadder than you could've imagined surviving, angrier than you could imagine at all, bewildered that something so horrible could happen so quickly and eliminate from the earth someone you love. And every morning you wake up knowing you're a day further from them, and that that keeps going forever.

If the killer is arrested, you enter the criminal justice system, hoping for some kind of justice. It's impossible to know then that most likely nothing that comes of the case will help much with your pain, and a lot of what you will have to go through to get any result at all will make you feel worse, because you're not really part of what happens. You might even find out that prosecutors don't have time for you, and even if they listen, they can't make any decisions based on what you say. And it's very likely that whatever sentence the killer gets isn't going to be enough for you, even if it's life in prison and especially if, as happens in many cases, the killer pleads guilty to a lesser offense and gets only a few years. The reality is, so many murders go unsolved, that you're actually fortunate if, in your loved one's case, you know who the murderer is. In many cases the body is never even found.[1]

In my father's case, the state of New York deemed his killer "not responsible by reason of mental disease or defect" and put him in a high-security hospital for a few years and then began the process of gradually releasing him: furloughs, moving him to a "¾ way" house on the edge of the hospital grounds where he could live for free while working and living in the community. Eventually he was given his entire, unsupervised freedom.

Almost twenty years after my father's death I spoke out against the death penalty and was involved in two campaigns to prevent its return to Massachusetts. I opposed the death penalty (and still do) not because I feel sorry for murderers or even because I think every human is redeemable; I wish I did, but I don't. I don't debate that there are people who "deserve" the death penalty—some people do things so horrible they "deserve" whatever happens to them. But I'm against the death penalty because of what it does to us: wastes our money; infects our justice system with racism, classism, and politics; and, in the end, turns us into killers. To put it on the personal level, the man who killed my father deserves, in my mind, whatever happens to him. But it's not worth the damage I would inflict on myself and my family to give it to him.

Out of these thoughts emerged the idea to write about the death penalty system when it worked and about the effect this process has on all the people involved in a case. I decided I would chose two death penalty cases at random (so there could be no question of my having picked one to make a point) and write whatever I found out about them. To find random cases, I picked three inmates from a death row pen pal website and wrote to them, explaining my idea and that if they agreed to work with me I would get to see their entire file, would interview as many people involved in the case as possible, and would write what I found to be the truth. Since most of the more than three thousand people on death rows across the country are guilty, I assumed I'd be writing about guilty men.

An inmate from Pennsylvania, Nick Yarris, answered my letter. He wrote that he didn't want to do the project—he was running out of appeals and didn't want to fight his case anymore—but he would give my letter to someone who might. (Two years later Yarris was exonerated by DNA evidence and released from death row.)

Shortly after that I received a letter from Walter Ogrod, who wrote that he was innocent. I didn't believe him, but since my rule was to follow the case of whoever wrote to me, I did just that. Soon, I began to think he might be telling the truth. That was in 2001, and I've been on the case since.

In the interim, I published an article about the case in a local paper in Philadelphia in 2004, and in 2008 took a job as an investigator at Innocence Project New Orleans, where I did finally learn something about murderers. It turns out there's not much to understand. Most are too angry, too drunk or high, too narcissistic, too crazy, too damaged, too some or all of the above to think about what they're doing. A few are psychopaths, people who have no feelings for others but can fake them. I once asked the former head of the New Orleans Police Department's homicide division: out of all the murderers you've been in a room with, what percentage were evil (psychopaths) and what percentage were just idiots (the rest)? Ninety-seven percent idiots, he said.

The problem is, this isn't satisfying; the crime of murder is so big we want the suspect to fill up the required space, and our system encourages this because once the victim is dead the entire process is geared to the suspect: who is he, what did he think, why did he do it, did he understand it, and so on. Popular culture is obsessed with the psychopaths, the devious geniuses, but the reality of murder is so grimly different.

In writing this book I also didn't end up learning anything about the death penalty when it "works." Instead, I've learned how deep the culture of "win at all costs" is in DA's offices, and how DAs and judges tend to reflexively dismiss all questions about a case once a verdict has been reached. I have developed an even greater respect for the lawyers, investigators, journalists, and inmates around the country who do the work of challenging wrongful convictions full time. And I have come to dislike the phrase "The truth always comes out." It does not; it has to be pried out, and when it comes to our criminal justice system you can bend iron with your hands just as easily.

This book recounts the story of a 1988 murder and the ensuing investigations and trials. I wasn't present for any of that; when my research into the case began in 2001, it was already five years after the verdict in this case. I published new evidence about the case in my 2004 article in the *Philadelphia City Paper*, and additional new evidence has come out since then, mostly due to the work of Walter Ogrod's excellent defense team. I am not privy to their files and have seen only the public briefs they have filed on Walter's behalf, some of which include my earlier work on the case.

In a case as complicated as this one, the various participants see things differently to begin with and change their stories over time; memories fade and, science confirms, change over time. Where two or more stories disagree or someone's story changes over time, I have relied on the account given closest in time to the event in question, cross-checked with whatever evidence there may be. Significant disagreements about important events have been highlighted in the text and in the notes. Dialogue in quotation marks is taken directly from an interview with someone present for the conversation, if that conversation is supported by other evidence, or from a transcript of the conversation or another direct source. Any thoughts or feelings attributed to people in the book are as they were told to me or recorded at the time of the event. I have tried to portray the thoughts and feelings of those involved as accurately as possible and to make it clear when I'm offering my own opinion or insight.

PART I

MURDER

I

BARBARA JEAN

BARBARA JEAN HORN WOKE UP on the morning of July 12, 1988, on a mattress on her living room floor next to her parents, Sharon and John Fahy. The living room was the only room in the house with an air conditioner, so they all slept there; the day before, the temperature had reached one hundred degrees, and though today wasn't supposed to be quite as bad, it was already hot.

Sharon and John had rented their small row house in a neighborhood of similar small row houses the previous fall. Authors Michael and Randi Boyette describe these houses as a "Philadelphia institution . . . endless monotonous ranks of tiny working-class homes, jammed shoulder-to-shoulder like people crowded on a bus, with flat tar roofs and postage-stamp yards (or none at all). . . . In blocks little more than 500 feet long and 150 wide—less than two football fields—builders managed to pack as many as sixty tiny houses. . . . Things such as front and back yards and streets wide enough for two cars to pass one another were a luxury that few could afford."[1]

The Fahys' house, 7245 Rutland Street, had a pink awning and a few square feet of yard, separated from the sidewalk by a hedge. Other than that, it was exactly like the houses around it: three bedrooms upstairs, a living room that opened to the dining room and a kitchen on the ground floor, and a basement, all crammed into eleven hundred square feet. Four-year-old Barbara Jean had two of the bedrooms—one for sleeping, one to play in, with a full toy kitchen set up.[2] The walls were thin, the doors flimsy; if anyone in adjoining houses talked too loudly, walked with heavy steps up the stairs, or flushed the toilet, you could hear it all.

The Fahys thought the house was perfect for their small family. Sharon, who had brown hair, a quick mind, and a deep laugh, worked at a customs brokerage firm downtown and liked to get to work by 8:00; that morning she got ready for work, kissed John and Barbara Jean, and left the house at 7:00 AM, walking up quiet Rutland Street in the cloudy, humid morning to catch her bus.

John had been unemployed since January and stayed home to take care of Barbara Jean, who was quiet for another hour and a half, waiting for him to wake. At about 8:30 AM, she turned on the TV and started jumping up and down on him. He dressed in a maroon sleeveless T-shirt and cutoff jeans and picked out Barbara Jean's clothes so she could dress herself: pink shorts and a pullover top with pink, yellow, and green pastel stripes. She wore earrings with yellow stones. John put her hair in a ponytail.[3]

John was slim and strong, a former marine with light brown hair and tattoos all over his arms. He ate Lucky Charms and watched TV with Barbara Jean; as a stay-at-home dad, he had chores to do and knew Sharon would be calling to check on him, which she did at about 9:00 AM. Between 10:00 and 10:30 AM, as John watched TV and did chores, Barbara Jean went down the block to her friend Nicole's house. Nicole was nine years old and liked to brush and braid Barbara Jean's hair. Nicole's grandfather, an off-duty police officer, was putting up a new porch, and Barbara Jean watched the workers for a few minutes, maybe hoping for Nicole to come out, before going home.[4]

When Sharon called again at about 11:00 AM, Barbara Jean got on the line.

"Where are you, Mommy?" she asked.

Sharon said she was at work and would be home a little later.

"Can I have a freeze pop?" Barbara Jean asked.

"After lunch," Sharon told her.

"Bye!" Barbara Jean said. She handed the phone to John and ran to the front door.

"Hi Charlie!" she called through the screen to her best friend, six-year-old Charlie Green, across the street.

At lunchtime John and Barbara Jean walked a couple of blocks to Yang's grocery to pick up milk, cigarettes, and rolls for supper. There wasn't anybody around. Back home, John made Barbara Jean a tuna sandwich and poured her a glass of milk, and they watched TV in the air conditioning. Barbara Jean went outside to look for someone to play with and after a few minutes was home again. She tried to get John to play, but he had too much to do and sent her to watch television upstairs.

Over the course of the afternoon, Barbara Jean looked for other kids without any luck; she'd try John again but he was busy, so she'd go upstairs or play on their lawn, where John had set up a kiddie pool. At 1:00 or 1:30 PM she went down the block to Nicole's house again and stood at the edge of the lawn, picking at the grass. When Nicole's mom, Margaret, came out, Barbara Jean walked away without saying anything.[5]

She went home and played by herself in the front yard.[6] She wasn't supposed to cross Rutland Street without John's permission, but at around 2:00 PM she knocked on Charlie's door; Charlie's mother told her he wasn't home. She also knocked on Casey and Shannon's door a few houses south, but their mom, Kathleen, told her they were having quiet time. She went home.

At about 3:00 PM, after more reminder calls from Sharon, John got started on his main chore of the day, cleaning out the fridge. Barbara Jean asked if she could help, but John thought she'd be in the way, so he told her to go outside and play. She took her sandals off and went outside. She had her bucket of toys. It was hot and quiet. She played by herself; maybe she splashed in the kiddie pool.

John liked to listen to TV as he worked, so he turned the TV in the living room to a soap opera his mother had watched when he was a kid, put the sound up loud so he could hear it in the kitchen, and got to work.[7]

Half a block away, Nicole's mother, Margaret, was sitting on her porch, rocking her new baby, when she saw Barbara Jean across the street—on Charlie Green's side of Rutland Street—being led by a man in a navy blue T-shirt and work pants with a funny, side-to-side, kind of bouncy walk. Barbara Jean's ponytail was bobbing; she seemed maybe scared or excited. The man had her by the elbow and turned toward her once, as if saying something, but was too far away for Margaret to see his face.

"Oh," Margaret thought, "that's nice. She's so bored her daddy's gonna take her to the mall." She looked down at her infant son for a moment, and when she looked up Barbara Jean and the man were gone. Margaret figured they'd turned left into the little alley up by the bank at the north end of Rutland.

At around 4:00 PM John heard *Oprah* coming on as he restocked the now-clean fridge. He realized he hadn't seen Barbara Jean in a while and went to call for her. He saw her sandals by the front door and called for her from the front steps, looking up and down Rutland Street. Nothing. He went back to restocking the fridge, but when he finished she still wasn't home so he went to the front yard. Just outside the hedge separating their lawn from the sidewalk he saw some of her toys—plastic cars, plastic people, a plastic duck.[8] John felt the first strains of panic: she never walked away from her toys like that.

Her friend Anthony's father was outside but hadn't seen her. He offered to help knock on doors. Barbara Jean never went in anyone's house, never even crossed tiny Rutland Street without asking permission, John thought. Then, suddenly: maybe she was upstairs; maybe she'd come in and gone up to play with her Barbies and he didn't hear her. He was up the stoop in two strides and up the stairs in three more, but she wasn't there.

He went outside and called her name, then crossed the street and knocked on little Charlie's door. Charlie's mother, Linda

Green, said that Barbara Jean had been by earlier looking for Charlie but he was at the rec center swimming. She'd seen Barbara Jean playing by herself on John's front lawn at around 2:00 PM but hadn't seen her since.[9]

John called Barbara Jean's friend Meghan's mother; Barbara Jean had been by there earlier, too, but she hadn't seen her since.

A few houses south, on little Charlie's side of the street, Kathleen Ritterson, eight months pregnant and wearing a back brace from a fall at work, was napping on her couch. Her daughters, Barbara Jean's friends Casey and Shannon, woke her up and told her Barbara Jean's daddy was at the door. He asked if Barbara Jean was there; Kathleen told him no and asked if he'd checked at the Greens'. He said he had, and a couple of other places, too.

Kathleen knew John was usually attentive to where Barbara Jean was, so it must've been terrifying for him to have no idea. She told him to wait a minute, that she'd get dressed and help him look. They decided to search around the block in opposite directions. Kathleen went slowly, given her pregnancy, back brace, and the two little girls she had with her. As she finished her route she saw John, even more agitated than before, going up and down the block, knocking on doors. Kids were helping him.[10]

John searched the neighborhood, up to busy Cottman Avenue, into stores; he asked a salesman in a bedding store if he'd seen Barbara Jean. No luck. He went back to his stoop and sat and hoped she'd just come home. But she was nowhere. Barbara Jean was nowhere. It was 4:55 PM.[11] He had to call Sharon.

Sharon was chatting with a friend when her desk phone rang. "You gotta come home," John said. "I can't find Barbara Jean."

"What do you mean?" Sharon asked. "Where was she?"

"She was out playing."

"Who was she playing with?"

"I don't know."

"What were you doing?"

"I was cleaning the fridge," John said.

"Well, did you check at Meghan's? Did you—"

"Sharon, just come home," John said.

Sharon was supposed to work late to earn some overtime and then meet up with her sister, Barb, after whom Barbara Jean was named. She called Barb to say she couldn't make it, she had to get home, Barbara Jean was missing. Barb lived nearby and said she'd go help John look.

Sharon left her office to catch the bus, thinking of what she'd say to Barbara Jean, who she was sure would be home by the time she got back.

———————

At 5:30 PM, inside 1409 St. Vincent, a block and a half southwest of Barbara Jean's house, Stanley Zablocky's wife looked out the front door and told her husband someone had left a box in front of the house. Mr. Zablocky decided he'd better see what it was before he took his bath. His wife stood in the doorway and watched as he walked to the curb and lifted a flap on the box.

"Oh my God!" he yelled. "Call 911! There's a baby in the box!"[12]

A neighbor who heard Zablocky yelling came over, pulled up a flap, and saw a small child lying facedown in a fetal position with a trickle of blood coming from her mouth. He started running back to his own house to call the police.[13] At that moment a squad car came into the next intersection, Loretto Avenue and St. Vincent Street, so Mr. Zablocky and his neighbor flagged the officer down and told him there was a baby in the box. The officer looked in and saw the child, partially covered by a green plastic trash bag, with dried blood on the back of the head and bruises on the neck and shoulder. The child's hair was wet and pushed forward, so he thought it was a boy. He felt the neck for a pulse but couldn't find one. He radioed a supervisor, requested that homicide be notified, and helped cordon off St. Vincent Street. Officers stood watch over the crime scene, waiting for the mobile crime lab and homicide detectives to arrive.[14]

John Fahy got home from another search at about 5:45 PM and stood on his front stoop, looking up and down the block, terrified, wondering what the hell to do next.

Half a block north, in the parking lot of the AM/PM mini-mart at the corner of Castor and Cottman, Sharon's sister Barb was standing next to her car, crying hysterically, looking up and down Castor. She'd been driving around the neighborhood for half an hour, searching, and had no idea what else to do.

A police van that had just been at the crime scene on St. Vincent Street pulled into the lot, and one of the officers asked Barb what was wrong. She told him her niece had been missing since 3:00 PM. He thought the missing little girl and the child in the box were probably the same person and relayed a description of Barbara Jean to the police at the scene, but officers on St. Vincent still thought the child in the box was a boy. The officer decided to go with Barb to her niece's house to get pictures. They left the AM/PM parking lot and drove slowly the wrong way down Rutland Street, half a block to John and Sharon's house.

When John saw Barb and the police van coming down the street the wrong way, he *knew* he'd fucked up. As he went inside the house he punched the door, breaking a pane of glass.

Sharon got off the bus at about ten minutes to six and walked the couple of blocks home, still considering what to say to Barbara Jean, who she was sure would be there by then. She came around the corner and saw the police van in front of her house and walked faster. When she got inside John was there with Barb and a few police officers.

"I don't know where she is," John told her. "I checked everywhere, I don't know where she is."

An officer asked for a picture of Barbara Jean, but all Sharon could do was stare out the back window in the dining room, trying to figure out where her daughter could be.[15] Two officers filling out forms asked for a description. They said again that they needed a picture, so Sharon went upstairs and got them two.

Outside, the street was filling with people talking about what had happened, repeating rumors, trading guesses.

The mobile crime lab and homicide detectives Maureen (Royds) Kelly[16] and Frank Miller arrived at the St. Vincent Street crime scene at 6:45 PM. The child in the box, a girl, was formally pronounced dead at the scene at 6:52 PM. She was three and a half feet tall, forty-three pounds, naked, wrapped in a garbage bag. She had five blunt trauma injuries caused by what the medical examiner would guess was a two-by-four plank of lumber, something lighter than a baseball bat or tire iron.[17] She had four lacerations on her scalp, two to the back and two to the left side of her head, and a bruise on her left shoulder. There was no sign of sexual abuse, and swabs taken of her mouth, anus, and vagina showed no sperm. She had no old injuries except a scabbed-over scrape on her right knee, suggesting she hadn't been an abused child.

Detective Kelly was sure this was the missing little girl whose frantic aunt had talked to police up at the mini-mart. It was time to talk to the parents.

Kelly and Miller went over to the Fahys and found John and Sharon at their dining room table, looking through pictures of Barbara Jean, trying to find a good one for the police to use. Kelly took Sharon to the living room and sat her on the sofa with Barb and Barb's husband, who had recently arrived. Miller took John into the kitchen.

Kelly told Sharon a child had been found in a TV box a few blocks away. She wasn't sure it was Barbara Jean but said they would find out as fast as they could.[18]

In the kitchen Miller said, "We found her, she's dead, and you did it," and pounded his finger in John's chest.[19]

Sharon heard John scream.

"You're out of your fucking mind," John told Miller. He couldn't believe Barbara Jean was dead, his mind was in chaos, she couldn't be dead, they couldn't be accusing him, it was all nuts. *Nuts.*

2

JOHN AND SHARON

JOHN AND SHARON MET IN the spring of 1983 at the Wanamaker's department store where they both worked—Sharon pricing merchandise, John unloading trucks. Sharon was twenty-one, the youngest of nine siblings (including a twin brother) in a close family from Oxford Circle, not far from Rutland Street. Her father left when she was twelve or thirteen, and she grew even closer with her mother and siblings. Some of her sisters wanted to go to college, but without their father around there wasn't enough money. Sharon never wanted to go to college. She wanted to get married and have kids, so when she graduated high school she got a job.

John was also one of nine children (second youngest) from Northeast Philadelphia; he'd joined the marines out of high school and served for three years, mostly driving trucks. He was twenty-two when he met Sharon. She was dating someone at the time, but John knew when he saw her that she was for him. He cultivated a friendship, taking lunch breaks with her and a couple other friends, hanging out with her when he could.

Sharon's relationship with her boyfriend ended because she wanted marriage and kids and he didn't. She found out a couple weeks later she was pregnant and called him; he wanted her to have an abortion. She wasn't doing that. She told him she wouldn't bother him and thanked him; they parted on good terms but didn't stay in touch. She'd always be glad he was part of her life because she got to have Barbara Jean.

By May of that year, Sharon was getting big and gave notice at Wanamaker's. John wasn't going to let himself be out of sight, out of mind, so on her last day, May 17, 1983, he walked her to the bus and asked if he could call her. She said that'd be fine. He called that night and visited her. She was surprised he wanted to get involved right away. By October he was living with her at her mother's house in his own room in the basement. Her mother quickly grew to love him.

Sharon had always wanted a daughter to buy dresses for, to braid her hair. As her due date approached, she decided that if her baby was a girl she was going to name her Barbara Jean, after her sister. Little Barbara Jean arrived at 5:23 PM on October 18, 1983, weighing five pounds, twelve ounces, nicknamed "Peanut" by the hospital staff.[1] Sharon and John weren't married yet, so she gave the baby her own last name, Horn.

Sharon stared at Barbara Jean in disbelief that she could make something like this, that this little girl had grown inside of her. John had wondered sometimes how it would feel to be a stepfather, but from the moment he saw the baby it wasn't like that—she was his daughter from the get-go; there was never anything "stepfather" about him.[2] She slept through the night from two weeks old and put on weight so fast that by three months she was too chubby to close her arms in a hug.

Sharon got her job at the customs brokerage firm downtown, and John worked construction or warehouse jobs, whatever he could find. They were married in March 1985 at St. Martin of Tours, Sharon's parish growing up, and paid for their own reception at a nearby Knights of Columbus Hall. More than a hundred people came.[3]

Around their first anniversary they split up. Sharon moved in with one of her sisters and John went to live with a buddy and then back with his mother, but within a few months they were back together. In the summer of 1987 they were helping a friend clean up a row house on Rutland Street she and her husband rented out; they thought it would be good for their little family, asked if they could rent it, and moved in that September.[4] They didn't meet many people on their block before cold drove everybody inside.

John and Sharon enjoyed the house and loved being parents. But John was drinking almost every day—Southern Comfort mixed with anything, and beer. He used crank, a cheap, crude form of speed, to stay awake and keep drinking.[5] He wanted to be clean, a good husband and father, but struggled with the combination of self-loathing, boredom, and addiction that makes people medicate themselves into an alternate universe.

Sharon smoked a little pot and occasionally used crank. When John stayed out late drinking, she went to bed thankful they didn't have a car so at least she didn't have to worry about him crashing. She didn't back down from telling him what she thought of his behavior; it might be 4:00 AM and he might be drunk, but she was going to say what she thought. The arguments sometimes led to throwing things, pushing, even to John smacking her.

The spring of 1988 brought people on Rutland Street out on their stoops in the evenings to drink beer, chat, and watch their kids pedal and run up and down the block. Barbara Jean was going on five, bright, with a wide smile and long brown hair cut in bangs. She had a vivid imagination, could entertain herself easily, and was strong for a little kid: John, the former marine, believed in push-ups for discipline, and Barbara Jean, who had her moods like any child, did her share.[6] She could be a little shy at first but quickly outgoing; she pushed boundaries but knew that when her parents said "no," they meant it. She loved riding her bike, rollerskating, jumping rope, and playing with Barbie dolls; she really wanted a scooter, and her parents were thinking about getting her one for her birthday.[7] She liked to watch herself sing and dance in a mirror in the living room, songs from *The Sound of Music* and *The Wizard of Oz* and Madonna's "Open Your Heart." She loved the television shows *Alf* and *Rags to Riches*; the night before she died, she told her parents she wanted to be on TV someday.[8]

Barbara Jean made friends quickly on Rutland Street and could almost always find someone to ride bikes or play Barbies with. Her best friend on the block was little Charlie Green across the street, whom everyone called "Charliebird." They got along well from the first time they met, and he treated her like a little sister, helping her learn her way around the neighborhood.

One day Charliebird saw John's marines tattoo and said his dad had one too, so John, the type who said hi to everyone, met Charliebird's parents, Chuck and Linda Green. Chuck was known as "Sarge" because he'd been in the marines in Vietnam; he had a Time Life book about the war with a picture in it that he said was of him. He was enormous, six feet tall and probably three hundred pounds, with tattoos all over his arms, a long ponytail, and a full, wild beard. He could be loud and aggressive and said he'd been kicked out of a violent biker gang. He had a long criminal record of drug and assault charges, collected disability payments, and carried a walking stick, explaining that part of his heel had been shot off in Vietnam. He dealt crank and other drugs, sometimes to John, and inked tattoos in his basement.

Charliebird's mother, Linda, was heavy and short; everyone called her "Turtle." She made trips into the city to bring back big wheels of government cheese and tubs of peanut butter. She had a loud voice and when she wanted her son home was known to stand on the front porch and yell, "Charliebird, get your fucking ass in here!"[9] Charliebird would run home fast to avoid being hit. The Greens' daughter, Alice,* was thirteen and babysat for some of the neighborhood kids, including Barbara Jean. She drank and smoked and was dating a twenty-year-old.[10]

Sarge and Linda drank and used pot, crank, Valium, heroin; cars would pull up and idle as someone dipped inside to score drugs from Sarge. The Greens had parties, the scrum of motorcycles taking over their lawn, the sidewalk, lining up along the street, rumbling houses when they started, each thrust of the engine

---

* The first name of the Greens' daughter is a pseudonym to preserve her privacy.

noise blending with the music and the noise of people laughing, yelling, or fighting. Later, stories of the parties and crowds at the Greens' would get exaggerated, but neighbors were alarmed by them.

John wasn't one for the biker parties but would cross Rutland Street to drink beers with Sarge while their kids played. He thought Sarge was a drunk and a bit of a loser but felt bad for him; he'd been wounded in Vietnam and seemed on the whole pretty harmless. They bonded over having been in the marines, and Sarge gave John some Marine Corps stickers and a poster.

Sharon, more guarded than John, had strong instincts about people and didn't like the Greens. They were wasted all the time. Linda would even send Charliebird across the street with a note asking if Sharon had an extra joint lying around. And Sharon didn't like not knowing who lived at the Greens'—there were always people moving in and out, biker friends of Sarge's, she figured. John would tell her Sarge wasn't so bad, Charliebird and Barbara Jean were good friends, and Linda needed a friend. *I don't need friends like that*, Sharon would think.

One weekend that spring Sharon came home to find that Alice had given Barbara Jean a full makeup job—eye shadow, blush, everything. Sharon was furious and told Alice never to do it again and told Barbara Jean the same thing. Sharon thought people let their kids grow up too fast, and she wasn't going to let that happen to her daughter.

Trying to be friendly, she did agree to go over to the Greens' with John one evening for a beer. But from the moment she walked into their house her nerves were on edge. The living room was filthy, dust and dog hair everywhere; the dining room had a mattress on the floor and garbage bags full of the Greens' stuff lining the walls. The bathroom upstairs was filthy, too, the sink broken off the wall and sitting on the floor.

Sharon sat on the edge of her chair in the living room, watching her daughter and Charliebird jump on the disgusting mattress, thinking it was time to leave, it was too chaotic; trying to figure out how Linda had broken their vacuum cleaner, which John had lent her, because she'd sure never run it.

It was the only time Sharon ever went in that house, and her instincts were clear. At home, out of Barbara Jean's hearing, she told John, "Don't you *ever* let her in that house, ever again in your life."

By the summer of 1988 Sharon wouldn't even say "hi" to the Greens, but John tried to keep the friendship up. One night toward the end of June, Sharon came home from work to find John, Sarge, and Linda sitting in her living room watching *Full Metal Jacket* while Charliebird and Barbara Jean played. Sharon tried to be polite, but the room was tense; the Greens knew Sharon didn't like them, and John knew Sharon was pissed off the Greens were there. Sharon didn't think *Full Metal Jacket* was appropriate for Barbara Jean and took her upstairs.

John looked over at Sarge, who was passed out in his chair, and thought about how pissed Sharon was. He told Sarge it was time to go, but Sarge didn't move. John slapped him on the chest and told him to wake up.

Sarge woke up. He slammed his walking stick against the ceiling, then did it again. John grabbed the stick and backed him out the door and down the front steps, then threw the stick at him and said, "Don't ever come over here again."

Upstairs, Sharon heard the banging. She didn't go downstairs. The next morning she found little blue pills scattered all over the couch, Valiums maybe, something Linda spilled the night before. She yelled at John: What if Barbara Jean had gotten some of those pills?

A few days later Sarge knocked on John's door and asked for his marines poster and stickers back. John gave them back, and Sarge handed him a biker's memento: a small grim reaper pin with the phrase FINAL NOTICE on it.

3

INVESTIGATION

WHEN A CHILD IS MURDERED, detectives check the parents first, and on the night Barbara Jean was killed, John—at five feet seven, about 160 pounds, short brown hair parted in the middle, a mustache, and a Philadelphia accent—generally matched a description of the man who'd been seen carrying the box that police were then developing from witnesses on St. Vincent Street. And John had a cut on his hand from punching the door.

The detectives put Sharon in a cruiser, allowing her sister and brother-in-law to ride with her. John rode in a separate car with two detectives, one sitting in back with him. In the homicide offices at the Police Administration Building downtown, called "the Roundhouse" because it's shaped like a pair of handcuffs,[1] the Fahys were put in separate interview rooms. Sharon said she had to get home in case Barbara Jean came back. A detective said not to worry, there was an officer at the house if that happened. The detective asked what she'd done that day, about her relationship with John, if there was any way he might've hurt Barbara Jean.

"No," she said. "There's no way. If I thought for a minute he could've done it, you wouldn't have to worry, I'd kill him myself."

Was there anyone who didn't like her or John, anyone they were fighting with? She mentioned the Greens and that John and Chuck had a falling-out a couple of weeks before.

Down the hall, Detective Miller read John his rights and asked if he wanted a lawyer. John said he hadn't done anything, so he didn't need one. Miller had him detail his day, then do it again. Then Miller accused him of the murder.

"You're out of your fucking mind," John told him.

Miller questioned him about his life and marriage. He wasn't always proud to answer but told the truth about his drinking, his fights with Sharon, how sometimes the situation could get out of hand, that things got thrown or there was some pushing.

Miller asked if he'd ever hit his wife and he admitted he'd smacked her.

"I'll tell you the truth," John said. "My daughter is dead. I want you to get the guy who did it. I don't wanna be a problem for this, I don't want you to waste a lot of time with me, I know I did nothing wrong. I want you to find out who killed her."

Miller brought in pictures of Barbara Jean, dead; John identified her. Miller told him again he did it. John took a lie detector test, and Miller told him the results were inconclusive; they shouldn't have given it to him just then because he was too upset. But detectives can and do lie about lie detector results during interrogations, so John may well have passed it.

The detectives pressured John for hours, but he never wavered.

Up on Rutland Street, Margaret Kruce, the neighbor who'd seen Barbara Jean at around 3:00 PM walking with a man she took to be the little girl's father, was shown a photo of John and said it wasn't him. Also, none of the St. Vincent Street witnesses had seen any tattoos on the man with the box, and John had seven on his arms.[2]

Miller and Kelly released John and Sharon close to midnight. John's mother came to the Roundhouse to get them and took them back to her house. They went upstairs and lay in bed, not saying much other than that they couldn't believe Barbara Jean was gone. Impossible. They just lay there in the dark.

John felt he was outside himself watching this whole other thing go on. *Crazy, just fucking crazy.*

For detectives, good information and leads were coming in. Barbara Jean had to have been killed between 3:00 PM—when she was last seen alive—and, say, 5:00 PM, since the man with the box had first been seen at 5:12. (The medical examiner would put the time of death between 3:30 and 4:30 PM.) There were rumors about someone in a black van trying to dump a TV box at Kutner Buick, a car dealership on the corner near where Barbara Jean had been left, but the narrow time frame for the crime suggested she'd been killed in the neighborhood. There wasn't time to take her away, kill her, and bring the body back. And why do that anyway?

The most promising leads came from four witnesses who had seen the man carrying the box on St. Vincent Street. These four all described a Caucasian man in his late twenties or early thirties, between five feet six and five feet eight, 160 to 180 pounds, with short dark blond or light brown hair, wearing shorts and a T-shirt. They disagreed about what color his T-shirt was, what kind of shorts he wore, and whether or not he had a light mustache.

The first of these witnesses, Michael Massi, a sixty-year-old car salesman, had been reclining in his chair in a cubicle in Kutner Buick on the corner of St. Vincent Street and Castor Avenue, taking a break in his twelve-hour workday. At a few minutes past 5:00 PM he'd been facing north, looking out a floor-to-ceiling window when a man walked past, going north on Castor Avenue, carrying a box for a thirteen-inch color TV with a garbage bag sticking out of the top. The man crossed St. Vincent Street and paused in front of the church on the corner, putting the box down to rest; he stood with his back to Massi for about twenty seconds, looking around, panting, then hunched over and dragged the box backward five or six steps down St. Vincent Street. He was five feet six or five feet eight, Massi thought, medium build, hair on the darker side and cut close to his head. Massi didn't get a good look at his face but saw enough to know he was no kid, probably thirty-ish.[3]

At 5:12 PM, off-duty fireman David Schectman, leaning against the tailgate of his 1980 Chevy station wagon in front of his house on St. Vincent Street, checked his watch, then looked back at his newspaper. His wife, Lorraine, who had multiple sclerosis, was sitting in the passenger's seat, ready to leave for her 5:30 PM doctor's appointment as soon as their kids got home from summer camp.

Schectman glanced up at the intersection, half a block east, where his kids' camp van would turn onto St. Vincent Street from Castor Avenue. A few people were waiting at the bus stop on the corner in front of the church, and as he looked, the man carrying a box for a thirteen-inch color TV came into view and put it down to rest for a few seconds. Schectman went back to his paper. When he looked up again, the man was coming toward him on St. Vincent, alternately carrying the box with both arms and dragging it by a garbage bag sticking out of the top. As the man approached, he put the box down to rest and looked up. He was maybe five feet six or five feet eight, with sandy blond or brownish hair.

"What do you have in the box?" Schectman asked him.

"Some old junk," the man said.

"Trash pickup is Tuesday," Schectman said.

"I thought it was Wednesday on this street," the man said. He made no attempt to hide his face, and had a medium-pitched voice and Philadelphia accent. He picked up the box and started up the steps leading to Schectman's backyard.

Schectman thought maybe he was from the church at the corner and was trying to go through the backyard to get back there.

"Hold on," Schectman said. "It doesn't go through."

The man turned around and came across the lawn. When he reached the sidewalk, he put the box down, dragged it a few feet, and tried to push it into some bushes between Schectman's house and the next house over.

"You can't put that in there," Schectman told him.

The man was agitated. He picked the box up and tried to go up the walkway two houses down but saw Schectman looking at him so continued west on St. Vincent, carrying and dragging the box, stopping several times.

As Schectman finished speaking to the man, Chris Kochan, fourteen, came east down the sidewalk on his bike to deliver

Schectman's *Daily News*. As Kochan approached, the man was bent over, dragging the box; he stepped aside so Kochan could squeeze past. Kochan gave Schectman his paper and settled his bill. They chatted for a minute or two, Schectman telling him about the man trying to put the box in his backyard. Kochan watched the man drag the box along the sidewalk until he left it on the curb next to a metal garbage can and walked away, not hurrying. Schectman and Kochan watched him cross the next street, Loretto Avenue, and continue west. It was 5:23 PM.

Kochan finished talking to Schectman and rode back the way he'd come. He passed the TV box but didn't see the man who'd been carrying it.

The camp van with the Schectman children arrived, and they left for Lorraine's appointment at 5:26 PM. David pointed out the box, now sitting in front of 1409 St. Vincent, to his wife. She asked if he wanted to see what was in it. He said no.

That night, Schectman told police he'd seen and talked to the man with the box for eleven minutes. Since the man had been only a day off in telling Schectman he thought Wednesday was trash pickup day on that street, detectives thought he had some knowledge of the neighborhood, probably lived or worked nearby. This made sense because they thought Barbara Jean must've been killed indoors, or someone would've seen the murder or heard her screaming.

More clues: Barbara Jean's wet hair suggested the body had been washed, maybe to clean off evidence, and her being naked made sexual assault a possible motive. Also, technicians pulled one fingerprint from the box and one fingerprint from the garbage bag, and the TV box had a serial number they could use to trace it to its owner.

––––––––––

That night detectives also interviewed a fifth witness who'd seen the man with the box. This was Peter Vargas, who'd been installing an air conditioning unit in 7259 Rutland that day and was in the alley behind the house—the same alley that ran behind Barbara Jean's house—that afternoon getting something from his truck when a man carrying a TV box approached, the muscles in his forearms straining from the effort. Vargas's description of the man was similar to the other witnesses: five feet nine to six feet, 165 to 175 pounds, with brownish-blond hair parted in the middle, a medium complexion, and a slight mustache. His description of the man's clothes was different; Vargas said he'd been wearing blue jeans, a plaid flannel shirt with the sleeves rolled up over a white T-shirt and a pack of Marlboros in the left breast pocket, and white sneakers. A cigarette dangled from the man's lip, and he asked Vargas to light it. Vargas did, and the man continued on his way north up the alley.[4] This story never fit with any law enforcement theory of the case, and Vargas never testified.

The one witness whose description of a possible suspect was slightly different was Margaret Kruce, who'd described the man she'd seen walking with Barbara Jean at 3:00 PM as five feet ten or so, not fat but with rolls over his belt, his hair dark brown and kinky, wearing a T-shirt and blue work pants or shorts. But after Margaret told police on the night of the murder that it wasn't John, she was never interviewed by anyone from the DA's office about what she saw; like Peter Vargas, her story never fit any prosecution theory of the crime.[5]

The day after the murder, a police artist met with the Schectmans to create a sketch of the man with the box. Michael Massi said the sketch was very accurate, especially the hair.[6]

Later, prosecutors would try to dismiss all the eyewitnesses as mistaken and even to keep the police sketch out of the trial. But at the time, the investigation was off to a good start.

4

AFTERMATH

THE DAY AFTER BARBARA JEAN'S MURDER, the sun rose and the heat of the Philadelphia summer brewed; the temperature would reach one hundred degrees. John and Sharon had one thing they had to do: go to the medical examiner's office to formally identify Barbara Jean's body. When they got there, they were shown a picture of her on a closed-circuit TV screen. Sharon noticed her little mouth was open and wanted to hold her again but was told that was a bad idea. She didn't insist—she wanted Barbara Jean to feel like Barbara Jean in her arms but knew that after we're gone our bodies don't feel the same.[1]

That day, both major newspapers in Philadelphia had front-page headlines about the murder: DEAD CHILD FOUND NAKED IN CARTON in the *Philadelphia Inquirer* and CHILD'S SLAYING HAS NE [NORTHEAST PHILADELPHIA] IN PANIC in the *Daily News*.

As the medical examiner performed the autopsy on Barbara Jean that morning, four homicide and four burglary detectives canvassed Rutland Street. At 7244 Rutland, Linda Green answered the door with Walter Ogrod, her housemate. With Linda standing there, Walter told the detective he'd been home the day before and had gone out on some errands at about 2:45 PM, returning at about 3:30. Pretty soon after he got back, John Fahy knocked on the door and asked if anyone had seen his little girl. He and Linda had told him no, and John went off looking.[2] Walter was twenty-three but looked younger, chunky at six feet two, 220, with jet-black hair over his collar and a speech impediment; he didn't match the descriptions of the man carrying the box.

Kathleen Ritterson, the pregnant mother of two of Barbara Jean's friends who, with her daughters, had helped John search the neighborhood, had slept little on the night of July 12, worrying about her own kids' safety and how to tell them their playmate Barbara Jean was gone. When she took her girls outside for a swim in a kiddie pool the next day, reporters were jogging up and down the street, asking to talk to people. Later, a detective knocked on her door and she told him what she'd seen and heard. He said he was sure if they stood on the corner and threw a stone they'd hit the killer's house.

The neighborhood was changed from a place where families sat on their stoops in the evenings to a place of "total panic";[3] everyone was scared: the murderer could live on the block and be thinking he got away with one and could get away with another.[4] A nearby day care center canceled outdoor play because people were stopping to stare at the kids through the green chain-link fence; the owner also didn't want children watching police stop traffic to distribute the sketch of the suspect, or garbage collectors going through trash cans for clues, or reporters and cameramen circling, looking for stories.[5]

Newspaper stories about the murder included important details: Barbara Jean was found in a fetal position, killed by blows to the head; there was no evidence of sexual assault, and her body had apparently been washed after she was killed. Both major papers included descriptions of the man carrying the box and photos of the police sketch of the suspect alongside photos of Barbara Jean.

By the afternoon of July 13, flyers of the sketch were being distributed all over Northeast Philadelphia and shown on local TV news. At rush hour, a dozen police officers joined the eight detectives canvassing the neighborhood with pictures of Barbara Jean and of the sketch. A detective told the *Inquirer* it was the kind of case every cop would work for free.[6]

Rumors spread: it was a serial killer; John Fahy got too angry and hit her too hard; Sarge Green killed her to get back at John because John owed him drug money; a black van had pulled up to the car dealership on the corner and someone inside asked if he could dump a box there, but an employee told him no and he drove off. Someone else saw someone drag a box from a black van on St. Vincent Street, near where the body was found.[7]

By the evening of July 14, police had passed out nearly a thousand flyers of the sketch and received more than two hundred tips. A woman called to say that on the twelfth she was parked on St. Vincent Street behind a male in a station wagon; he was about five feet eight, medium build, wearing a white T-shirt and blue jeans and struggling with a TV box, he looked nervous, and she thought he was stealing the TV—and then she hung up. Several people called about a man named Vinnie who owned a Monte Carlo. A woman called with the license number of a black van, driven by a man who matched the sketch, that she'd seen on July 11 and again after the murder. Another caller had seen a black van with tinted back windows and a white and red license plate (maybe Virginia?) in the area of St. Vincent Street at about five or five thirty on the afternoon of the murder.

On the fifteenth the *Daily News* offered a $4,000 reward.

For most people on the block, including the Fahys, one thing seemed sure: if a stranger had come into the neighborhood and killed Barbara Jean, he had something to do with the bikers at 7244 Rutland. There'd been a murder there two years earlier, and now the biker parties, the fights and drugs . . .

As detectives and reporters swirled through the Fahys' neighborhood in the days after the murder, Sharon and John stayed in a fog with the help of a friendly nurse, who gave them Ativan.[8]

The police might have cleared John as a suspect, but he knew what people were saying. Sometime after the murder he went home to pick up clothes and decided to get a haircut. In the barbershop near his house, news about the murder came on TV and the barber said, "Oh, they're gonna get the stepfather for that. You know he did it."

John started crying and went outside. The barber came out to apologize; John had been there many times and had even brought Barbara Jean in, the barber just hadn't remembered.

And in his own mind, it was simple—he'd been watching her; he'd let her down. And she was *dead*.

More than five hundred people came to Barbara Jean's viewing on Friday, July 15, at St. Martin of Tours, the church where the Fahys had been married and Barbara Jean had been baptized. Barbara Jean was laid out in white, lying in a small white coffin surrounded by flowers, including a heart made of pink carnations.

"There is a cloud of confusion, a cloud of darkness," the priest said in his homily.[9]

John and Sharon sat in a daze beside the altar, greeting the line of people, which stretched to the rear of the church. God didn't mean much to them just then—if he existed he would've protected Barbara Jean, maybe made John go outside to look for her a few minutes earlier. If he existed they didn't want anything to do with him.

———————

As of July 20, police had received more than four hundred tips: A deliveryman reported that in the middle of all the police activity at the Fahys' house on the night of the murder he'd delivered a pizza to a man a few doors away who looked just like the sketch. A three-page letter, with supporting astrology charts, suggested the murder may have been committed for satanic reasons. Another letter described a man in a black van eyeing the writer's daughter, who was three but looked five, at around 1:30 PM on July 12. A woman who turned out to have a long history of mental illness claimed to have seen Barbara Jean in a department store that afternoon with a man who matched the sketch; a few minutes later, she said, she walked by a black van on the street and heard the sounds of someone being beaten inside. A man who lived just down the street looked exactly like the sketch; a security guard at Temple University looked like the sketch, had a dark blue or black van, and dyed his hair shortly after the murder. A bus driver had snapped at a caller's five-year-old daughter and made an obscene gesture.

The police put ten or twelve officers in the field every day, following up every tip, no matter how far-fetched,[10] hoping to ease fears and talk to as many people as possible who'd seen something the day of the murder. Media pressure to solve the case was building: the man with the box had been right there on a busy street in the middle of rush hour without trying to disguise himself, had been seen by many people, and had just disappeared.

A *Daily News* article that ran under the headline YOU WONDER IF IT'S HIM: FEAR HAUNTS NEIGHBORHOOD IN WAKE OF KILLING described Rutland Street as a ghost town with empty kiddie pools and abandoned front stoops. A second article spread the fear city-wide: Barbara Jean was one of five children killed in Philadelphia between July 11 and July 19, and a police officer was quoted as saying he'd never seen so much violence against children in eighteen years on the force.

For the police, it was a high-profile case of the worst kind, the kind that scared parents in their homes and, therefore, politicians in their offices: voters who feel unsafe may think their leaders soft, and soft leaders do not win reelection.

Then a break: on July 21 police connected the serial number on the TV box to a family living at 7208 Rutland Street, about half a block south from the Fahys, near the corner of Rutland and St. Vincent on the Greens' side of the street. The house belonged to Joseph Ward, who lived there with his wife, elderly mother, and younger son. The box was for a thirteen-inch Hitachi color TV that Joseph's older son had bought four years earlier, and though he'd moved out a few months earlier he'd kept the box stored in his parents' basement.[11]

Joseph and his wife had been in Atlantic City the afternoon of the murder and his mother in Florida, leaving his younger son, Wesley, a college student, alone in the house. It seemed suspicious that Wesley had decided to put a long-stored box out for trash collection the very afternoon of the murder, after the trash had already been picked up.

Reporters, TV cameramen, and dozens of neighbors stood outside 7208 Rutland Street on July 21 as police "tore it apart."[12] Some in the crowd were relieved the killer had finally been caught; others were skeptical. Ward's neighbors couldn't believe he would do something like that and said he didn't look anything like the sketch.

Detectives took Wesley Ward down to the Roundhouse to interview and photograph him. Ward told police he had been at class on the day of the murder, a claim they couldn't confirm because the professor hadn't kept good attendance records. They took samples of what looked like blood from the basement where the box had been stored but lacked hard evidence linking Ward to the crime and let him go at 7:00 PM.[13]

Another possible break came on August 1 when David Schectman identified Raymond Sheehan, a suspect in the recent rape and murder of a ten-year-old girl not far from Rutland Street, as the man who'd carried the box.[14] Police took Sheehan's fingerprints to test against the fingerprint found on the TV box, but there was no match.

The most promising suspect seemed to be Ross Felice, a twenty-three-year-old who lived a couple blocks from where the box was left. He'd come to the attention of Jonathan Jones, a homicide detective who lived in the neighborhood, on the night of the murder by going up and down Rutland Street until 10:00 PM, asking too many questions about what detectives knew, like he *wanted* to be seen. Even after the police left, he kept going.[15] Then, the next day, police started getting phone calls telling them Felice looked exactly like the sketch.

Two of the witnesses from St. Vincent Street, Chris Kochan and Lorraine Schectman, would eventually pick Felice as the man who'd carried the box, but in August, David Schectman identified Felice's brother, Michael.[16] Police searched the apartment the Felice brothers shared with their mother and took samples that looked like blood from a rug, a shower curtain, and a few other places. They interviewed Ross Felice twice and even followed him for six months; the detectives working the case wanted him charged, but the prosecutors said they didn't have enough evidence.

Nothing taken from either Felice's apartment or the Ward home was linked to the crime; trash bags from Wesley Ward's house and from the Felice apartment were not similar to the bag found wrapped around Barbara Jean. The fingerprint on the TV box did not match Ward or either Felice brother, and a palm print taken from the box had no identification value.[17]

Sharon spent a lot of time in Barbara Jean's room, which she and John left just as it was, a Cabbage Patch doll tucked into bed. Sharon could smell her daughter there.[18] They left Barbara Jean's playroom untouched, too, the toy kitchen and the computerized picture on the door of Barbara Jean over the words "I Love My Daddy!" Even if it was hard to see her things, Sharon wanted to remember her daughter playing there.[19]

It was good to be back with Barbara Jean's things, but being home was also horrible; they felt isolated in the neighborhood, and nobody talked to them. Maybe no one knew what to say or maybe they thought John did it, but Kathleen Ritterson was the only one who knocked on the door sometimes to see how they were doing. Not that they wanted to talk to their neighbors. They didn't trust anybody.

The sketch of the killer was up everywhere, more than three thousand in the windows of Laundromats, convenience stores, hair salons, and other businesses around Northeast Philadelphia. John helped distribute the flyer, but he and Sharon hated seeing the face.[20] And the horror wasn't just seeing the sketch, it was seeing men who looked like it. They *knew* they were living in sight of the murderer, so everybody was a suspect. Everybody. Someone fidgeting on the bus would cause Sharon to wonder why and think, *Oh God, he looks like the sketch* and follow him home. Once she asked John to come, to see if he thought so, too. John went to bars, got drunk, and picked fights with people who reminded him of the sketch. Detectives kept telling him Ross Felice was the killer,[21] so John put out the word he was looking for Felice; once he even saw Felice, who ran away.

One little girl's mother who was putting together a memorial plaque for Barbara Jean at a local community center asked Sharon for some pictures, so she and her sister Barb took some over. The woman's husband was drunk and took them to his basement to show them where he'd ripped up some carpet and done some work on the storage area beneath the stairs. *Why was he redoing the carpet in his basement just then, and why was he insisting they see it?* Sharon wondered. She brought it up with John, and together they remembered a day that spring when that little girl had been at their house playing with Barbara Jean and when John went upstairs to ask if they wanted mac and cheese and hot dogs for supper, the little girl had backed up against a wall like she was scared. Maybe her father had sexually abused her, they thought. Everything out of the ordinary seemed sinister; everyone around them was a suspect.

The Fahys still thought the murderer had something to do with 7244 Rutland. There was no way Barbara Jean would have walked off with a stranger without a fight, but she might have followed someone from that house if she knew him from playing with Charliebird.[22] With so many people coming and going from that house, Barbara Jean could've known someone they didn't.

In mid-August new flyers offering a $10,000 reward raised by a local businessman went up around the neighborhood. By then police had gotten more than a thousand tips. Detective Frank Miller, on the case from the first night, skipped his summer vacation and worked on his days off.

"We have significant pieces of the puzzle," the head of the Philadelphia Police Department's homicide division told a reporter. "The trail of that box is very important."[23] He also addressed the woman who'd called police on July 14 and described the man struggling with a TV box in a car on St. Vincent Street—since the line had gone dead at that point, the police needed the woman to call back. She never did.[24]

Sharon went back to work at the end of August. Her employers at the brokerage firm paid her for the time she missed. John got a letter from a man at an employment agency who'd read about Barbara Jean and wanted to help him get a job. Soon he was working at a metal shop.

At 5:45 AM one day, just after John left for his new job, the phone rang. Sharon answered it.

"I know who killed your daughter," a deep, male voice said.

"Hello?" Sharon said.

"I know who killed your daughter. Can we get together and talk about it?" the voice asked.

Sharon thought she was going to have a heart attack.[25] She hung up and took the phone off the hook until 6:30 AM, when John was supposed to call. She talked to her mother briefly, and then a few minutes later the phone rang.

"I want—" the voice started.

Sharon slammed the phone down.

The Fahys had a trace put on their line, and the next evening the man called again, asking Sharon obscene questions. A few days later a call came at 6:10 AM, even more obscene. Two more came that morning; Sharon wasn't terrified anymore, she was furious. One morning fourteen calls came between three forty and eight thirty.[26]

Police tracked the calls to a part-time cab driver with two prior convictions for making obscene phone calls.[27] John went to his house, thinking he would take care of the man himself, but when he got there it was obvious the guy was just a big, dumb loser who didn't know anything about the case. John went home.[28] Police arrested the man, who indeed knew nothing about the murder. He'd gotten the Fahys' number out of the phone book.[29]

John's new job didn't work out. He was grateful for the opportunity but felt like everyone knew how he'd gotten there and was looking at him all the time.

———————

On September 8, two local organizations held a child safety forum at a local church. Barbara Jean was the second child murder victim in a year and a half in the neighborhood; the first was Heather Coffin, the ten-year-old who'd been raped and strangled in her bedroom in February 1987. Raymond Sheehan, a suspect in that case, was one of the men David Schectman had identified as the man carrying the TV box.

Twenty-five people showed up to the safety meeting, along with five police officers and an assistant district attorney.

"We have Barbara Jean picked up off the street in broad daylight," an audience member said. "We have Heather Coffin killed in her own home at night. The horror is, these kids are dead. Does anybody have anything encouraging to tell us? What do we do?"

"Keep your child secure," an officer from the Philadelphia sex crimes unit told the audience. "Keep your child supervised. Keep your house supervised. And keep your fingers crossed."[30]

In other words: We have no idea what to tell you.

In October the *Inquirer* ran a story featuring Barbara Jean and Heather Coffin. It included pictures of both little girls, the TV box on St. Vincent Street, and the sketch of the man seen carrying the box.[31]

November came. Sharon just couldn't understand why it was so hard to find the killer. It was driving her crazy; days went by and nothing was different.[32]

One of the detectives on the case flew to Los Angeles to tape a segment of *Unsolved Mysteries*, a new TV program designed to generate fresh information about difficult cases. The segment on Barbara Jean aired on November 16, with photos of her supplied by John and Sharon.

"Every parent's worst nightmare is the loss of a child to a violent stranger," the host, Robert Stack, said while introducing the segment, which included details of the day of the murder, a shot of the police sketch, and information about the $10,000 reward.

Hundreds of tips came in. None led to anything.

The evening after the *Unsolved Mysteries* segment aired, John was watching TV in his living room when he heard cursing and punching outside. Sharon, upstairs, didn't care what happened to anybody on that block and called to John to leave it alone. But John opened the door and saw Sarge Green beating somebody across lawns and down Rutland Street; the guy looked like a teenager, and Sarge, this big biker, was pounding him. They fell to the ground and Sarge kept pounding him.

John thought the size difference was too much. He called 911 and went out to break up the fight. By then it was over and Sarge went back in his house.

The other guy came toward John and asked, "Can I come in?"

It was Walter Ogrod, but John didn't know him other than that he was one of the people who lived with the Greens. John pointed to a brick wall a couple of houses away, told him to sit there, that the police were on the way, and went inside.

When the police came Sarge was arrested and charged with aggravated assault. The police report noted that Sarge "did punch [Ogrod] numerous times about the head, throw him down a staircase, then knock him to the ground, kicking him about the head and body." Ogrod was taken to the hospital "for possible fractured orbital socket, concussion, facial lacerations, and human bite."[33]

The next time John saw Sarge, he asked what the fight was about.

"You don't wanna know," Sarge told him. "It's none of your business."[34]

So the fall went. Everyone on Rutland Street felt suspicious and isolated, John and Sharon most of all.

During the last week of November, two detectives were assigned to watch Ross Felice.[35] On the afternoon of January 13, 1989, they brought David Schectman to a school gym where Felice liked to play basketball. When Felice saw Schectman and the detective, he put a hand up to hide his face and walked quickly away. Schectman said Felice was the man he'd seen carrying the box,[36] but it was his third ID after Felice's brother and Raymond Sheehan.

In June detectives tried again. Felice was due in court for jury duty, so they brought Lorraine Schectman in her wheelchair to the hallway outside the courtroom and asked her to tell them if "anything interesting" happened. When Felice came out and saw the detectives and Lorraine, he put his head down, turned away from them, and went back in. He came out again, went back in again; through a window a detective saw him pacing. He came out again and got in line for the water fountain, trying to shield himself behind a larger man.

"The guy that keeps looking at me, I think that's him," Lorraine said. She leaned over the arm of her wheelchair to study Felice for a minute and told the detective, "That's him."[37]

Both identifications by the Schectmans have a big problem: Felice knew he was being followed and knew he was a suspect, so if he acted strangely when the Schectmans saw him it might well have been because he knew what was happening. Mrs. Schectman may have even picked Felice because he kept looking at her.

Detectives wanted to arrest Felice, but they didn't have enough.

––––––––––––

As weeks passed, John and Sharon would hear on the news that Barbara Jean's case was going cold. John didn't wait to hear from detectives. He called them every day, and they told him there was a guy down the block (Felice) who matched the sketch. What about the Greens' house? John would ask. No, don't worry, we're following this guy from down the street—he looks exactly like the sketch, the detectives would say.[38]

John got a job and went to AA meetings sometimes but couldn't quit drinking. Grief split him from Sharon as his drinking and temper got worse. He felt failures building up on him: he knew he wasn't helping his wife, knew he couldn't, knew he was a loser who let his daughter get killed, couldn't even keep a job, couldn't do anything. Just a loser. He drank more, dousing the pain, then trying to kill it. Then he was drunk 24/7 and feeling like shit for being drunk and feeling his family looking at him like he was shit because he was drunk, and the pain was still there anyway. It just blended; everything got worse and worse.[39]

After a while Sharon didn't even argue with him anymore when he came in at 4:00 AM. She'd just think, *There he is, drunk again.* She leaned on her friends and family and worked as much overtime as she could. She didn't want to be around kids. A close friend at whose wedding Barbara Jean was supposed to have been the flower girl got pregnant, but it was hard for Sharon to be around her; she was glad for her friend but jealous about the baby.

In the fall of 1989, the Greens and everyone else who lived in 7244 Rutland moved out. The Fahys again begged police to search the house; once those people moved, valuable evidence could be lost. But the detectives didn't want to hear it. John thought about searching the abandoned house himself for any of Barbara Jean's clothes. But he figured if he did find anything, the police would say he had the evidence and pin the murder on him.

By March 1990, 7244 Rutland had become a haven for squatters, the windows broken out, living room walls covered with graffiti, beer bottles and trash scattered on the floor. The city sent a crew to clean the house out and seal it with sheet metal, plywood, and cinder blocks.

John saw the clean and seal crew and called detectives again.

"You gotta get over here," he said. "They're cleaning that house out. If somebody in that house did it, there's evidence in that house and it's gonna be gone."

"John, it was [Felice]," a detective told him. "We're gonna get the evidence."

It's nuts, John thought. *They're just boarding it up, don't want to hear nothing, just feed us enough information to keep us quiet. They didn't want to listen. Did not want to listen.*

Detectives were convinced that people with potentially crucial information about the case weren't helping them, so in 1990, Assistant District Attorney Joseph Casey led a grand jury inquiry into Ross Felice and Wesley Ward. The grand jury could force reluctant witnesses to testify and offered John and Sharon hope. The jury did convene, but no indictments resulted.[40]

It was hard for the Fahys to see Barbara Jean's case mentioned on a list of unsolved crimes in a June 1990 *Daily News* article, along with the observation that as each year passed, the chances of solving the old cases got slimmer.[41] But they weren't letting the case go cold. John continued to call detectives frequently, asking for updates.

Sharon was determined that whoever killed Barbara Jean wouldn't ruin her life any more than he already had; she thought she and John would get through it if she just worked and worked. She told John many times he couldn't let the killer ruin his life, too, but she could see the murder was killing him.

For a couple of years John and Sharon felt they were living in the same house without really being together but tried to hold it together. In 1991 they moved out of Rutland Street and in with her sister, Barb, who'd separated from her husband. John lost his latest construction job just before Christmas and didn't tell Sharon for a week. When she found out, she'd had enough. He'd been trying AA meetings off and on for eleven years and was only getting worse; he'd stop for a couple weeks only to drink again whenever he was around liquor. She loved him but couldn't do it anymore and told him, "Go."

John moved in with his mom, but she was almost eighty and couldn't deal with him the way he was—out of work, drinking. Finally she told him, "You're not doing this to me; you're not staying with me."

John didn't know what he was supposed to do. Sharon didn't want him anymore, his friends didn't want him around, even his mom didn't. Nowhere to go, not working, he was feeling suicidal, even homicidal. He wanted to take his anger out on somebody, anybody—someone needed to pay for what happened to Barbara Jean.[42]

5

DETECTIVE PERFECT

IN FEBRUARY 1992, NOT LONG after John and Sharon split up, John heard Barbara Jean's case had been transferred to new detectives again, so he called them.

"Well, you're the new guys," he said. "When do you want to meet?"

"Come on down tonight," the detective said.

John and Sharon, though separated, went to the Roundhouse together.

The new detectives on the case were Marty Devlin and Paul Worrell, part of the Special Investigations Unit (SIU) of Philadelphia homicide. Marty Devlin was known as one of the smartest and hardest-working detectives in Philadelphia. He was short and cocky and wore Ray-Bans, loud Hawaiian-style shirts, and a mustache. He had twenty-seven years of experience, five in homicide, and after all those years as a cop knew, as a fellow detective put it, "as much about character and personality as any good shrink."[1] Devlin didn't give up on a case until his superiors forced him, and interrogations were his specialty; he could convince anybody, even the worst murderer, that he was his best friend, his only hope, and that he should tell him what happened. Devlin's intelligence, hard work, and high clearance rate—95 percent, one of the best rates on the force[2]—had earned him the nicknames "the Golden Marty"[3] and "Detective Perfect."[4]

A detective's clearance rate is the most important number by which he or she will be judged. Because homicide detectives "catch" their new cases in turn (when a new homicide comes in, the next detective up takes it), the law of averages says that sometimes you get a "dunker" or "smoking gun"—a killer standing over a body with a gun—and other times you get a "whodunit" with no witnesses and no evidence, impossible to clear. Statistically this should even out over time, so Devlin's unusually high clearance rate sticks out.

One of Devlin's most controversial cases—most successful, from his point of view—was still recent when he was assigned to Barbara Jean's murder. On the night of April 9, 1990, according to five eyewitnesses, Roy Shephard, a worker at Jacko's Steak Shop in North Philadelphia, shot another worker named Christian Bradley in the face and then shot himself in the head. Another coworker, panicking, picked the gun up and threw it out a window. But Devlin thought the disposal of the gun and the location of Shephard's wound on the left side of his head (as opposed to the right side, where right-handed people usually shoot themselves) indicated that something was going on, so he brought the eyewitnesses in to the Roundhouse for individual interviews, several of which went through the night. By the time Devlin was through, four of the eyewitnesses—including two teenaged girls whose interviews started at 1:15 and 1:20 AM—had changed their story: they now said that after Shephard shot Bradley he dropped the gun and the owner of the shop, Jack Combs, came in from the kitchen, picked the gun up, and shot Shephard. One eyewitness refused to change his story, and one fifteen-year-old whose interview had started after 1:00 AM retracted her statement immediately, begging Devlin to accept that the shootings had been a murder-suicide. But Devlin used the new version of events he'd gotten from the four witnesses, and Jack Combs was convicted and sentenced to life in prison.[5]

That case was a kind of Ultimate Devlin: applying pressure in all forms, friendly, helpful, aggressive; going all night, getting the statements he wanted and the information he needed. More recently, in October 1991, just a few months before taking over Barbara Jean's case, Devlin had solved the rape and murder of a seventy-seven-year-old woman by getting the suspect to confess. The alleged killer, Anthony Wright, a twenty-year-old with a seventh-grade education, recanted his confession soon after, but would be convicted of the murder in 1993 only to be exonerated by DNA testing and freed in 2016.[6]

Devlin's partner, Paul Worrell, had twenty years on the force, six in homicide. He was tall, soft-spoken, and solid, wore gray suits and played the good cop to Devlin's bad cop when they worked an interrogation that way.

The two men, both Philadelphia natives, were new to the SIU and new partners when they were assigned Barbara Jean's case in early 1992 but had known each other for more than fifteen years.[7] They'd first met as young cops in the mid-1970s[8] and had both come of age in a police department famous, under Chief and later Mayor Frank Rizzo, for its brutality and coercive techniques. Rizzo had risen through the ranks of the police department to become chief in 1967. One defense lawyer describes Rizzo's standing instructions to police at the time as "Get the confession by any and all means, and I'll back you if you go over the line," and in 1977 the *Philadelphia Inquirer* won a Pulitzer for a series of stories about dozens of suspects being threatened with pistols or beaten to force confessions from them. Some suspects had been taken from the Roundhouse to the emergency room for broken jaws or fractured skulls before being taken back to booking.[9]

When the murder rate in Philadelphia skyrocketed in the late 1980s due to a sharp rise in the use of crack cocaine and the violence that came with it, pressure on the police department to clear cases and bring the murder rate down intensified. As Paul Solotaroff wrote in a *Rolling Stone* article in 2015 about the Anthony Wright case, "For [cops] weaned on Rizzo's bruised-knuckles ethos, this meant doubling down on the strong-arm stuff, and no worries if an innocent kid got swept up in the net. The jails, after all, were full of such cases. What did one more come to, for the greater good?"[10]

Devlin and Worrell's unit, the SIU, had been started informally in the late 1970s and officially founded in 1980 to work high-profile and cold cases like Barbara Jean's that took more time and attention than homicide detectives taking cases in their regular turn could provide.

"It's very important to solve a murder within the first hours," a lieutenant who ran the SIU in the early 1990s explained to the *Philadelphia City Paper* in 1994. "You can never recreate a crime scene. Witnesses forget what they saw or become hard to find. That's why it is so important to solve crimes right away, and that takes a lot of work. As the number of killings increased, it became harder to work on the older ones or those that take more time."[11]

Known as the "Wacker Squad" because it attracted detectives with "wacky" personalities, the SIU was successful, solving nearly four hundred murders in a four-year stretch in the late '80s and early '90s, making Philadelphia Homicide among the best in the country during that period.[12] Devlin's cockiness was evident around the time of Walter's case when he posed for a "Wacker Squad" profile in a local paper, walking down the street wearing his Hawaiian shirt and sunglasses, a shotgun resting on his hip.

When Devlin and Worrell took over Barbara Jean's case in early 1992, they thought the original detectives had been too fixated on the sketch, too interested in Ross Felice. Barbara Jean had to have been killed nearby by someone she knew, they thought, so they would focus on her block unless something convinced them the murder happened somewhere else.[13] They wanted to know who lived nearby: Was there somone on the block Barbara Jean had been comfortable with? Were there any trouble houses on the block?

It had been almost four years since the murder, so new evidence in the case was unlikely. In order to solve it, they needed a confession.

Cue Detective Devlin.

———————

John and Sharon arrived at the Roundhouse in the evening of a cold day at the end of February, expecting to meet the new detectives and get an update on the case. Instead, they were put in separate interview rooms and interrogated, just as they had been on the night of the murder.

Detective Devlin told Sharon she knew John killed Barbara Jean and was covering for him. She said no. Devlin insisted.

"Listen to me," Sharon fumed. "I am not even with this man right now. If I thought he killed my daughter, I'd kill him. He'd be dead. Get that through your head: I'm not protecting him for anything. I would not protect him."

"You're protecting him," Devlin insisted.

"You don't understand," Sharon said. "I would not protect somebody that did that, I don't care who he is. There's no way."

Devlin and Worrell pressured her for hours without any luck.

Sharon couldn't believe it.

"You gotta be kidding," she told them. "This is almost four years down the line here, and you're gonna tell me we're back to this?"

With John, Devlin and Worrell started friendly, taking down his information, listening to him describe the day of the murder. They left the room for a while, and when they came back, Devlin said, "Here's the problem. You changed your statement [from 1988]. You're a fucking liar. You fucking did this."

"No way," John said.

"You're lying to us now, just like you were lying to us then."

John couldn't believe it.

"You listen to me, you fucking assholes," he said. "You go get the fucking file, you bring it in here, and you show me where

I changed my fucking statement. That was the worst day of my life. I know what the fuck happened on my end. I ain't changed nothing."

Devlin insisted John was lying, but it was a bluff; John's story was the same.

"I can't believe we're four years in and this is where we're at again," John told Devlin. "You're pointing the finger at me? Fuck you. You ain't pinning shit on me 'cause it's the easy fucking way out for you."

Devlin and Worrell worked back and forth between the Fahys, sometimes leaving one alone for a while to work together on the other one, sometimes splitting up to speak with them individually. But neither John nor Sharon would change their story, so after several hours Devlin let them go.

"We're getting a lawyer," Sharon told John as they left the building. "Because if they think they're just gonna wrap this up in a neat little bow and pretend that you did it after all this time, they're crazy."[14]

The Fahys' lawyer called the detectives and told them that from now on they wouldn't talk without him present. A couple days later the detectives asked for a meeting and explained to John and Sharon that the tough interview was part of starting an investigation from scratch, going over every detail, reinvestigating every possibility. That's how they did these things. But they'd known as soon as Sharon and John left that John had nothing to do with the murder. No hard feelings?

John and Sharon hated Devlin but didn't care about that. The way John saw it was, *Look, you don't know me, I don't know you, I don't care how you treat me—just find whoever killed Barbara Jean. Just find him.*

No hard feelings, the Fahys agreed, but they were angry that after four years the police were back at square one: no leads, no information, nothing. Sharon told the detectives again to look at 7244 Rutland and at the house down the block where, a few days after the murder, the drunk father had shown them where he'd ripped out the carpet in his basement.

After their new interrogations by Devlin and Worrell, the Fahys remained separated. John went through an outpatient rehab program and on March 30, their anniversary, called Sharon to tell her he'd been sober forty days. Sharon was torn but felt he'd start drinking again if she gave in.

"Just leave me alone," she said. It was the hardest thing to do. She hung up the phone and cried at her desk at work.

John went to a bar and got drunk. When he sobered up he knew he had to go to an inpatient clinic. He called Sharon to make sure his insurance was in place, then went back to his AA group and told them he needed to go away. They sent him to a rehab place, a cross between hospital and camp. During detox John roomed with a religious former cop who kept telling him that if he wanted the police to find the killer, if he wanted to heal himself, he needed to get on his knees and pray. For days the guy just annoyed John, but eventually he decided to try it. He got on his knees and prayed. It was April 5, 1992.

6

WALT

AFTER INTERROGATING THE FAHYS, Devlin and Worrell claimed later, they considered the neighborhood. The Fahys had urged them to look at anyone who'd been living at 7244 Rutland, now boarded up by the city after being used as a drug flophouse. From neighbors they'd heard rumors that Sarge Green, one of the inhabitants, had killed Barbara Jean because John Fahy owed him money for drugs.[1] And the detectives knew 7244 as a trouble house because in 1986, two years before Barbara Jean's murder, Maureen Dunne, the sixteen-year-old daughter of a fellow detective, had been murdered in the basement. One of their colleagues in the small SIU office, Detective Edward Rocks, had overseen the taking of the crime scene photos in the Dunne murder and had worked as well on Barbara Jean's murder in 1988.

If Devlin and Worrell looked at the Dunne murder file, they would have read about Walter Ogrod, the young man who lived with the Greens at 7244, who'd been a key witness in that case. Later, this would become an important point in the case against Ogrod, but Devlin and Worrell swore they never did.

Devlin and Worrell did hear about Ogrod from some of his neighbors, who called him "Crazy Walter" and described him as strange, "off"; he talked funny, kept to himself, was "retarded" or something.[2]

Though the detectives would later deny that they considered Ogrod a suspect, he did fit several of their criteria for a suspect: he was weird, his house was nearby and was a trouble house, and Barbara Jean would've felt comfortable there because of her friendship with the Green children. Later, Devlin and Worrell would admit only that when they realized Ogrod had only ever been spoken to once about Barbara Jean, the quick interview at his door the day after the murder, they decided they should speak to him again.

———

Walter Ogrod was born February 3, 1965, at St. Vincent's orphanage in Philadelphia. His father was sixteen, his mother fourteen; she left the facility a month later. Walter was adopted at three months old by Walter and Olga Ogrod. Walter Sr. (they had different middle names, but I'll use "Jr." and "Sr." for clarity) was forty-two, a World War II veteran who'd participated in the liberation of a concentration camp and worked as a draftsman, designing chemical plants and refineries. Olga was thirty-six, a secretary in a furniture shop and a dressmaker and artist. They'd met at a dance at the Ukrainian club on Franklin Avenue in the early 1950s and after getting married bought the tiny row house at 7244 Rutland Street. Art and design were Olga's passions; twice she designed the first-prize-winning bonnet for the annual Atlantic City Easter Parade, and at one point a local department store was interested in some of her dress designs. But Walter Sr. didn't want his wife going into business, belittled her frequently, and, she told her brother, beat her. Olga's family felt her creativity threatened him. She was also schizophrenic and was hospitalized in 1954 after cutting her wrists.

The Ogrods had tried for years to have a baby before deciding to adopt, and for a time Walter Jr.'s arrival seemed to improve the marriage. He was the star of the family, a cheerful baby who loved to hug.[3] Two years later the couple adopted another infant, Gregory. But as the boys grew, the marriage disintegrated. According to what Olga told her family, if Walter Sr. saw another woman he found attractive, he would point out some way Olga should try to be more like her. Olga had plastic surgery on her nose to try to please him. He hated that she was an artist and mocked her in front of the children. One day when the boys were about five and three, she was teaching them to paint and he went into a rage, yelling that he didn't want them learning that art garbage and stomping his foot through the table on which they were working. When the boys misbehaved, she said, he beat them, sometimes with a slat from a wood floor.

Olga's stories to her family became even more ominous. She described Walter Sr. as hyperreligious, lighting white candles all over the house, getting on his knees and praying for hours, telling Olga she would burn in hell if she left him. The end finally came in 1970 when, she said, in a rage, he pulled a gun. Olga took the kids and moved, and found work taking shopper surveys at a nearby mall. Walter Sr. agreed to pay thirty-five dollars a week in child support but did so only sporadically. Olga couldn't afford a babysitter, so on days she couldn't be home to meet her boys after school they had to wait on the front porch—rain, cold, or snow, they were forbidden to leave the stoop. Olga got much of their food from a local church, and the family went to bed hungry many nights. One year she pawned her wedding ring to buy coats for the boys. She argued bitterly with Walter Sr. about who owned the house on Rutland Street, claiming she'd contributed most of the down payment. This became one of the fixations of her life, and as her mental state worsened, she filed multiple lawsuits.

Walter Jr. and Greg dressed in worn-out clothes, didn't have bikes, and were outcasts in their new neighborhood, not invited to join the neighborhood kids in their games.[4] It didn't help that Walter Jr.'s black hair always seemed greasy, he had a speech impediment, and he seemed mentally slow and clumsy. And he behaved strangely—lying on the ground and spinning around in circles or making guttural noises. He didn't like to be touched and would pull away when his brother tried to hug him. If he fixated on something, he couldn't let it go. If the ice cream truck came and Olga had no money, Greg, two years younger, would understand but Walter Jr. would scream "I want ice cream!" over and over, crying.

The neighborhood kids thought Olga was strange, too. They'd see her, tiny and frail, dressed all in black, walking quickly from her apartment to the bus stop, never stopping to talk. They thought she was a ghost. John Fahy was one of the neighborhood children who remembered her drawing while riding the bus, how strange that seemed.[5]

Walter Jr. and Greg went to Catholic school for a few years and then to public school when their father stopped paying the tuition. Walter lived in a world of perpetual self-defense, consistently picked on at school, where he got in fights to defend himself, and physically and emotionally abused by his mother at home. She'd hit him, throw him into walls, tell him that he was nuts like his father and that she should have him put away. She took him to doctor after doctor; she'd yank him out of school, telling him he couldn't learn, then put him in another school, then take him out again for long stretches.[6]

Sometimes Olga took the boys to an artists' colony where she went to sell her drawings. As they got older her artwork became increasingly bizarre—she painted tortured faces and affixed human hair, eyelashes, and fingernails to her canvases. She increasingly focused her delusions and paranoia on Walter Jr., saying he was trying to kill her. Sometimes she'd lead him to a table, point to a lamp, and convince him it didn't exist.

One friend of Walter's, William Daka, was a few years older and saw Walter getting picked on every day, called names, teased, and beaten up. William thought Walter was too easy a target, too slow and odd and unable to fit in, so he began to intervene. Otherwise, he thought, Walter would've been beaten up every day.[7]

At home Walter acted out, kicking and screaming, knocking holes in walls, smashing in a door. Sometimes when Olga couldn't control him, Greg would watch her take an eyedropper and put a few drops of something in Walter Jr.'s orange juice. Walter Jr. would calm down. Greg stopped drinking orange juice. Other times Olga would call her brother John, who, frustrated at being woken up in the middle of the night again, would arrive to a familiar scene: Walter Jr., a big kid for his age, kicking and screaming, his speech impediment giving the screaming a harrowing quality. John would wrestle him to the ground and sit on him until he calmed down, sometimes spanking him with an old fraternity paddle. Once he hit Walter Jr. with a belt and the buckle caught Walter Jr.'s eye.[8]

Walter Jr.'s behavioral problems weren't as bad at his father's house; he got along well with his father, who dressed his boys in nice clothes, though he made them change back into their old clothes before returning to their mother's. And Walter was still picked on by neighborhood kids. He fought sometimes, but fighting wasn't his first choice; he wanted to be liked and accepted and would do anything most kids said, believe anything they told him.[9]

Olga was deteriorating mentally, filing more lawsuits against her ex-husband and against anyone she thought wronged her, fighting back against a world she was sure was out to get her. In September 1975, she checked ten-year-old Walter Jr. into a psychiatric hospital, telling the staff he assaulted her. She claimed he kicked and bit her, but doctors observed that he had no aggressive interactions with anyone other than her, and noted Olga's psychiatric history. Walter Jr. stayed for a month, being treated with psychotherapy and medication, and was released with a diagnosis of hyperactivity, minimal brain damage (which seems to translate roughly to "something not quite right"), and adjustment reaction of childhood.[10]

On April 12, 1976, after another call from Olga, Uncle John wrestled Walter Jr. into a car and took him to the emergency room at Nazareth Hospital. Olga, screaming and waving her arms, told the staff her son was violent and abusive, had threatened to kill her, and she wanted him locked up in a state home forever. The doctor on duty observed that Walter Jr. seemed fine and suspected instead that Olga was mentally ill and had been abusing her son. He didn't want to send Walter Jr. home with her but couldn't get in touch with Walter Sr., so he checked the boy into the hospital.[11]

All Walter Jr. knew was he was supposed to see his grand-mother that night, then they were driving up to the emergency room and his mother was saying he needed to be admitted.[12] He ended up spending a month at Nazareth Hospital under the care of a psychiatrist, Dr. Peter Ganime. Ganime called Walter Jr.'s school and was told that the staff there had never seen any of the violent behaviors Olga described, but that they had seen bruises on him and suspected he was being abused. Ganime tried to meet with Olga, but her behavior was erratic; she missed a scheduled appointment, then called twice demanding to see him immedi-ately, and when he couldn't, refused to accept another appoint-ment time, then eventually accepted it, then didn't show up again. Ganime came to believe that Olga was paranoid schizophrenic and suffered from Munchausen syndrome by proxy, a condition that causes mentally ill parents to project their illnesses onto their children.[13] Essentially, Olga was seeing her own paranoid schizo-phrenic horrors in her son.

Dr. Ganime was able to meet with Walter Sr., who struck him as gentle and kind, showing no signs of the violent nature Olga described. Walter Sr. told him about Olga's 1954 suicide attempt, her endless lawsuits, her paranoia, his concern that she was driv-ing Walter Jr. into mental hospitals.[14] After the meeting Ganime was able to have a phone conversation with Olga, but when he recommended Walter live with his father she refused adamantly, saying she preferred to have him in a mental institution for the rest of his life.[15]

The doctors at Nazareth described Walter Jr. as showing no signs of psychosis—he was not mentally ill. They described him as being of limited intellectual capacity and diagnosed him with anxiety neurosis and what we now call attention deficit disorder. When it was time to leave Nazareth, Walter Jr. had to go in front of a judge to choose which parent to live with; he picked his father. When Olga visited the hospital and heard about this, she tried to attack Walter and had to be escorted from the building. Greg stayed with his mother, so the brothers did not spend a lot of time together after that.

Walter Jr. moved in with his father, who enrolled him in the Ashbourne School for learning disabled and troubled children. He got along well with staff, though they noted he was immature—if another student yelled, for example, Walter Jr. yelled, too.

As a teenager Walter Jr. was extremely self-conscious about his acne, his speech impediment, and his weight, refusing to ever wear shorts even on the hottest days because he thought his legs looked gross. He couldn't process other peoples' words very quickly, and when he tried to respond, his speech sounded funny. He couldn't get other students' jokes and they teased him for it, and for being fat and clumsy.[16] He had trouble understanding and expressing his own emotions and with perceiving others' emotional cues. He knew people thought he was a freak.[17] He would throw the other students' contempt back at them, responding to their taunts by telling them he was the smartest kid in class. (This trait is common enough in people with autism spectrum disorder to have become known as "Asperger's arrogance.")[18] The school staff told him to let them handle it when he was bullied, but he'd grown up defending himself, so that's what he did. He could throw other kids around or sit on them; he was once suspended for a day for pushing a kid who called him fat. In another fight he fractured his wrist and in two others got concussions.

Still, at Ashbourne Walter Jr. was industrious and made good academic progress; by age fifteen he was working at an eighth-grade level.

In the late 1970s, Walter Sr.'s diabetes and kidney problems worsened, and by the early '80s he was going blind. Walter Jr. got a learner's permit early so he could drive his father on errands and to dialysis appointments; he helped with his father's stomach drainage bag, drew his insulin for him, helped with injections, wrote checks and signed legal documents for him, and, as Walter Sr. worsened, explained everything to him. Walter Sr. retired in 1982 and lived on Social Security disability benefits.[19]

Walter Sr. worried what would become of his son after he died. At Walter Jr.'s appointments with Dr. Ganime, Walter Sr. would pull the doctor aside and tell him he was terrified that soon he wouldn't be able to care for his son and the boy would have to go live with Olga, who wouldn't be able to handle him, so he'd end up back in an orphanage. Walter Sr. said he'd been in an orphanage when he was a child and couldn't stand the thought of his son ending up in one. He knew he wouldn't live long and suffered from despondency, insomnia, anorexia, intense anxiety, and depression. Walter Jr., equally worried about his father, was anxious and depressed to the point of "desperation."[20]

In 1982, when Walter Jr. turned seventeen, a possible solution presented itself: the army. Walter Sr., the World War II veteran, hoped the army would teach Walter Jr. how to take care of himself. Dr. Ganime wrote a letter of support, and Walter Jr. enlisted and was sent to Fort Dix in New Jersey for basic training, scheduled to become a truck driver. On just his second day he was admitted to the base hospital with a bad reaction to an immunization. By the end of the second week, other recruits were treating him as their "errand boy" and he'd been in two fights with a recruit who bullied him.[21] He was sent back to the hospital, where he told the doctors that other recruits were scapegoating him and wanted to hurt him, that he couldn't concentrate and felt confused. He said he was "lonesome, wondering, don't know what to know."[22]

He spent six weeks in the hospital. The nurses were struck by his immaturity, noting that he butted into other peoples' conversations, mocked other patients, and liked to stick his face right next to someone who was trying to read the paper. The doctors diagnosed him with "Mixed Personality Disorder manifested by extreme dependency, immaturity . . . [an] intrinsic belief that he is different from other people, poor history of socialization, poor ability to handle stress." His "impairment for further military duty" was "marked" and for "social and industrial adaptability" was "definite."[23]

Walter Jr. was granted a medical discharge and went back to his father and grandmother. He did the one thing he could always do: work hard. He joined a lawn service company a friend from the Ashbourne School, Richie Hackett, had started, and by 1984 they had 120 landscaping and snow removal clients. They had leaf blowers, fifty-inch mowers, and a couple trucks they used as snow-plows in the winter.[24] Walter Jr. was the workhorse—most people thought Richie took advantage, letting him do the hard work.

In 1984 Walter Jr. got his certificate of completion from the Ashbourne School, graduating only two years late. He was proud he'd gotten the high score on an aptitude test two years in a row and had lost out on being class valedictorian by only one point. He worked long hours with the landscaping company that summer and took care of his father, who, as Walter described it to me later, looked like an AIDS patient. It hurt seeing his father like that, going blind, going in and out of the hospital for months at a time.

Walter Sr. died at fifty-eight in October 1984.

Walter Jr.'s anchor was gone; he was lost.

"I went for months—I kind of wasn't there," he remembered.[25]

Walter Jr. would have two periods of relative stability in his life. The first one had just ended, and it would be a long, difficult path to the next.

7

GREG AND MAUREEN

AFTER WALTER SR.'S DEATH IN 1984, Walter Jr. was on his own. He had a place to live—Walter Sr. left the house to his sister, Walter Jr.'s aunt, but on the condition that Walter Jr. could live there if he let his brother, Greg, move in. He also left Walter what must have seemed like a lot of money—$35,000. It was Walter Sr.'s dying effort to create a stable family for Walter.

Greg was seventeen, two years younger than Walter but socially confident and popular. He moved in and took charge of the house. A wild teenager, he now had a house and a pliant older brother who was always happy to spend money on beer. The house became a hangout for Greg's friends; he threw loud parties, cars came and went at all hours of the night, and the noise and loud music annoyed the neighbors. One night Greg, drunk, fired a rifle out of an upstairs window.

Walter tried to join the party sometimes, standing around, holding a beer; he wanted to approach girls but felt fat and ugly and knew he couldn't understand their social cues. He smoked pot a couple of times and tried cocaine, but the drugs didn't help; he didn't like the parties or the noise. The neighbors yelled at him about the noise because they knew him, not Greg, but he had to get up early in the morning for his landscaping job and worked long days, so all he wanted to do after work was watch the nice color TV he'd bought for the living room and go to bed early. But he couldn't even do that because there were always so many people hanging out, listening to music. Eventually Walter and Greg made a deal that he could watch one show on the color TV in the evening, then he'd close himself in his room and watch the rest of his shows on his little black and white.

Walter tried to make friends, buying beer for the house, loaning money or his Trans Am to pretty much anyone who asked, giving people rides. Greg took the Trans Am to get cigarettes once and didn't come back for three days. Walter was pissed but just asked him that he not do that again. Another time a friend took the Trans Am, got in an accident, and returned it to Walter to pay for the damage.

Greg didn't put in as much money for utilities and rent as he could have, which made Walter angry, but he made up the difference and his inheritance dissolved steadily, spent on food, utilities, gas, beer for the house, and loans that would never be paid back. In 1985 Greg and Richie, Walter's landscaping partner, talked him into buying a run-down, barely inhabitable bungalow in Wildwood on the Jersey Shore so they could have parties there, too. Richie was supposed to put up half the money, but the night before the sale he said he didn't have his half, that Walter should go ahead and put up all the money but keep Richie's name on the title, and he'd pay him back. Walter did. Richie never paid him back.

For a couple of summers Greg's parties moved to the Shore and Walter became more of an errand-boy, shuttling people down to the bungalow even if he had to return immediately to Philadelphia to go to work or, if he was at the Shore, driving round-trip to Philadelphia to pick someone up.

Walter wanted friends and spent his money to get them, but most of the people who hung out at Rutland Street or at the Shore and drank his beer and "borrowed" his money didn't even like him. People treated him like a personal servant and made fun of him; he never seemed to fully understand that he was the butt of their jokes. They remember him as "weak and simple," "a little retarded," a "big dumb kid," a "lamb among sharks" who would "do anything we asked him to."[1]

"I'm not proud of the way I treated Walter," Greg said much later. "It was just too easy to abuse him because he was so gullible. He'd believe anything he was told and do anything we asked of him. We all took advantage of Walter in every way imaginable, yet Walter seemed oblivious to it all."

But Walter wasn't oblivious. He knew then that he didn't have good social skills, that he had what he calls his own "problems," and that he didn't read people well. He knew people thought he was slow and weird, he just thought he could get them to like him. He was Charlie Brown, trying to kick the football over and over as Lucy pulls it away. He was easily manipulated, immature, and socially awkward; his psychiatric, school, and army records paint this picture of him. Today there's a much better chance a child like Walter would be recognized as developmentally disabled and treated appropriately, and Walter's record shows that when he got that kind of support he did fine. But when he didn't, he floundered.

For a while Walter kept his life steady in the midst of Greg's party scene, working hard to keep up the landscaping business. But in the summer of 1985 a strain of malevolence emerged when Walter's landscaping partner, Richie Hackett, started burglarizing houses with a couple of friends, calling it "nightshopping." He targeted a house near a landscaping client, got arrested, and spent time in jail and then in a work-release program, leaving Walter to run the business himself. When Richie finished the work-release program, he asked if he could stay with Walter, promising to pay rent and contribute to the bills, and Walter agreed. Richie never paid rent, though he did help with the bills occasionally. He also talked Walter into loaning him money for new equipment for the landscaping business at the same time he took out a bank loan to buy himself a new twenty-one-foot boat.

Greg and Richie had bitter arguments over who was taking advantage of Walter and grew to hate each other. Greg was dealing drugs, bringing a tougher crowd around the house. By late June 1986 Greg and one of his associates, Marvin Spence, were having frequent, nasty arguments about drug money Marvin owed Greg. Marvin broke into 7244 Rutland through the back door to the basement one night and stole some stereo equipment; a week later he offered to sell it back, but Greg wouldn't pay. Greg and Walter moved a transmission in front of the broken basement door to block it. (Both brothers and another resident of 7244 Rutland all say the transmission was still there on the day of Barbara Jean's murder, two years later.)

Richie and Marvin didn't get along at first but, realizing they both hated Greg, joined forces to get rid of him. On the night of July 30, 1986, Walter watched *The Tonight Show Starring Johnny Carson* with Richie and Rob Fritz, another friend from the Ashbourne School who was staying there for a while and helping on some landscaping jobs. Rob went to bed about midnight, Walter when the Carson show ended half an hour later; as he went to bed Greg and his new girlfriend of a few months, Maureen Dunne, the petite sixteen-year-old daughter of a Philadelphia Police detective, were getting home.

Maureen's parents had a strict curfew, locking the door at 11:00 PM even if she wasn't home, which meant she spent some nights with Greg in his basement bedroom. That's where they were at 4:00 AM on July 31 when Marvin Spence and two accomplices used Richie's key to get into the house and attack them with knives from the kitchen, a crowbar, and a tire iron. Greg fought back, grabbing the tire iron from an attacker and chasing them upstairs.

The banging and screaming woke Walter up. He looked out his bedroom window and saw the attackers running away across the front lawn. He ran downstairs and Greg ran out the door, chasing the attackers. When Greg came back he leaned in the archway in the living room, bleeding all over, saying, "They stabbed us, Maureen's downstairs, help us, help us!"

Walter called 911 and put Greg on the sofa. Greg was crying. Walter went to the basement stairs to check on Maureen, went partway down and looked over and didn't see any movement. He ran back upstairs and called 911 again.

"This is a cop's kid!" he yelled.

Maureen was dead. Greg survived. Richie and Marvin had hired two men to help kill Greg, and too bad for Maureen if she got in the way. At the time of the attack Richie was waiting up the street in his truck to serve as getaway driver. It took police a few days to figure out Richie's role in the plot. Walter had seen the attackers running away and became an even more important witness in the case when he saw blood on a door in the landscaping company office a few days after the murder and notified police.

Richie, Marvin, and their accomplices were arrested and convicted; Richie and Marvin were sentenced to death in 1988, the same week that Barbara Jean was killed; the other two men got long prison sentences. Walter, despite seeing the attackers and finding the blood in the office, was never called as a witness. A detective told Greg that Walter just wasn't competent to testify.[2]

A week after Maureen's murder, Heidi Guhl, a friend of Greg's and Maureen's, went by 7244 Rutland Street to pick up some clothes for Greg. There was still dried blood on the doors, bloody handprints on the walls, and fingerprint dust everywhere. Greg's mattress, soaked with blood, was still in the basement. Heidi felt bad for Walter; he seemed at a loss as to how to clean up, and she couldn't imagine what it was like to have to see that crime scene all the time.[3] Another friend who went by a few weeks later noticed blood still on the door. Greg moved out when he got out of the hospital, and almost none of the people Walter had thought were his friends came around anymore.

The landscaping company went out of business. Walter took various jobs, first at a used-car rental place, then a roofing company, carting shingles, ripping out old roofs. The other employees teased him about being slow and gullible, so he brought a newspaper to work to hold open in front of him during lunch so no one would speak to him.[4]

Around this time Walter, who'd lost his virginity at seventeen and had had sex maybe a dozen times with about eight different women, the "relationships" rarely lasting more than a week or so, had the longest dating relationship of his life, a couple of months. He was twenty-one, she was seventeen, and they didn't sleep together. Walter thought it was going well until he found out she was seeing two other guys at the same time.

He took in housemates to help with his finances. There was still dried blood on the basement walls when Adele Boyle and her middle-school-aged daughter, Melanie, moved in a few months later.[5] Linda Green, a friend of Adele's, started coming around after fights with her husband; according to housemates, Linda was foulmouthed and mean and looked drunk or high all the time,[6] but she eventually convinced Walter she and her two children had nowhere else to go. They all moved in and were joined in the fall of 1987 by Linda's husband, Sarge, the Vietnam vet who claimed to have been kicked out of a violent biker gang.[7]

The Greens agreed to pay fifty dollars a week in rent but stopped after a few weeks. They turned 7244 Rutland Street into a party house again, opening it up to their biker friends, and again Walter couldn't stop it. Melanie, the middle-schooler, remembers the grown-ups were always drinking and doing drugs and yelling at Walter, who spent most of his time in his room with a dresser barricading the door. She couldn't understand why he let all those people in his house but knew that even kids like her and Alice Green could ignore him if he told them to do something.[8] Melanie and her mother moved out shortly thereafter.

A seventeen-year-old runaway who spent about a month at the house was scared of the Greens and could tell Walter was, too; she watched Walter try to stand up to Linda about something, and Linda cursed him out until he went to his room. (This same young woman had a drug problem and used to "ransack" Walter's room when he was out, looking for money; she never saw any pornography, certainly no child pornography—a point that would be of great importance later.)[9] Neighbors, too, were scared of the Greens and would get cursed out if they brought up the noise. As many as twenty-five people would cram into the tiny house at a time, drinking, doing crank and meth, shooting heroin.[10]

A friend of Sarge's named Tom, a thin guy with a ponytail, moved into the basement; he smoked pot and did coke with Sarge, didn't have a job and, as far as Walter could figure, probably did something illegal for a living. The house got even more crowded when, in mid-1988, another friend of Walter's from the Ashbourne School, Hal Vahey, moved in. Hal thought Sarge was a "dirtball," that Linda was mean. She was always home watching TV, only going out for alcohol or something to eat. Sarge, too, rarely left the house and spent his days nodding off on the couch.[11]

Walter and Hal had bedrooms upstairs; Sarge usually slept on the living room sofa, Linda and Charliebird on the mattress on the floor in the dining room. Alice had a bedroom upstairs but kept her clothes in the dining room. Everyone could hear everything; from the living room you could hear someone using the bathroom upstairs or people having a conversation or using the laundry machine in the basement. People were always coming and going, showing up to drink or do drugs or get a tattoo from Sarge. Walter hated Sarge but admitted he did great tattoo work.

This was the house Sharon Fahy sat in so uncomfortably one night in the spring of 1988: filthy, chaotic, and claustrophobic, with five adults, three of whom were unemployed and around all day, two kids, and Hal's and Walter's dogs all living there. Graffiti, including swastikas sprayed by some of the bikers, covered the walls of the living room. Dog hair and dishes and food wrappers and beer cans and cigarette butts and ash were everywhere. The basement was full of junk, the broken back door still blocked by the car transmission.

Walter wasn't able to do much about what was happening in his house. He'd tell Sarge he wanted his freeloading family out of there, and Sarge and his friends would beat him up.

The Green children tried to spend as much time as possible away from the house; twelve-year-old Alice's twenty-year-old boyfriend was too scared of Sarge to come around much, so Alice went to him as often as she could.[12] Sometimes she'd go out all night.

Sarge and Linda would go out to parties, leaving their kids without anyone to look after them. One weekend they left on a Friday and hadn't come back by Monday. Alice got Charliebird ready for school, but around noon the school called looking for Charlie's parents because he was sick. Walter went down to the school and signed for him; the Greens were just getting home when Walter and Charlie did.[13]

In the summer of 1988 Walter was working for an aluminum products company as an installer, trying to keep his life steady. He was usually up by 6:00 AM so he could be at the office by 7:30 or 8:00; when there wasn't enough installation work, he passed out flyers.

On July 12, the day Barbara Jean was murdered, Walter got to work at about eight thirty, a little later than usual. His boss handed him a newspaper-boy bag loaded with flyers, a Walkman, and a photocopy of a street map with the target neighborhood highlighted.

Walter passed out the flyers and got back to the office in the late morning. He waited until twelve thirty or one for the owner to come back and give him more flyers or pay him before giving up and catching the bus home. When he got to his stop, it was a little after two o'clock and hot. Walking down Rutland Street, he didn't see anybody. The front door to his house was unlocked; Linda was sitting on her mattress on the dining room floor, watching a small TV. Walter was in a relative truce with the Greens so he said hi and asked where the kids were; usually Charliebird was running around and Alice was there, sometimes with her boyfriend. Linda said they were at the rec center a few blocks away.

Walter went upstairs, put on a T-shirt and jeans, and walked up to the Clover department store for shampoo and some other things. He was gone maybe half an hour. When he got home Sarge was in the dining room talking to Linda, who was still sitting on the mattress on the floor.

Walter said hi to Sarge, put his shampoo upstairs, and sat with Sarge in the living room watching TV. Linda stayed in the dining room. The front door was open to let in some air. A little later, John Fahy came to the screen door, worried, and asked if any of them had seen Barbara Jean. They said they hadn't, and he went off looking. Linda went back to the dining room; Sarge and Walter went back to watching TV. They didn't talk about John's visit.

Alice and Charliebird came home, and not long after that the cops came down Rutland Street the wrong way. People were coming out of their houses, saying Barbara Jean was missing. Walter went outside with the Greens. A neighbor who had a police scanner said the police had found a body.

At supper that night Walter and the Greens talked about who could've taken the little girl; they found out for sure the body was Barbara Jean on the late local news.

The next day Walter went to work as usual and got home in the late afternoon. He and the Greens heard the rumors about a man carrying the body in a TV box, about someone seeing Barbara Jean being taken away, about a black van pulling up to the car dealership to get rid of a box. When a detective knocked, Walter and Linda answered and told him they'd been home watching TV the day before and hadn't seen or heard anything. Walter looked nothing like the descriptions police had of the suspect. The detective thanked them and went to the next house. It was the last time police talked to Walter until April 1992.

8

INTERROGATION

IN AUGUST 1988, needing steadier work than passing out flyers, Walter enrolled in truck-driving school. It ran five days a week, 7:00 AM to 7:00 PM, for eight weeks, and in mid-November he passed his driving test. That night he got home at about 9:00 PM and found his front door locked. He banged on it and yelled. Walter's uneasy summer truce with the Greens was long over. He'd had two serious fights with Sarge in the previous couple months, and that night Sarge was still angry about a fight they'd had two days earlier. Sarge opened the door, they got into it again, and Sarge beat Walter out of the house and down the street. This was the fight John Fahy heard from his living room and came out to break up, after which Sarge was arrested and Walter was taken to the hospital with fractures and bite wounds.

Sarge spent a couple weeks in jail, and with a restraining order forbidding him from returning to Walter's, went to stay with a friend. He would eventually plead guilty to simple assault but skip his April 1990 sentencing hearing, so a warrant was issued for his arrest—the warrant that was still outstanding when Devlin and Worrell interviewed him in 1992.

In October 1989, Walter's aunt evicted him and the Greens from 7244 Rutland, and he moved in with two friends in an apartment in Glenside, just outside of Philadelphia, ten or fifteen minutes away. After earning his tractor-trailer license, he'd driven part time for UPS for a while before getting a full-time driving job, which he lost when he scraped his truck against a low archway in the road. After that he picked up work where he could. His landlord in Glenside had a chandelier company and gave Walter the overnight shift cleaning chandeliers at the Four Seasons hotel downtown.

Walter's roommates moved out in 1990, and in September of that year he got a job driving a delivery truck for Bake Rite Rolls; it was, as Father John Bonavitacola, a priest in the Philadelphia prison system who got to know him later, put it, a "big deal" for him.[1] He paid off his driving school loans and paid back some money to his brother, Greg. By 1992 things were going well; he was still with Bake Rite, getting twenty-five cents a mile. He could afford the apartment by himself and had upgraded from an old hatchback Greg had given him that was missing a floorboard—it was like driving the Flintstones' car—to a '78 Chrysler Newport. He worked a lot and was often too tired after work to go out, but he had a few friends.

After all his childhood and adolescent difficulties, compounded by his ASD,[2] Walter had managed to stabilize his life again with a good job and a good routine.

———

In late March 1992, about a month after reinterrogating the Fahys, Detectives Devlin and Worrell located the Greens living in Coatesville, an hour or so outside Philadelphia. They went to speak to the couple on March 30. Sarge was in bed when they arrived; his health had been deteriorating, and he was still sick following his most recent stay in the hospital. Devlin and Worrell had done a background check on Sarge Green, so they would have known he had an outstanding warrant for skipping the sentencing hearing.

Alice Green answered the door and the detectives barged in, but they saw right away that Sarge, six feet tall and heavy, with the tattoos and wild hair, didn't fit any of the developed descriptions in the case.[3] He told them he'd been friends with John Fahy, they'd hung out drinking beer sometimes, and he thought John was a good father. He said he'd been home all day the day of the murder, sitting on his couch, zoned out on painkillers. That wasn't much of an alibi, but he was definitely not the guy who'd carried the TV box around the neighborhood.

Alice, seventeen now, said she'd babysat for Barbara Jean occasionally and had seen John Fahy use crank and sometimes hit Barbara Jean to discipline her. She said when she got home at about 2:00 PM on the day of the murder, her parents were there and Walter Ogrod came in a little later. He went out again at 2:30 or 3:00 PM for about half an hour and was in the living room later when John Fahy knocked on the door asking if they'd seen his daughter; both of her parents said the same thing about Walter's whereabouts that afternoon.[4] (In subsequent interviews, however, Alice would remember being at the rec center until later in the afternoon.)

The detectives eased up and said they were just reinterviewing everyone in the neighborhood. Alice asked them why didn't they go talk to Walter Ogrod—he'd lived there too. She got Ogrod's address from a friend who still knew him and called them with it. On April 1 Devlin and Worrell drove out to Glenside with their supervisor, Sergeant Larry Nodiff, to talk to him. They would later claim it hadn't occurred to them yet that Walter could be a suspect, though detectives don't usually take supervisors with them to speak to informational witnesses.[5]

They got to Walter's apartment above the chandelier shop next to the railroad in Glenside at about five in the afternoon and knocked. No one answered, so they approached the shop owner, Walter's landlord, Howard Serotta. Worrell knew the arrival of a homicide detective could be startling, something that never happened to most people. He reassured Serotta that Walter wasn't in any kind of trouble, they just wanted to talk to him.[6]

The detectives asked Serotta what Walter was like, what his routines were. Then, oddly, according to Serotta, one of them asked if Walter had a weight set. The question stuck out in Serotta's memory because he was, as Worrell had thought he might be, surprised to be talking to a homicide detective—especially about Walter, who seemed like a nice, quiet guy. And since the detectives never followed up with Serotta, it was the only time he ever talked to them.[7]

The detectives, on the other hand, would swear they never asked Serotta about a weight set, that they couldn't have because they didn't know about the weight set in Walter's basement until he told them about it a few days later. This would become a key issue in the case for two reasons: 1) if detectives asked Serotta about the weight set, they were asking him about what they would later allege was the murder weapon, something supposedly only the killer knew, two days before they claim Walter told them about it; and 2) this would also prove that the detectives had thought of Walter as a suspect several days before they interviewed him, which, for technical reasons, would make Walter's entire interview with detectives a few days later inadmissible.

Serotta told the detectives Walter's car was in the parking lot, so he didn't think he'd be gone long, and they were welcome to wait. The detectives decided not to; clearly they were in no particular rush to speak to Walter. Devlin and Worrell had the next couple of days off, so Worrell wrote, "Call Sunday after noon re: John Fahy" on the back of a business card and left it for Walter. He felt sure Ogrod would know who John Fahy was.[8]

On the afternoon of April 1, the day the detectives came by, Walter had returned from work, taken his dog for a two-hour walk, and then gone out again, this time for one of his twice-monthly trips to the comic store. He'd been collecting since he was a kid—*Batman vs. Predator, Superman, X-Men, Star Wars.* On his way home he'd picked up his weekly Chinese food supper, wontons, and when he got home Mr. Serotta gave him Detective Worrell's card. Walter didn't recognize John Fahy's name and thought it must have something to do with Maureen Dunne's case. He called the homicide office but was told Worrell was gone for the day. The card said to call on Sunday, so he put it aside.

On Saturday, April 4, Walter got up at 8:00 AM, walked his dog, watched TV for a while, and showered. He got to his Bake Rite job at about 1:00 PM and had to wait three hours for sourdough rolls to come in from another bakery. He got on the road at about 4:00 PM and drove his regular route, twenty-five stops dropping off rolls and picking up empty pallets at fast-food restaurants stretched over 303 miles in and around the Philadelphia suburbs. He got back to Bake Rite at 4:30 AM on Sunday, April 5, put in his paperwork, and was asked to drive another route, a short one of eighteen miles. He returned to Bake Rite from that route at 10:30 AM, put in his paperwork, and went home, stopping on his way for groceries.

He got home a little before noon, exhausted but glad to have put in more overtime; he was saving money to buy himself an actual new car to replace the Newport. He made himself something to eat, took a shower, and dialed Detective Worrell. When he got Worrell on the phone, he asked who John Fahy was. Worrell explained that John Fahy was Barbara Jean Horn's stepfather and that the detectives were speaking to everyone from the neighborhood who might know anything about the case. Walter asked if they could talk on the phone, but Worrell said no, he had to come in. Walter said he was tired and asked if he could come in another time.

"We want to solve the case," Worrell said. "A little girl was killed. We just want to ask you some questions. We will be in and out quick."

Walter relented and drove to the Roundhouse, arriving, he has maintained, at around 1:30 PM. By this point he'd been awake for almost thirty hours. He went to the front desk and asked for Detective Worrell. The officer said Worrell was expecting him and would be down shortly.

Worrell came down, introduced himself, and took Walter inside. Walter asked if Worrell knew Detective Clark, one of the detectives who had interviewed him about Maureen Dunne's murder. Worrell said that he remembered the case and that Clark was doing all right. Walter claims he went to the logbook and asked for a pen to sign in, but Worrell told him he didn't have to.

"I signed it every time I came here before when I talked to Clark," Walter said.

"You don't need to. You'll only be here a few minutes," Worrell said.

Worrell led Walter to the elevator. The elevator doors closed. Walter didn't see sunlight again until the next morning.

———————

The detectives' version of that Sunday, April 5, is that when they got to work on that day they already had two phone messages from Walter, who then called again before Worrell could call him back. Walter made an appointment to come in around 6:00 PM but unaccountably showed up at 3:45. Worrell signed Walter in (Walter's name appears on the Roundhouse log sheet, signed in at 3:45 PM in Worrell's handwriting), took him upstairs, sat him on a bench outside the homicide offices, and told him to wait because Detective Devlin was out running errands and they were required to have two detectives present for the questioning.

Whatever errands Devlin may have been on, making a suspect wait is the first step in an interrogation, establishing that he is under your control and letting his nerves about the interview build.[9] Walter spent close to two hours in the waiting area outside the homicide offices; there was a bench, some empty magazine racks, wanted posters on the wall. After about forty-five minutes of reading posters, Walter walked down the hall, found a detective, and asked him to tell Worrell that he'd been waiting a while, was really tired, and would come back another time. He headed for the elevator but just before reaching it felt Worrell's hand on his arm, steering him back to a bench. He said he was tired and wanted to go home. He waited again, bored and dozing on the bench, for another hour. Then he found Worrell again and told him he was going home. Worrell said they were ready for him and led him to Interview Room D. By Walter's timeline, it was about 3:45 PM; according to Devlin and Worrell, around 5:30.

The interview room was small with a grayish interior, a one-way mirror in one wall, and just enough space for a table with a chair on either side. To one side was another chair, a metal Windsor chair that was bolted to the floor, with handcuffs dangling from one of the arms.[10] Walter sat in one of the regular chairs.[11]

Devlin and Worrell asked basic questions at first, writing down his information: height, weight, address. They then started what they would call the "oral" part of the interview, meaning the part they didn't transcribe. These questions were general—how long he'd lived on Rutland Street, who'd been living there at the time of Barbara Jean's murder, how long he'd been living in Glenside.

They explained that they had asked him down to talk about Barbara Jean Horn. They were talking to all the witnesses again and wanted to know what he knew. Walter said all he knew was she was found in a box on St. Vincent Street. Neighbors supposedly saw the man walking down the street with the box; he'd heard something about someone seeing the man with the box from a church across the street and something about a man trying to dump the box in the Dumpster behind the car dealership. And a sketch of the man had been put up all over the neighborhood.

Walter hadn't recognized John Fahy's name, but the detectives asked if Walter knew the little girl's stepfather. What he was like? How did he get along with Barbara Jean, with his wife? What did Walter know about his drinking, drugs, his family? Had he done anything that made him seem like he might harm someone?

Walter said he'd never seen Fahy treat Barbara Jean any way other than a good father would. He hadn't known John was the child's stepfather until after the murder; he thought her parents were husband and wife and she was their child. He said that John was a nice guy as far as he knew, that he would come over and have a couple of drinks with Mr. Green every once in a while.

These general questions took about half an hour, until about 6:00 PM according to the detectives, 4:15 according to Walter.

———————

From this point on, the two versions of what happened in that interrogation room split, but not entirely, shadowing each other, twisting around each other at key moments.

According to Walter, when the detectives finished the general questions he told them to call him if they thought of anything else. He stood up to go but Worrell closed the door.

"We think you might know something," Devlin said in a helpful tone, pulling his chair up very close to Walter. "We think you might have done it, and you're blocking it."

Walter says he asked for his phone call, but Devlin said they would get to that later.

For the detectives, the interrogation moved to the next level of control. A Philadelphia homicide detective who worked with Devlin and Worrell in the early '90s (or may have been Devlin himself, since he was among the detectives interviewed) explained these control techniques to author Arthur Magida:

> *[The suspect] wants coffee? Fuck it, you get it for him. He needs to go to the bathroom? Fuck it, you go with him. You go right to him and bluff: "We know you did it. And we know how you did it. You either come clean now or we get you anyway. It's that simple. We know what happened, and we're your worst nightmare." You might even say a neighbor saw what happened. You go right up to the point of not being believable—and you try not to cross it.[12]*

This vivid description of how to establish control, given by a detective years later, matches Walter's version of his interrogation exactly.

According to Walter, Devlin then put a photograph of the TV box in front of him.

"Here, take another look at the box with Barbara Jean in it," Walter remembers Devlin telling him, sitting close in the small interview room, sliding a picture at him on the table. "Here's what she looked like. Do you remember putting her under the sink and washing her off? Do you remember the trash bag you put over

her? Do you remember putting her in the box? Does this help
you remember?" Devlin asked. "Does it bring back any memories?"

"No, man, I didn't do it," Walter said. He told them he wanted
the phone.

Devlin said, "Look, we'll get to that later on. We just want to
help you remember."

They brought out two more photos, one with Barbara Jean in
the box, a garbage bag over her body, her head showing, and the
other with the bag removed.

"You killed this girl, man, and we want to help you," Devlin
said. "You killed her. We want to help you remember it. We want
to see you get some help, and we want to put this to rest. You seen
Barbara Jean that day. Mrs. Green wasn't in the house. Barbara
Jean came over for Charlie. You let her in."

"No," Walter said.

"You must have because nobody was around. Mrs. Green wasn't
there," Devlin said.

"She was. She was home that day," Walter said.

The detectives knew this was true—Sarge, Linda, and Alice had
all told them they were home that afternoon.

"We have neighbors say they saw you let Barbara Jean in the
house," Devlin said.

This was a bluff; no one saw Barbara Jean go into Walter's
house that day.

They showed Walter picture after picture, again and again,
Barbara Jean, the box with the cover on, without the cover.

"Why'd you hit her, man?" Devlin asked. "Why'd you kill her?
What happened? Did you do anything to her? Did you have fun
with her?"

"No, I didn't," Walter said.

"Well, why'd you bring her in the house?" Devlin pressed.
"What did you do with her clothes? She was a child—why'd you
do it? You took her downstairs because if somebody walked in you
didn't want them to see you."

"No, I didn't take her downstairs," Walter said.

"Yes, you did, man. You took her downstairs to have a little fun."

"No, I did not."

"No clothes," Devlin pressed. "She was raped."

"No, I did not rape her."

"You took her downstairs. You had fun. Something happened and you killed her."

"No, I did not," Walter said.

Devlin pressed harder.

"You know, you need to go to a place where they can give you a little help. You know what I mean? You seem like you're a little off. Did you ever see a doctor?'

"Yes," Walter said.

"Is there a reason you seen him?"

"Things and all."

"Well, what is wrong with you?"

"Nothing," Walter said. "I need help now and then, but that's it. I'm not gonna deny it."

Devlin and Worrell pushed: *Here she is. Look at her. She was raped! You went nuts and beat her up. How the hell else did she get beat? It makes sense. What did you hit her with?*

"I wouldn't do that," Walter told them. "If I did, I would've killed myself."

Walter's statement, written by Devlin, says, "I feel like killing myself over this."

Devlin threatened him: if he didn't confess they'd put him in a cell with "a bunch of niggers" and tell them he'd raped and killed a black girl. When he dozed they prodded him awake. They gave him coffee, five, six cups. They told him they were going to be all night so he might as well eat and gave him a cheesesteak. Walter was terrified and now hadn't slept in thirty-six hours, and as the interrogation dragged on, deepening panic and exhaustion clouded his mind; eventually, the detectives' insistence that someone had seen Barbara Jean go into his house that day had him wondering if he could have done something so horrible and blocked it out. He didn't remember it, but someone saw him let

Barbara Jean in and she'd been killed; he stared at the pictures of the dead little girl and started crying. As he described it to me later, his thoughts began to cascade: *Someone raped that little girl. It was horrible. Someone killed her, look at the pictures, someone seen me let her in and then she was killed. I must have done it. But how could I do that? How could I—but she was killed in my house, I let her in—she was raped. . . . How could I do that? How could I do that?*

The detectives pushed him through a description of the murder and its aftermath. They drew a map of the neighborhood and told him to trace his route with the box. He got it wrong.

"No," a detective told him, "people saw you here. You must have gone this way."

They asked leading questions and gave him the answers when he didn't know or answered incorrectly: "Imagine in your mind what she was probably wearing. . . . Her hair was wet. Did you wash her? . . . You needed to hide her; you needed something to put her in. Where did you get the box? Well, it came from down on the corner, you went down there to get it . . ."

As he sat in Interview Room D that night, Walter Ogrod was a case study in risk factors for giving a false confession: he was immature, twenty-seven but with the maturity of a teenager; he had ASD, so couldn't read social cues and information from the detectives' faces; he suffered from excessive social anxiety, always wanting to please others so they'd like him; he was more suggestible, more easily manipulated, than 95 percent of the population (as he would score later on the Gudjonsson Suggestibility Scales, a test designed in the 1970s to determine how likely a person is to change a story under pressure).[13] And his life experiences had reinforced these issues—his schizophrenic mother convincing him a lamp didn't exist, the years of being teased and beaten, of "friends" relentlessly manipulating and using him. In the words of a doctor who examined him years later, Walter was a "ripe apple" who had been "primed his entire life to be easily misled and manipulated."[14]

In addition, he hadn't slept in a day and a half, which meant that his ability to make decisions—especially those that required integrating his understanding of what was going on and his emotions, something he had very little ability to do in the first place—was even more severely impaired.[15]

And he was sitting across from Marty Devlin, a detective famous for getting "tough" confessions, whose only real chance to clear the Barbara Jean Horn murder was to get a confession. Devlin had gone after the Fahys hard and would use his skill on Walter, too; as he'd told John and Sharon, putting pressure on people who might know something was part of the process.

Devlin and Worrell's interrogation of Walter, as described by Walter, followed an interrogation technique known as the Reid Technique. Invented in the 1940s by John Reid, a private polygraph expert, to replace the then-popular Third Degree, which called for suspects to be threatened, or beaten, into telling the truth (or at least whatever would make the beatings stop), Reid's idea was to use psychology instead of violence or intimidation to get suspects to confess.

The Reid Technique eventually became standard practice in homicide divisions across the country, and anyone who's watched a TV show about homicide detectives has seen it in action: at its most basic, it consists of the detectives convincing the suspect that they're his only hope, that if he tells them the truth—or what they want to hear—they can help him, but if he insists on denying it they can't. They tell him he wasn't a bad person, didn't mean it, maybe there was a reason for what happened; this is called the "out," the aspect of the story that will show that the suspect wasn't as bad as he seemed. Detectives are trained to use threats, lies, friendship, whatever it takes to get the suspect to talk.

The Reid Technique breaks interviews into two parts: the Behavioral Analysis Interview (BAI) and the interrogation. The BAI is the informational conversation meant to gather basic facts from the subject—where he lives, his background, and so on. Walter and the detectives both describe this happening in their interview; the detectives called it the "oral" part of the interview. The BAI also allows the detectives to assess how the suspect talks and acts to see if he's being truthful. During the BAI interrogators can also use "behavior provoking questions" like, "What do you think should happen to the person who did this?" These are designed to anger the subject or throw him off balance while the detective assesses his honesty.

The next stage of a Reid Technique interrogation comes if the detective thinks the subject is a suspect in the crime. If that happens, the Reid Technique teaches detectives to assert intense pressure on the suspect. First, the detectives confront the suspect with how serious the crime is and how confident they are that the suspect did it (maximization); then they offer the suspect "themes" or "alternate questions" designed to let him save face and soften the consequences of what he's done (minimization). We've all seen this on TV, a confident, aggressive detective convincing a murderer to explain what he did in the best possible light so he won't seem like such a monster in front of a jury.[16]

Under the Reid Technique, then, much depends on a detective's ability to tell if his subject is telling the truth, because a truthful subject's insistent denials of guilt can be indications of innocence, while a guilty suspect's denials should be ignored. And good homicide detectives rely on their ability to know when someone is lying. As David Simon memorably explained in his 1991 book *Homicide*, "to homicide detectives the earth spins on an axis of denial in an orbit of deceit. . . . It is a God-given truth: Everyone lies."[17] Detectives learn to trust instincts and experience to know when a suspect is lying, and, since people lie for all kinds of reasons, to know when that suspect is lying about the murder and not about something else like drugs or infidelity that, unless it's directly related to the murder, doesn't interest him.[18]

This means, Simon went on, that a homicide detective's thinking during an interview usually runs something like this: "Are they lying? Of course they're lying. Everyone lies. Are they lying more than they ordinarily would? Probably. Why are they lying? Do their half-truths conform to what you know from the crime scene or is it complete and unequivocal bullshit? Who should you yell at first?

Who should you scream at loudest? . . . Who gets the speech about leaving the interrogation room as either a witness or a suspect?"[19]

Detectives therefore take a great deal of pride in their ability to tell when someone is lying. This was the psychology at which Devlin was considered a genius; he or one of his colleagues in the homicide division later explained to author Arthur Magida that detectives know more about psychology than a psychologist and can tell from a suspect's body language, eye contact, or turn of phrase whether he is guilty or not.[20]

A problem can arise, though, when a detective with a big ego, convinced he can read minds, fixates on the wrong person, trusting his instinct even if the evidence doesn't point to that suspect. Marty Devlin had no training in interrogating people with ASD, so maybe he took Walter's odd mannerisms and inability to express emotions in a typical manner as indications of guilt. Maybe Walter wasn't showing the emotions Devlin and Worrell thought he should be showing. Whatever it was, Devlin decided Walter was lying and began to apply pressure, the kind of pressure that can cause false confessions.

This is how false confessions happen. Once a detective fixes on an innocent person as a suspect, the fixation leads to "anchoring heuristics," the trait that makes all of us, once we're convinced of something, more likely to see evidence that supports our claim,[21] and as a detective's suspicions harden into belief of a suspect's guilt, he can develop tunnel vision and "confirmation bias."

Once a detective thinks a suspect is guilty, the Reid Technique offers a wide array of coercive techniques to pressure him to confess: promising leniency or threatening harm; lying about evidence; presenting the "out" so suspects feel that their only chance for survival, particularly in a case that might carry the death penalty, is to admit to the crime.

One problem that arises in false confessions is that in the course of the interrogation a detective eager to get the truth—the confession he wants—can "contaminate" the statement by discussing details of the crime that were never made public. These kinds of details are the best proof that a confession is true, so crucial to investigations that in the early 1930s, after more than two hundred people came forward to confess to kidnapping the Lindbergh baby, police started intentionally withholding information about crime scenes from the press so they could judge confessions on this basis. Contamination can happen intentionally, the detectives feeding information to the suspect, or by accident: for example, a suspect seeing crime scene photos during a long interrogation can pick up details that, repeated back to the detectives an hour or more later, seem like things only the killer would know. Detectives can also accidentally provide this kind of information to suspects by asking leading questions or posing "alternate theories" as to how the crime happened.

One basic tactic of the Reid Technique is to lie to the suspect. Detectives will say that a friend or accomplice gave the suspect up, that there's physical evidence connecting him to the crime—anything. The courts have ruled this kind of lying acceptable. With John Fahy, Devlin bluffed by telling John his statement didn't match his version from 1988; with Walter, the lie was that a witness saw Barbara Jean go in his house.

These kind of lies can lead to false confessions. Even John E. Reid and Associates, the modern-day company that provides training in the Reid Technique, warns that lying to suspects can lead to false confessions. And innocent suspects who are immature, malleable, or sleep deprived, have a low IQ, or are too intellectually limited to stand up to pressure are even more likely to confess falsely.[22]

When false confessions do happen, they happen in one of two ways: some people confess falsely under police interrogation just to get the interrogation to end, thinking that since they're innocent they'll be able to clear the situation up later. Other people become convinced under the detectives' pressure that that they must have committed the crime but can't remember it. The latter is what Walter says happened to him: after hours in Interview Room D he began to believe, as the detectives were telling him, that he'd murdered Barbara Jean and was blocking it out.

I asked him what it felt like to believe that.

"When I started believing it I was, like, 'How could I do that? How could I do that?'" he told me. "They're saying, 'You enjoyed it, you liked raping that girl.' It felt horrible."

Was that when he started crying?

"I started crying before," he said.

One phrase that Walter said Devlin used—he wanted Walter to "imagine in his mind" what happened during the murder—was familiar to me from Robert Mayer's book *The Dreams of Ada*, about a false confession case out of Ada, Oklahoma. In that 1984 case, detectives, trying to solve a months-old disappearance for which they had no clues and no leads, subjected an intellectually disabled man named Tommy Ward to a full Reid Technique interrogation. The detectives made Ward wait for an hour and a half prior to questioning, as Walter had—"common police procedure prior to the questioning of a suspect," Mayer points out, to "let him get nervous." When the interrogation started, Ward, like Walter, insisted on his innocence; like Walter, he was confronted with pictures of the missing woman (though not, in Ward's case, pictures of her body, which hadn't been found yet) and with evidence invented by detectives; like Walter, Ward told them, "If I thought I did something like that, I'd kill myself"; like Walter, the detectives asked him if he had mental problems; like Walter, he was threatened, told that if he didn't come up with a good explanation for the crime he'd face the death penalty.

"What do you think happened to [the victim]?" the detectives asked Ward.

"I don't know," Ward told them.

"Use your imagination," the lead detective urged. "What do you think?"

The detectives offered him his "out": What if she'd been killed by accident? Could he imagine that? Could he imagine where she might have been buried? Eventually, after hours of interrogating Ward and urging him to use his imagination, detectives had a confession. Like Walter, important information did not check out—the body was not found where Ward supposedly said he'd dumped it, and an accomplice he named was proven innocent. Like Walter, at Ward's trial the prosecutor admitted some things in the confession weren't accurate but insisted that it was, nonetheless, true. Ward and a codefendant, Karl Fontenot, who had likewise given a confession that didn't match any facts of the case (or Ward's confession), were found guilty and sentenced to death.

The same detectives and prosecutors used the same device—false confessions cultivated from a defendant's imaginings about the case—to "solve" another Ada murder a year or two later; that second crime was the subject of John Grisham's book *The Innocent Man.* The defendants in Grisham's book, Ron Williamson and Dennis Fritz, were eventually exonerated by DNA testing.

In Tommy Ward's case, the victim's body was eventually found—miles away from anywhere Ward or his codefendant had been or had mentioned in their confessions—and she'd been killed not by stabbing or burning, as the defendants had said, but by a single gunshot to the head. There is no DNA to test in the case, and Tommy Ward and Karl Fontenot, their sentences reduced to life in prison, are still incarcerated.

While writing his book, Mayer spoke with a potential juror named Barry Anderson:

"You can get anyone to confess to anything," Anderson told Mayer. "I know. I was in Vietnam. Everyone has a different pressure point. But if you want, you can get anyone to say anything."

"Were you a prisoner of war in Vietnam?" Mayer asked.

"No," Anderson said. "I interrogated prisoners of war."[23]

It's is hard to believe someone would admit to a crime he or she didn't commit, especially one as horrifying as killing a child. *No way,* we think; *I don't care what you did to me, if I didn't do it I would never say I did.*

But it happens. As of this writing, about 25 percent of the 325 DNA exonerations in the United States involved false confessions or admissions.[24]

The result of Walter's interrogation by Devlin and Worrell was a sixteen-page document, written out by Devlin and signed on every page by Walter. It told a story of a spur-of-the moment decision to sexually assault Barbara Jean that went wrong:

The day Barbara Jean died she came over to my house and knocked on the front door looking for Charlie Bird. He was six. He wasn't in the house but I let Barbara Jean in anyway. Now usually Linda is right there in the Dining Room but she must have stepped out for a short while or was upstairs or something because it was only me and Barbara Jean in the living room. I got the idea to ask Barbara Jean to come down the basement with me and she followed me down the basement.

When we got down the basement I asked her if she wanted to play doctor and she said yes so I started to take her clothes off. I can't really remember what she was wearing but I think it might have been like a one-piece thing. I'm not real sure about that. I remember she didn't have nothing on her feet. Anyway after I got her undressed I started stroking her shoulders and her back. Then I started to rub her feet. After that I asked her if she wanted to see between my legs and I pulled my pants down around my ankles and knelt down. I was getting hard by now. I pulled Barbara Jean over to me and I was like holding her real tight and rubbing against her leg. Then I was like trying to force her head down towards my penis. I liked [sic] pushed her face onto my penis and that's when she started to scream. I don't know what happened to me then I just went crazy. I remember picking up what felt like a pipe at the time and I just started hitting her in the head. The best I can see it in my mind is that I was holding her head down and hitting her with this pipe. It might have been my small "pull down" bar to my weight set. I hit her at least four times maybe more. She didn't move after that.

It also described the aftermath:

I got real scared after that. She was bleeding and I didn't know what to do. I grabbed some kind of cloth that was down there and

I held it on her head to [til?] I could get her over the the [sic] basement tub and when I got her by the tub I turned on the cold water and I either put her in the tub or held her under the faucet to clean her off. After that I think I left her in the tub and went out the back door to the garage and I opened the garage door to look in the garage to see if there was something inside to put her in. I found a green or blue trash bag and I went back in the basement and wrapped the bag around her to cover her and then I carried her out the back door to the garage. I didn't want nobody to find her in the basement. After I got her in the garage I put her down and covered her up some more with clothes in the garage and I left the garage closed the door and went looking for something else to put her in. I walked up my back driveway towards St. Vincent St. and I saw this box in the back of this house near the corner so I grabbed it.

I took the box back to the garage and I put Barbara Jean in the box and I put the bag on top of her and closed the box. Then I took the box out of the garage. I was going to just put the box out in the trash maybe a couple of houses away from mine but then I realized that the trash had already been picked up. Then I started looking for a place to dump the box. I walked up to St. Vincent Street turned onto St. Vincent. I was going to put the box in the dumpster that's located behind Kutner Buick but there was [sic] people by the dumpster so I couldn't. Thats [sic] located right there by my driveway and I could have tossed the box right over the fence if those people weren't there. So I had to walk down St Vincent street and across Castor av [sic] to the other side but there was [sic] people waiting for the bus on the corner by the church so I crossed over St Vincent to the other side of St Vincent where Kutner Buick is also located and I walked a couple of steps down Castor and I decided to turn around because it was so busy on Castor Av [sic] and so I turned the corner of St Vincent and Castor walked a little ways and crossed over St Vincent again. By this time the box was really heavy. It wasn't at first but by this time it was getting heavy I had to put it down. Then I picked it back up and went

*a little further and put it back down by some trash cans. Then I
went back home.*[25]

When the statement was finished, the detectives had Walter
sign a waiver of his Miranda rights in the form of a questionnaire
that they read to him.

According to Walter, Devlin read the first question to him,
offering the answer as well.

"Do you understand you have a right to keep quiet and you
don't have to say anything at all? Put 'yes,'" Devlin said.

"Yes," said Walter.

"Do you want to remain silent?" Devlin asked.

"Yes," Walter said.

"No," Devlin said. "We got this statement here. We have that
signed. You didn't want to remain silent. Put 'no' then."

When they got to the part about having a lawyer present Walter
said again that he wanted his phone call.

"Well, we have the statement," Devlin said. "You signed it. You
didn't want a lawyer."

"I want a lawyer," Walter said.

"No, you didn't have a lawyer here. You sign this, you get your
phone call."

————————

Devlin and Worrell's supervisor, Sergeant Larry Nodiff, called Joseph
Casey, the assistant district attorney who'd overseen the grand jury
investigation into the murder. Casey got out of bed and got to the
homicide office at about 2:30 AM.[26] It was extremely unusual to get
the ADA on a case out of bed in the middle of the night, since the
charging DA, whose job was to sign off on charges overnight, had
already accepted the charges. But Casey spent the rest of the night
in the homicide offices, reviewing Walter's statement for any "legal
issues" that might come up.

Walter was taken downstairs and booked for murder in the
early morning of April 6. Passing a window on his way down, he

saw outside for the first time since the previous afternoon; it was light out. He'd lost all sense of time. He'd been in homicide at least fourteen hours, most of it in an interrogation room, and hadn't slept in almost two full days.

——————————

Peter Blust's phone rang at about seven thirty that morning. Blust was a lawyer who'd met Walter a couple years before when Walter was doing some roofing work on Blust's neighbor's house. Walter struck him as slow, very earnest, childlike, and had asked his advice a dozen times or so on some student loan issues. Blust felt sorry for him.

Now Walter was on the phone, frantic.

"Pete—Pete—Pete—they're telling me I killed this little girl and just don't remember it, I have a mental block about it," Walter said.

"Whoa, whoa, what are you talking about?" Blust asked.

"I'm in jail! I'm in jail!" Walter said.

Blust got him to slow down and describe his interrogation.

"Walt, why didn't you call me?" Blust asked.

"I kept telling them I wanted to call you but they wouldn't let me," Walter said. "They said, 'Oh, sure, we'll make an appointment with your attorney, and in the meantime we'll arrest you and put you into the general population, but you probably won't last because when this gets out, they'll kill you in there.'"

Blust didn't know about the Reid Technique but didn't think Walter capable of murder and definitely didn't think he had the brains to make up a story to explain away a real confession so quickly.[27] He told Walter he'd be down as soon as he could.

Walter was put in a cell in the Philadelphia Detention Center and fell asleep.

9

LOOSE ENDS

SHARON FAHY WAS STILL HOME on the morning of April 6 when one of the detectives called to tell her they'd arrested Walter Ogrod for Barbara Jean's murder.

"Who?" Sharon asked.

One of the people living with the Greens at the time, the detective explained.

Sharon called her job to say she wasn't coming in. *Who do I talk to now?* she wondered. *Who do I call?* She wanted to call John but didn't have the number—she'd sent him off to rehab with best wishes but without much hope that he'd really stop drinking. But this was the kind of news that could change everything for him. She called John's mother, who worried the news might send him out drinking again but gave Sharon the number.

She called and left a message with John's counselor and had to wait an hour and a half, going nuts, for John to call back. Finally he called and Sharon gave him the news: Walter Ogrod had been arrested for the murder.

"I don't know who that is," John said.

Father John Bonavitacola, the director of prison chaplaincy services for the Archdiocese of Philadelphia, made a point of checking on newly arrested inmates charged with major crimes or crimes against children to make sure they'd been treated properly by the police and were safe from other inmates. When he arrived to visit Walter on the morning of April 6, there was a copy of that morning's *Daily News* on the guard desk, the whole front page taken up with the news of Walter's arrest and a picture of the original police sketch.

"I'm here to see that guy," Father John said, pointing to the *Daily News*.

The guard told him which cell Walter was in, and Father John walked down to it. Walter was asleep, but Father John could see he didn't look anything like the sketch. He went back to the guard's desk.

"Woody," he said to the guard, "I misunderstood. Which cell is Ogrod in?"

"No you didn't," she said. "Everyone says he doesn't look anything like the sketch."

Father John went back to Walter's cell. Walter was exhausted, in shock, incoherent, possibly on the edge of a breakdown, and insisting he was innocent.[1] Later that day Walter told doctors at the prison hospital he hadn't slept in two days, that he'd felt suicidal when he first got to jail but wasn't anymore. He said he was innocent.[2]

Heidi Guhl, a friend of Greg's who'd been a regular at 7244 Rutland until Maureen's murder, heard about an arrest in Barbara Jean's murder on TV.

Oh God, they finally got him, she thought.

A picture of Walter appeared on the screen.

No way, Heidi thought. *No way. They got the wrong guy.*

She called Greg. They knew Walter was a pushover and couldn't stick up for himself, but confess to murder? They went to see him as soon as they could.

"Why are you so stupid?" Greg yelled at him. "How could you sign that?"

"They said I could go home if I signed it," Walter said.

"Walt, you signed a confession to murder," Greg yelled. "You ain't going home."

That morning, Devlin and Worrell searched 7244 Rutland Street. They didn't find any evidence of Barbara Jean's murder but weren't surprised, given it had been four years.

Devlin, Worrell, and Sergeant Nodiff also went back to the Greens'. They needed the Greens to corroborate their story and had some leverage: Sarge was looking at jail time on the outstanding warrant from when he'd skipped his sentencing for beating Walter up in November 1988. When Devlin told the Greens they'd arrested Walter, Alice didn't think it made any sense. She didn't like Walter but didn't think he was capable of that kind of thing. Plus her parents had been there all day, and she'd gotten home sometime that afternoon; how could it have happened in the house?

Her father felt the same way. He'd been there all afternoon; if something had happened he would've heard it and killed Ogrod himself.

Alice told the detectives she hadn't gotten home on the afternoon of the murder until later in the afternoon; this was a small change from her story in 1988. She told them how obnoxious Walter was—he'd spanked her when she was walking through the house dressed only in a towel, said rude things to her friends. But she still didn't think he could've killed Barbara Jean; he wasn't smart enough or slick enough to pull something like that off. The detectives asked if Walter had ever gone in the basement and she said he had, to do laundry and use the gym set.

Sergeant Nodiff, who hadn't been in the interrogation room when Walter's statement was taken and who'd been concerned enough about it to call in ADA Casey at 2:30 AM to review it, apparently was still wondering. He asked Alice if Walter was the kind of person who would confess to something he didn't do. She said no.[3]

The detectives got a story from Charliebird, now ten: Walter once showed him pornographic magazines and told him how to use "jerkoff cream."[4]

(Walter denies this. He says he absolutely never showed Charlie magazines, let alone said anything to him about jerking off. If Charlie saw pornographic magazines, Walter insists, they were the biker magazines Sarge left all over the house.)

When the detectives told Linda her childrens' new, damning stories about Walter, she said she'd never heard them before. She said she'd never seen Walter with any blood on him that day and that his behavior was normal all day, even after Barbara Jean's body was found. When the detectives asked if Walter ever impressed her as having "an unusual interest in children" she said, "No, not really; he really had no time for kids." She also said she'd seen Walter's pornographic magazines in his closet and it was all "normal"; she'd never seen any child pornography in the house.[5]

What if Sarge didn't hear anything on the day of the murder because he was passed out on the couch? the detectives asked. What if Linda hadn't heard anything because the air conditioner in the dining room, which rattled like some ancient warplane, blocked the noise?

Possible, the Greens agreed. But it didn't make much sense to them.

With that, the detectives had all they were going to get from the Greens. It didn't exactly explain how Walter could've beaten a little girl to death in the middle of the afternoon in a tiny house with at least two other adults and two large dogs in the living room without anyone hearing or seeing anything—not Barbara Jean coming in, not Walter taking her to the basement, not the beating or screaming, not the dogs barking or the foundational house buzz of the garage door raising and lowering as Walter supposedly came and went, looking for garbage bags in which to hide the body, not any change in Walter's behavior even as more people came home and talked about Barbara Jean and the people and police filled the street outside, talking about it.

The information from the Greens didn't exactly explain any of this, but it would do.

Other than the follow-up visit to the Greens and the minimal search of 7244 Rutland, Devlin and Worrell made little effort to corroborate Walter's statement. They didn't take his photo to the witnesses for identification; they didn't use luminol, a blood-detection agent that even years later can show where blood was spilled, to search his basement; they didn't test the scrapings from under Barbara Jean's fingernails to see if there was skin that matched his. They never spoke to Hal Vahey, Walter's friend who was living at 7244 at the time of the murder, who got home a little later that afternoon and would've told them that Walter was home at around 5:00 PM, the same time the man with the box was walking on Castor Avenue, and that Walter seemed normal, not excited or stressed. Vahey also would've told them that he and many other people did their laundry in the basement of 7244 and that after Barbara Jean's murder it looked just the same as it always had—junk everywhere and a transmission blocking the back door, no blood, no signs of struggle or of sudden cleaning. Vahey also would have said that his Doberman, Angel, was a "well-trained and protective" dog who would've heard a child screaming in the basement and barked "loud and long" until someone checked it out. No one in the house that day remembered the dog acting strange that afternoon.[6]

Something else the detectives didn't do was unusual: they didn't search Walter's apartment in Glenside. Though he'd moved there a little more than a year after the murder, he still might have had the weight set or the pull-down bar from it, which they claimed was the murder weapon. Wouldn't they want to look for some trophy of Barbara Jean, or, God forbid, some other victims? Or maybe child pornography or some other evidence of a deviant interest in children?

All of these would be good reasons to search Walter's apartment. Walter's landlord, Howard Serotta, shocked as he was by Walter's arrest because Walter had never seemed like a violent person, understood this. He assumed the detectives would be back to search the apartment, so he waited a few weeks to clean it out but never heard from them. The only police he heard from after the arrest were local animal control officers, asking about Walter's dog. After a few weeks Serotta finally did clean out the apartment, wondering again as he did why the detectives had asked about a weight set. He found nothing of interest—no weight set, no kids' things, nothing suspicious. He found a lot of *Star Trek* books and magazines and he found some pornography, none involving children.[7]

Devlin and Worrell didn't search for evidence everywhere they could have, but they did try to find people with bad things to say about Walter. Several neighbors had already told them he was weird, but they needed more than that. Devlin and Worrell pressured Dawn Vahey, Hal's sister, to give them a creepy Walter story but she was adamant that he didn't look anything like the sketch, so the detectives gave up.[8] And after Robert Fritz, Walter's friend who'd been living at 7244 when Maureen Dunne was murdered, got a phone call from Walter in jail, two homicide detectives—Fritz couldn't remember their names—came to the Pet Center, where he worked. They told him he and Walter had spoken about the murder. Fritz told them no, they'd talked about school and old friends. The detectives insisted he and Walter *had* talked about the murder and took him down to the Roundhouse to scare him. They told him what Walter must have said to him about the murder and he told them again that Walter hadn't said anything about it. They pushed, said they didn't believe him, but finally he got so upset they let him go.[9]

As an expert homicide investigator hired by Walter's defense on appeal wrote years later, "Given the hedging language of [Walter's] statement itself, the fact that portions of it were not consistent with known facts, and the lack of corroborating evidence, the police should not simply have closed the case upon receipt of Mr. Ogrod's 'confession.'"[10]

But that's what they did.

Peter Blust made it to the detention center to see Walter on the evening of his arrest. Walter told him he'd been forced into giving a false confession. The next day, feeling very much in over his head in a capital case, Blust reached out to private eye and former Philadelphia homicide detective Joe Brignola, who'd served a subpoena for him once. Blust asked to meet that night.

They met at a McDonald's near Brignola's house. Blust explained Walter's situation, and Brignola asked who the cops involved were; when Blust told him he said, according to Blust, that given the detectives involved in Walter's case he wasn't surprised that the confession had been coerced. Blust cracked a half-kidding joke that Brignola should wear a wire and engage his old colleagues in a conversation about Walter's statement.[11]

Brignola didn't offer any help. After the meeting he called his old friend, Joseph Casey, the prosecutor, and told him about it.[12] Casey took advantage of this heads-up and would be ready to discredit Blust at a key moment.

A few days after Walter's arrest, Mark Greenberg was appointed to be his attorney. Greenberg was not a public defender; the Philadelphia public defender's office had a good reputation but didn't take homicide cases in 1992. Homicides were handled by private lawyers appointed by judges. The problem was that although a private lawyer hired to defend a wealthy client could expect to charge $50,000 for a capital murder trial, the lawyers appointed to defend poor defendants in capital cases got a $1,700 flat fee and $400 for each day in court—an average of $2,700 per case for cases that required, on average, five hundred hours of work. Also, it could take up to two years to get paid even this small amount, and there was so little money for expert witnesses that judges often denied defense requests for funding. Many experts wouldn't testify in Philadelphia cases anyway, because they knew their fees would be cut sharply or not paid at all.[13]

Not surprisingly, few lawyers were willing to take state-funded capital cases in Philadelphia in the early '90s; out of eight thousand lawyers in the city at that time, only eighty were qualified and willing to take on death penalty cases.[14] Mark Greenberg was young but had done capital murder trials before. He would work Walter's case essentially alone; the court authorized $300 for an investigator, and a private investigator put in eight hours and forty-five minutes of work; Greenberg was also able to hire a forensics expert to review some physical evidence in the case.[15]

The year after Walter's arrest, judges in Philadelphia admitted there weren't enough private lawyers willing to take death penalty cases and allowed the public defender's office to take one case in five. Each defendant who was assigned a public defender got two lawyers, a mitigation specialist (someone trained to investigate a defendant's background to provide reasons why he shouldn't be executed, if the case came to that), and an investigator, as well as a fund for outside experts and a staff psychiatrist to evaluate him. The importance of resources to mounting a strong defense became clear very quickly: between April 1993, when public defenders started taking murder cases, and July 1995, defendants with public defenders were not given a single death sentence while those represented by private attorneys were given thirty-three.[16]

Walter remembers the DA offering a deal, a life sentence if he pled guilty.

"Greenberg told me I could face the death penalty, and I said I'd rather be dead than plead guilty," Walter told me.

Later, one of Walter's prosecutors told me that was a standard deal they offered in murder cases. He didn't take it. That was the gamble of going to trial: his life would hinge on whether the jury thought he was a liar.

PART II

LIKE
TV STUFF

10

"OFF"

WAS WALTER OGROD A LIAR and a child killer or an absolutely innocent man? One key line in the statement Devlin and Worrell took summed up the whole question: Did Walter say, *I could never do that to a little girl—I'd kill myself,* as he claims, or did he say what Devlin wrote: *I want to kill myself for what I did to that little girl?*

Which was the truth?

The first time I spoke to Walter, I was struck by his speech impediment: while the detectives swore they'd never noticed he had one, it was bad enough to me that I had a hard time understanding him on the phone. I'd heard he had one growing up, and later read about it in his school and medical notes going back to when he was eleven.[1]

And if the detectives would lie about not noticing a speech impediment, what should I make of their claims that Walter never seemed tired, never yawned, though he'd been up for thirty hours by the time they interviewed him, or that they'd never noticed anything "off" about him? Everyone I'd talked to about Walter had said something like that: he was "off" somehow, "slow," that if you met him you might not pick up on it right away but sooner or later you'd understand. A few told me he was "retarded"; his brother Greg had described him as "not retarded but on the road there."[2]

The detectives, I thought, were not telling the entire truth about the interrogation. But that didn't mean Walter was.

When I began corresponding with Walter I assumed he'd try to manipulate me, to make me feel bad for him. But his letters had no emotional appeals, not even any emotion, really—no long, persuasive descriptions of key events or ideas or feelings that he'd had. There were few sentences about himself in the pages and pages of information and arguments he wrote about his case, and those came only when I prodded him.

Likewise, on the phone he wasn't articulate about himself or his emotions or his situation, but he understood his case well and could explain the problems with it in detail. He answered questions directly, stating facts; whatever it was that was "off" about him, it didn't seem to me to be his intelligence. Instead of emotion, he fixated on detail. If I asked him what he'd felt at a certain moment—when he was arrested, for example—he answered with a word or two. If I asked about some aspect of his childhood, he would give a word or two and then revert to talking about his case, urging me to find a particular document or person that would support one of his claims. Once, when I asked him how he was doing, he said prison was "depressing." Another time he said, "It gets a little monotonous in here." At first I thought he was just prone to understatement.

I asked him to tell his lawyer to let me review his entire case file and was a little surprised when he did. I ended up in a small conference room at his lawyer's office with six double-sized legal boxes piled on the oval table and floor. I read everything. I thought Walter could be telling the truth. But the idea of someone giving a false confession to the murder of a child is hard to take.

One spring at a conference I approached Peter Neufeld, one of the founders of the Innocence Project, to ask his advice about what I should look for in investigating the case, which documents I needed to get, what reports I was entitled to see, whom I should be sure to speak with. I explained Walter's case briefly and he told me I could send him a two-page write-up—"Two pages, not eight," he said—and he would look it over.

I sent him the write-up, and in a couple of weeks he called. He said that the detectives' story about Walter not being a suspect until he broke down and cried in the interrogation room was an "MO" he'd seen before in false confession cases—in fact, the Innocence Project had just freed an inmate from Pennsylvania death row in whose case the police had an audiotaped confession that Neufeld said was detailed, chilling, and (as DNA proved) false. He asked me jokingly if I'd made up the case, it was such a perfect example of a setup for a false confession. After I told him Walter's statement was in the detective's handwriting, he wouldn't even refer to it as a confession anymore and stopped me when I did. After more questions he said, "It looks like this guy might really be innocent. I don't know if we can prove it, but he could really be."

I thought, *We?*

Neufeld said I'd have to do the legwork on the case. They didn't have anyone available, but they'd help me, and I could tell people the Innocence Project was interested. This would prove incredibly helpful, a shorthand way of letting people know that my concerns about the case had something to them. And hearing from one of the most experienced innocence lawyers in the country that Walter's case was a "textbook" example of a false confession made Walter's version of events even more credible.

I met Walter in person a year after we began corresponding.

It was a long walk to the high-security visiting cells at the State Correctional Institution at Greene (SCI Greene), down bright linoleum corridors and through several series of iron doors. When I got to the visiting cell I pulled the door open and there he was: he looked the same as in pictures, his black hair greasy and messed, though now gray at the temples, his soft face with dark eyes and pale skin. We sat on either side of a small table divided up to the ceiling by Plexiglas with mesh on the sides so we could hear each other. He was wearing glasses with thick plastic frames and an orange jumpsuit, and his hands were cuffed in front of him. From certain angles, the way his lip curved into his soft cheek gave him a touch of the hallmark facial characteristics of people with Down syndrome. I hadn't noticed this in any pictures of him, so it suddenly made more sense that people who'd known him had thought he might be intellectually disabled: that quality of his face, along with his speech impediment, poor social skills, and malleability, had combined to give that impression.

We said hi and he said, "It's pretty empty in here and all," referring to the fact that we were the only two in the no-contact visitors area that morning. I told him he looked the same except for his gray hair, and he said, "I got gray?" Then he bent over, showing me the top of his head, and asked if he was losing his hair. I said he wasn't.

We talked for a couple of minutes, a conversation like our phone conversations: he answered my questions about his life in prison without much self-reflection or articulation of feelings and got back to the list of things he wanted me to look into, the documents and witnesses I needed to find.

At a pause I looked at him directly and asked, "Walter, did you kill Barbara Jean Horn?"

He looked back at me and said, "No."

"Do you know what happened to her?" I asked.

He looked away, then back, confused.

"Do you mean, like, what the trial said and all?"

"No," I said. "I know about the trials. But aside from all that, do you know what happened to that little girl?"

"No," he said.

He'd had plenty of time to prepare for that question, so I didn't give his answer much weight. But I had to ask him to his face, and he'd answered me directly.

Sitting in the visitor's cell, trying to establish a rapport with this person I'd read so much about for so long, I was struck by his lack of ability to connect even in the small ways we all do in conversation: someone tells you something, you have eye contact, body language, and gestures that communicate your feelings even more than your language does. But that level of communication didn't happen with Walter, and, as in his letters, not only did he not try to use emotion to get to me, I had to pry at his feelings and then only got them in one- or two-word answers: something "felt bad" or made him "pissed."

The longer I spoke with him, the more I thought he must have developmental disabilities. But that didn't answer the question of whether this hunched, handcuffed person was a murderer or a victim.

At one point I tried to come at the subject sideways by asking him about his sex life. He wasn't going to admit to an interest in underage girls if he'd had one, but I needed to at least draw him out on the subject a little. He told me he'd had sex with several women, a total of maybe a dozen times. I asked him if he'd ever been in love, and he told me the following story: One Halloween night years before his arrest he'd gone to a strip club in North-east Philadelphia called Visions and talked to a beautiful dancer named Autumn. He'd talked to her all night, she was special, and after that he went to see her dance a few times but never talked to her again. Then, years later, when he was in jail, some guy he knew was on the phone with a friend who was at Visions and she was there. The guy's friend at Visions told her Walter was on the line, and she remembered him, she couldn't believe it, she was too excited to talk to him just then and ran off to the bathroom, crying. But she'd told the guy's friend to tell Walter she would write to him. He got a letter from her, and they wrote back and forth a few times. Walter thought they were falling in love, but then she stopped writing.

Walter's idea of love, then, was something he'd felt about a stripper who'd been nice to him. But it was also a strange story: why would a stripper remember a customer for four years and write to him after he was arrested for murder? It didn't make sense, but Walter insisted it was true.

I spent my first day interviewing Walter going over his version of events, on the lookout for a change in his story of either the day of the murder or his interrogation by detectives, but his stories hadn't changed. I'd hoped it would be easier in person to get some better understanding of what he'd gone through from his perspective, but that hadn't happened either; he explained his days and memories like listings.

The contrast between the detail of his memories of dates and locations and his lack of ability to describe his own thoughts or feelings was striking. When I asked about his mother, he said, "She had her own problems and stuff." Even without knowing the medical terms for her "problems"—paranoid schizophrenia and Munchausen syndrome by proxy—there might have been a lot for him to talk about; he'd wanted nothing to do with her in her final years, and the last time he'd seen her, by chance on a bus, he'd ignored her. He learned only later that after his arrest she'd put posters up around town, trying to find evidence of his innocence, and had gone to see a local columnist to beg her to write about his case. (Instead, the columnist wrote about the obviously mentally ill mother doing the best she could for a murder-defendant son.)[3] Soon after that she'd died in her apartment, and her body went undiscovered for weeks.

I asked Walter about all that, but he didn't say much. On the other hand, when I asked him how long it took to drive from Rutland Street to the shack on the Jersey Shore he stood up, gesticulating with his cuffed hands on the Plexiglas, and for several minutes gave me street-by-street directions. Later he wanted to tell me every stop he made on the three-hundred-mile delivery route the night before his meeting with detectives. I told him it wasn't necessary. A few months later he sent me a map, hand drawn on six or eight regular-sized sheets of paper taped together, of his delivery route, with every stop and the number of pallets of rolls he'd left there.

In person, it was clear that Walter does have emotions, though he doesn't process and express them like most people. And that he has difficulty reading and responding to eye contact, gestures, tone of voice, and emotional cues.

It was also clear that he hated that people think he's stupid or mentally ill; he told me he was worried that someday he'd have an appeals lawyer who wanted him to plead insanity to get off death row.

"They'll try to say I'm mentally ill," he said. "They like to say everyone's a little screwy. I'm not going to say I'm mental. Because I didn't do it."

As I left the prison after my first six hours of talking to Walter, I was convinced it was impossible that Devlin and Worrell, who had him in the homicide office for at least fourteen hours, didn't notice that he was "off." But what did "off" mean? I didn't think he was slow—that wasn't the problem. He understood his case very well. But it was something.

That night in my hotel near the prison it occurred to me that Walter behaved like some of the students with developmental disorders that a friend of mine taught. He reminded me of the kids who had what was called, at the time, Asperger's syndrome (now part of autism spectrum disorder, or ASD), which is characterized by difficulty in picking up emotional cues, lack of empathy or emotional connection, and lack of ability to process emotions. I knew from Walter's medical records that some of the diagnoses he'd received as a child—organic brain dysfunction, ego weakness—corresponded with aspects of Asperger's syndrome, so I described Walter's behavior to my friend over the phone and she said it sounded like Asperger's but obviously couldn't diagnose him over the phone.[4]

I thought of the passage Devlin had written down at the alleged moment in the confession when Walter broke down: in addition to "I feel like killing myself over this," Devlin alleged that Walter had said, essentially, *You've got to give me a minute. You have no idea how hard this is for me, I never meant to kill that little girl.*

Walter was not capable of conceiving or expressing that many layers of emotional information—balancing an understanding of the detectives' frustration with an expression of his own powerful emotions and a plea for more time and stating it all clearly in a high-pressure situation.

Even with all of the problems with the case against Walter, I'd always wondered how some people could be so sure his confession was false. But it wasn't just that the language in the confession was smoother than Walter's or that he'd supposedly spoken coherently for more than two and a half hours without being interrupted. The detectives, I realized after meeting Walter, had put complex emotions and feelings in the mouth of a man whose brain didn't operate that way.

11

RELIVING IT ALL OVER AGAIN

AFTER ANOTHER TWO DAYS with Walter Ogrod, I felt I knew the case well enough and had enough doubts about his guilt that it was time to contact Barbara Jean's family.

I e-mailed John Fahy, explaining my project and asking if he and Sharon would be willing to talk. He replied that he had found a couple of my articles online and that I seemed to be anti–death penalty. He wanted to be clear with me that he and Sharon were pro–death penalty, but if I wanted to include Barbara Jean's story, they were willing to talk to me. I wrote back that I wanted to include their views, whatever they were. We set a day, and John wrote that when I got close on the morning of the interview I should call him at home to get directions.

"I'll be able to help you with that," he wrote. "Whatever you do don't ask Sharon or you'll end up somewhere in Central PA. (Ha Ha) Talk to you soon."[1]

John and Sharon had reunited after Barbara Jean's murder was solved and were living in a quiet, tree-lined neighborhood, in the house in which John had grown up. He answered the door, looking the same as he did in the newspaper pictures taken ten and fifteen years earlier. Sharon looked the same, too; what's most immediately striking about her is her smile, her deep voice and laugh, and her strength.

The living room was small with a thick carpet, a couch, and an enormous television. On the wall above the couch hung a framed portrait of John and Sharon and Barbara Jean, painted after the murder, they explained. I recognized the photo the painting had been based on: Barbara Jean, smiling, her hair in bangs.

A pillow on the couch had a poem embroidered on it:

If tears could build a stairway
And memories a lane
I'd walk right up to heaven
And bring you home again

We sat at the dining room table with our coffee. They explained that they had just moved in, that the house had been John's mother's house, the house John had grown up in, the house they had come back to the night of the murder after their interrogations by detectives.

When a child is murdered, the parents are the first suspects, and rumors about the Fahys had quickly spread through the neighborhood: John drank too much, had a violent temper, hit Sharon sometimes. He did drugs, they both did drugs, they did crank with the Greens; Sarge killed Barbara Jean because John owed him money for drugs. I wasn't sure how to address these rumors. I knew other people whose children had been murdered and who'd withstood the public rumors about what they had done wrong that had gotten their kids killed. It was recurring devastation for people already crushed by guilt that they hadn't been there at the right moment to save their children.

I explained how I had come across their daughter's case and that, if it was OK with them, I would tape the conversation, and everything they said would be on the record unless they told me otherwise. (They ended up going off the record once, to discuss one of the homicide detectives who worked the case immediately after Barbara Jean's death.)

Both of the Fahys had grown up with eight siblings.

"I'm going to guess the answer to this next question is 'yes,'" I said. "Are you guys Catholic?"

They both said "yes," and for the first time I heard Sharon's booming, hoarse laugh.

"With nine in a family, you'd think so," she said.

Sharon and John both have strong Northeast Philadelphia accents, the same accent Walter has (though he had the speech impediment on top of it): a sort of wide, sweeping pronunciation that flies past inconvenient consonants. Sharon usually pronounced her daughter's name "Barrajean," though sometimes when she was speaking more slowly it came out with the second *b*, "Barbrajean." They pronounce their last name "Fay."

John seemed sensitive and was able to laugh at himself. When I asked if he'd enjoyed being in the marines he answered, "They didn't enjoy me." He and Sharon laughed and he added, "I was a little too much to handle."

Sharon told me what Rutland Street was like back then, about warning Barbara Jean about strangers.

"Like, you would tell her certain things about, you know, people could hurt you, and things like that," she said. "But I think you'd try not to take her innocence away. You know, which is sad, because nowadays you have to."

"This summer was brutal," John said, referring to a series of high-profile child murders that summer, some in other parts of the country and a couple in Philadelphia. Kids snatched and murdered.

"Yeah, just on the news, every time you turn around there was another one," Sharon said. "It was horrible, reliving it all over again."

"Live it all over again," John echoed.

———

I had wondered how to ask the Fahys about the rumors about them using drugs, about John possibly hitting Sharon sometimes, but I didn't have to. When Sharon was telling me about Linda Green sending Charliebird across the street with a note asking if she had a joint, John said, "We weren't—like I said, we smoked pot, but we wasn't into pills or something like that. They were drug addicts."

"We did do crank every once in a while, too, though," Sharon said.

"Right," John agreed.

Crank is a cheap, crude form of speed with a strong high. In his book *Methland* Nick Reding describes the high as having five parts: the rush (euphoria); the high (hours of "exceptionally vivid confidence and sense of well-being"); the shoulder (when the high plateaus); the tweak (the "physical manifestations" and intense agitation that come when the drug has finally left the system); and the withdrawal.[2] John took the edge off his tweak and withdrawal by smoking pot.

"For me, it was, you know, you could do [crank] and stay up and drink more," John said. Most of the time, he explained, he'd set out to just have a drink or two. "Never happened, but that was my intention," he said. "But there were times when I set out to get hammered. 'A Southern Comfort, an Alabama Slammer, and a Michelob, keep 'em coming because I'm not driving,'" John would tell the bartender. "Bartenders used to go, 'I can't believe you.'"

"Yeah, we never had a car," Sharon said. "I was like, 'That's the last thing I need to worry about.'"

"I could drink, I could really drink," John said. "And there were times I would come in at four o'clock in the morning, no money left, drunk."

"I'm Irish and bullheaded," Sharon interjected, laughing. "Let's put it that way."

"Yeah," John agreed. "She's Irish, bullheaded, and she wasn't putting up with it. We'd get into fights, things'd get thrown, stuff would get said. I slapped her," he said. "And I knew when I drank it was a problem. But I didn't see the problem that it actually was. You know what I mean? I always put it off on, 'Well, if she would just leave me alone when I was drinking.' To me, that's common sense at that time."

So that was part of Barbara Jean's world, too—her stepfather's hard drinking, fortified with crank, that led to arguments, to fights, to him smacking her mother.

Later, I asked them how they felt about the death penalty. They said when they met with ADA Joseph Casey, he told them the case against Walter would be a capital case and asked if they preferred the death penalty or not.

"I said 'yes' right away to the death penalty," Sharon remembered. "Because I figured that was the worst thing. I'm for 'an eye for an eye.' Actually, I think they should get exactly what they gave to the other person. That's how they should get killed."

John agreed. "You wanna kill him, kill him," he said of Walter. "The death penalty's good. I like the death penalty."

I asked if they'd felt like their opinion about the death penalty mattered to Casey, or if he was just asking out of courtesy.

"I think if we'd have said, 'No, we are totally against the death penalty—we don't want anybody killed in the name of our daughter,' they would've said, 'OK,'" John said.

"You think?" Sharon asked. "I don't know."

In any event, there was no disagreement between the Fahys and Casey. Casey asked if they wanted the death penalty, they said they did, and Casey told them, "Well, that's what we're going to do, then."

"John wanted to be left in a room with him [Walter] with a baseball bat," Sharon said, laughing at the memory of her husband offering this plan to Casey.

"Quite honestly, that's what I told them," John said. "I said, 'Give me a baseball bat and about five minutes and we'll be done with this.'"

When I told the Fahys I had doubts about Walter's conviction, Sharon talked about a couple of things that had always stuck in her mind—not doubts, necessarily, but other possibilities that had never been cleared up: the house the TV box had come from, the strange interactions with some of her neighbors.

"I don't want it to be that, just to make us feel better, somebody gets killed for this and it's not the person who murdered her," she said.

"You want the right guy," I said.

"Absolutely," John agreed. "And I believe that Walter is the right guy."

He was tense but remained friendly.

I asked if they had a few more minutes to show me some pictures of Barbara Jean, and John went off to find them. And then there she was, in photo albums, in snapshots, the beautiful little girl with the great smile. John and Sharon teared up as they looked through the pictures.

I'd asked the Fahys to tell me what convinced them of Walter's guilt but learned several things from them that, I thought, supported Walter's innocence. First of all, they, too, didn't believe Barbara Jean could have been murdered in 7244 Rutland Street without the Greens, who were home all afternoon, knowing about it. This was a central claim of Walter's defense. The Fahys' explanation for it was that the Greens *did* know about the murder but covered for Walter. I found it difficult to believe that Sarge knew Walter killed Barbara Jean but continued living in that house with his own children and, given his antipathy toward Walter, never told the police, even he was arrested a couple of months later for beating Walter. Years later, Alice, their daughter, told me her father said if he'd known of the crime he would've killed Walter himself.[3]

I also thought their story of how they were interrogated by Devlin and Worrell in February 1992, a month before Walter's interrogation, supported Walter's version of events, especially since

Devlin had told Sharon that putting that kind of pressure on possible witnesses or suspects was part of the process of reinvestigating an old case. They'd pressured the Fahys so much, John and Sharon had left the Roundhouse thinking Devlin wanted to pin the murder on John. I didn't think Walter could have so accurately described an interrogation like it if he hadn't been through one.

John walked me to my car. It was late afternoon; the street was quiet. I thanked him again for talking to me. His eyes seemed full; I had the impression he wanted to tell me something. He looked past me for a moment, then back at me. Whatever it was, he held it to himself.

We shook hands and I got into my car and drove off, impressed by John and Sharon and that they'd made it through together. I didn't see how John could've had anything to do with Barbara Jean's murder. So many people described how frantic he had been that afternoon, searching for her, and he'd called Sharon at the same time the man carried the TV box down Rutland Street. He'd also followed up with detectives so many times over the years, trying to keep the case alive. As for the possibility of Sharon lying to cover for him, I believed what she'd told detectives in 1988 and 1992 and repeated to me that morning: if she thought for one second John had anything to do with Barbara Jean's death, she'd kill him herself.

12

FINDINGS OF FACT

THE FIRST AND MOST IMPORTANT ISSUE to be decided prior to Walter's trial for Barbara Jean's murder was whether prosecutor Joseph Casey could use Walter's statement to Devlin and Worrell at trial or if it had been coerced. In September 1993 Judge Juanita Kidd Stout held a hearing on this issue.

Judge Stout was one of the most distinguished jurists in Philadelphia. In her long career she had been an ADA in charge of a division of the DA's office, the first African American judge in Pennsylvania, the first African American woman to be elected to a judgeship in the United States, and the first African American woman to serve on any state's supreme court. She had gray hair pulled back tightly from her forehead and habitually leaned forward in her chair to look out over the courtroom with deep-set, intelligent eyes. Being five feet three inches, she sometimes had to sit on a pillow on her chair to see over the bench.

Stout was comfortable with high-profile cases, having presided over two of the biggest in recent Philadelphia history: the investigation into the infamous 1985 showdown between Philadelphia police and the radical MOVE organization that culminated in the firebombing of the MOVE house and the ensuing destruction by fire of an entire city block; and the trial, in absentia, earlier in 1993, of Ira Einhorn, a '60s radical who'd beaten his girlfriend to death. Einhorn somehow got bail on the eve of his trial in 1981 (his lawyer was Arlen Specter, the well-connected former DA who went on to become a long-serving US senator) and fled to Europe. The controversial trial in absentia resulted in a conviction, and Judge Stout sentenced him to life in prison; he was eventually extradited from France and convicted of the murder in a new trial in 2002 and is currently serving life without parole.[1]

For ADA Joseph Casey, fifty-three, with thinning gray hair and a middling reputation, this was a big case. He had a chance to win a high-profile case that had embarrassed law enforcement officials for four years, from when Barbara Jean Horn's body had been found two blocks from her house to the morning of Walter Ogrod's arrest. Casey had worked on the case since 1989, overseeing the 1990 grand jury that had failed to indict either of two other suspects in the murder, and now could get a death sentence for a vicious killer who had put the whole city on edge.

The most important issue at Judge Stout's suppression hearing was what was known as the "six-hour rule," according to which once Philadelphia detectives had a suspect in custody, they had six hours to interrogate him. Any confession that took longer than six hours to obtain was supposed to be thrown out—was, as Devlin himself described it, "not worth the paper it's written on."[2]

In the Ogrod case, the statement was even more important than usual—since there was no other evidence against him, if the statement were tossed, he would go free. And the statement presented a real six-hour rule problem for the prosecution; even by the detectives' account, Walter had been in the homicide offices for about fourteen hours, from his arrival at the Roundhouse at 3:45 PM on April 5 until being booked the next morning at about 6:00 AM. (If Walter's version is true, he arrived around 1:30 PM and was there more than sixteen hours.)

The detectives, then, had to whittle Walter's fourteen hours in the homicide offices into a six-hour confession. The first step in this process was to swear that they never thought of Walter as a potential a suspect, only an "informational witness," until the moment he confessed. This was crucial because the six-hour rule clock only started ticking when Walter became a suspect.

On the stand at the suppression hearing, Devlin gave the detectives' version of what happened the night Walter signed the statement. He admitted up front it was a crazy story that in some ways didn't seem to make much sense, but it went like this: Walter called homicide after noon on that Sunday, April 5, 1992, and made an appointment with Detective Worrell to come in for an informational conversation at 6:00 PM. It had *never occurred* to either detective—Devlin stressed for the first time of many—that Walter might be a suspect in the case. To the detectives' surprise, Walter showed up at 3:45 PM, more than two hours early. Worrell met him in the lobby of the Roundhouse, signed him in, and took him upstairs to wait on the benches outside Room 104, the homicide offices. Devlin testified he was out running errands at that time and protocol required two detectives in an interview, so Worrell waited for Devlin to get back before taking Walter to an interview room. The entire time he waited on the bench, Devlin explained, Walter was free to go, because he was not a suspect yet.

Devlin said he got back to the Roundhouse at around five thirty and Worrell put Walter in Interview Room D, leaving the door open because Walter was purely an informational witness— not a suspect. For the next half hour or so, the detectives conducted what Devlin called an "oral" interview, meaning he didn't write down what Walter said. He only began writing down the questions asked and Walter's responses just before six thirty.

During this conversation, one of Walter's answers concerned the detectives, Devlin explained: Walter said that on the day of the murder Barbara Jean had come to his house sometime between 1:00 and 3:00 PM, looking for Charliebird, and that he'd let her in, told her to "go talk to Mrs. Green," who was in the dining room, and gone upstairs.

Until that moment, Devlin testified, they'd never heard that Barbara Jean had been in any house on Rutland Street that day other than her own. He asked Walter if Barbara Jean had talked to Mrs. Green after he let her in, and Walter said he didn't know.

This, Devlin testified, was hard to believe, because if Linda had been in the dining room, as Walter said, he would've seen her from the front door and would know the answer to that question.

The information about Barbara Jean being in the house and Walter's apparent lie about seeing Linda bothered the detectives. Then, Devlin testified, Walter told them that when John Fahy came to the door later in the afternoon asking if he'd seen Barbara Jean, Walter told him he wasn't sure if he had or not. This answer bothered the detectives, too—what kind of person wouldn't tell the father of a missing little girl that he'd let her in his house a couple of hours earlier?

Devlin testified that he sensed that Walter was getting nervous and so asked him, "You're not telling us the truth. Are you, Walter?"[3]

Walter began crying convulsively, Devlin said. Devlin and Worrell decided to give him a chance to compose himself. It was 6:50 PM.

"You know, Walter, relax, take your time," Devlin told him.

Even at this point, Devlin swore, he and Worrell had *no idea* Walter might be a suspect.

Devlin said he got Walter a cup of coffee and Worrell took him to the bathroom. Back in the interview room Walter took his seat, sipping his coffee, eyes red and swollen, and before the detectives could say anything started talking, pouring out a long, rambling description of his childhood. Then Walter said he was going to tell them something he'd never told anyone, not even Dr. Ganime, his psychiatrist for many years.

Devlin said it still didn't occur to him or Worrell that Walter was a suspect, but they decided out of an abundance of caution to read him his Miranda rights. They gave Walter a printed card with the rights on it and had him read them aloud and initial each one. They did not make a note of this on Walter's interview record, nor did they record the time of day on his rights waiver—an odd thing to forget, since the entire point of a rights waiver is to prove a suspect understood his rights *before* he confessed.

Devlin testified that after signing his rights waiver, Walter seemed to want to cooperate, so they asked him the one question they had: What were you going to tell us? And, Devlin told the court, he wrote down verbatim what Walter said next: "This is going to be hard for me to say. Please be patient and let me take my time. I never meant to do anything bad to that little girl. I feel like killing myself over this. It's caused me a lot of stress. I'll tell you the best I can remember it."

Then, Devlin swore, Walter spoke for the next two hours and forty-five minutes, uninterrupted, describing the murder and the aftermath as Devlin transcribed every word, verbatim. The detectives never interrupted, Devlin explained, because they were nervous Walter would stop talking if they did.

When he finally did stop, they stepped into the hallway to consult with Sergeant Nodiff, their supervisor, then went back in for follow-up questions. Devlin asked Walter if he ejaculated during the sexual assault. Walter said he didn't remember, and Devlin asked him if he knew what the word meant. Walter said he did. Was anyone else in the house? Walter didn't see anyone. Had he talked to anyone while carrying the body around? He didn't remember doing that.

The questions continued, Devlin testified, but it became clear Walter wasn't going to cooperate anymore. They had him read a couple of pages of the completed statement out loud to make sure he could read Devlin's handwriting, and then he read the rest to himself, signing each of the sixteen pages as he went. They faxed the statement to the charging DA at 12:04 AM.

Devlin said he and Worrell were surprised by how relaxed Walter was once the confession was done. He was "a different guy . . . like he excised a demon or something."[4] They didn't even handcuff him. He put his feet up on the table, ate a cheesesteak, drank some coffee, and read the newspaper.

Sergeant Nodiff, Devlin said, called Joseph Casey at about 2:00 AM to come in and sign off on Walter's statement. He didn't say if they discussed why Nodiff got Casey out of bed to review a statement if it had in fact been accepted by the charging DA two hours earlier.

In his cross-examination of Devlin, Mark Greenberg focused on the detective's claim to have written down everything Walter said "verbatim." How could it have taken two hours and forty-five minutes for Walter, in a smooth, uninterrupted monologue, to say what amounted to a few minutes' worth of spoken words? Devlin explained that Walter had stopped often to cry. Had Devlin noted those pauses in his transcript? No, Devlin admitted, he hadn't made a note every time it happened; he'd noted it once at the beginning but not again, though it happened several times.

Eventually, Devlin admitted the statement was not verbatim. This was the first time the prosecution's case against Walter would shift, but not the last. Walter had been arrested and charged with capital murder because, the detectives swore, an unprompted confession had poured out of him and Devlin had written down every word. Now Devlin, pressed on this explanation, admitted it wasn't exactly true.

A few minutes later, under intense questioning from Greenberg, Devlin grudgingly admitted that he and Worrell had known every provable detail of the case—manner of death, that Barbara Jean was wet, that she was naked, etc.—before they ever talked to Walter.

Greenberg questioned Devlin about the justifications he was offering for producing a confession without a single provable detail that only the killer would know. Devlin grew testy.

"We did not know . . . the location of the murder," he snapped. "We did not know the instrument of the murder. We did not know who the murderer was."

But there was no other evidence for these things.

Greenberg came to the problems with the detectives' version of the interrogation, including their stated impressions of Walter at the time. Devlin said Walter had appeared normal and sober.

"Regular person, right?" Greenberg asked.

"Seemed to be," Devlin said.

"Yet, the first question on page fourteen [of the statement] that you wrote down, 'Do you know what 'ejaculate' means? Answer: 'Shooting your load so to speak.' What was it about Mr. Ogrod, Detective Devlin, that made you ask a twenty-seven-year-old to define what the word 'ejaculate' means?"

Devlin tried to dodge the question but eventually admitted, "To find out whether or not he knew what 'ejaculate' meant."

"Did you think that was such a word that would have difficulty for him to define?" Greenberg asked.

"I had no idea," Devlin said. "I had no idea."[5]

Greenberg asked if he'd noticed Walter's speech impediment or anything that indicated Walter might have psychological problems. No. Had he ever asked his supervisor if Walter seemed like the kind of person who might confess falsely? No. Did he now know his supervisor had asked Alice Green that same question the next day? No.[6]

Devlin came through his cross-examination well enough; no one could prove that he'd noticed Walter's speech impediment or that Walter was "off," so it would come down to whether the judge would call him a liar by throwing out Walter's statement. Not very likely.

————————

Greenberg called Walter's landlord, Howard Serotta, to describe his conversation with detectives on April 1, 1992. This would establish that the one remaining detail in the statement that supposedly only the killer could know—the murder weapon—had actually come from detectives themselves.

Serotta described his conversation with the detectives, them asking about the weight set; he said having a homicide detective show up was not an everyday thing and it was the only time he ever spoke with Philadelphia detectives about Walter, so he couldn't be mistaking it for a later conversation. He said he was very surprised when Walter, who seemed like a good person, was arrested, and he told of waiting a few weeks to clean out Walter's apartment, assuming the detectives would be back to search it. He said he eventually cleaned the apartment himself and didn't find anything of interest to the case—no weight set, no child pornography, no child's belongings.[7]

Peter Blust testified next, describing Walter's frantic phone call the morning he was arrested. This testimony was meant to support Walter's claim that he had been saying he was coerced and describing his interrogation in detail from within a few minutes of being booked; he could not, then, as the prosecutors would claim, have invented the story at his lawyer's suggestion a few days later.

But Joseph Casey, alerted to Blust by his friend Joe Brignola, had done his research. He got Blust to admit that his law license had lapsed and that he'd been arrested a few years before for drunk driving and being abusive to a police officer. This finished Blust as a witness, which meant that when the trial came, the jury wouldn't hear his corroboration that Walter had recanted his confession immediately.

Greenberg put Walter's psychiatrist, Dr. Ganime, on the stand to give some of Walter's background, explain Walter's deficiencies, and offer his opinion that the confession was not in Walter's style of speaking. This was the closest Greenberg came to putting up an expert to describe Walter as being at high risk for giving a false confession; given the limits to his resources, it might have been the best he could do. He never brought up Joseph Casey's post–2:00 AM trip to the homicide office.

––––––––

Predictably, Judge Stout ruled that the prosecution could use Walter's statement at trial, which would be in late October. But even as she ruled Walter's statement admissible, she undermined the detectives' version of events, writing in her "Findings of Fact/Conclusions of Law" that the detectives *did* ask Walter's landlord if Walter had a weight set—which would mean the detectives had their idea of the murder weapon before they talked to Walter. Joseph Casey realized the import of this finding and asked Stout to reconsider it. She said she would be happy to, but I can't find any record that she did, which means her original finding remains on the record.[8]

13

LIKE TV STUFF

WALTER'S TRIAL STARTED ON OCTOBER 21, 1993, three days after what would have been Barbara Jean's tenth birthday.

The TV box that had held her body was placed between the prosecution and defense tables with a garbage bag over it.[1] Judge Stout peered down from her bench; Walter, pale and bulky, his black hair greasy, sat with a legal pad in front of him.

John and Sharon sat in the front row behind the prosecution table, surrounded by two rows of family. They were going to have to testify, and it made them nervous.[2] Even at that point, knowing whom to blame for Barbara Jean's death, they felt they'd failed her.

Joseph Casey's case was the Devlin/Worrell statement, which was strong evidence, given how juries usually view signed confessions to murder. But the statement had its problems, too. To win, Casey needed to undermine the witnesses who'd seen the man with the TV box and focus the jury on how creepy Walter was and on the horror of the murder. If they felt Walter was the kind of person who could do such a thing, they'd convict him.

Casey began his opening statement by describing the Fahys moving into 7245 Rutland Street, meeting the Greens, and Barbara Jean becoming friends with little Charliebird. He explained that she'd been killed by six or seven blows that left four large lacerations on her scalp, a substantial bruise on her left shoulder, and two bruises on her back over her shoulder blades. She had lived for thirty to forty-five minutes after being struck, he said.

Casey next began the process of making the testimony of the witnesses seem vague. He only intended to call one of them, Michael Massi, the car salesman, who'd had the quickest, least-helpful look at the man with the box and was now willing to say he'd disagreed with the widely distributed police sketch of the suspect. But Casey knew Greenberg would call the other witnesses, so he undermined them generally, telling the jury that "a couple" of people saw a man carrying the TV box around the neighbor-hood and that the next day, in what he called "one those quirks of fate that ofttimes affects investigations," it ended up that only one witness, David Schectman, actually helped a police artist cre-ate the sketch of the suspect.[3] This same witness, Casey pointed out, identified three different men as the man he'd seen carrying the box.

Casey was arguing that both the witnesses and the police sketch were unreliable, as Detectives Devlin and Worrell had decided when they took over. Casey urged the jury not to be too hard on the original detectives: they'd done their best, they'd just spent too much time trying to track down someone who looked like the sketch.

Casey explained Devlin and Worrell's decision to refocus the investigation on Barbara Jean's block. As the detectives interviewed neighbors, he said, they heard over and over about the problems at 7244 Rutland Street. When they realized that no one who'd lived there at the time of the murder had been questioned prop-erly, they decided to start with the Greens, who put them in touch with Walter Ogrod. Ogrod came in as an informational witness, Casey said, but after a brief conversation burst into convulsive sobs. The detectives had no idea what was going on.

"Worrell and Devlin looked at one another and went outside and may have said some obscenity," Casey explained, "'What the F is going on?'"

Realizing how strange it must sound to the jury that two bril-liant, experienced homicide detectives swore they'd been entirely clueless even at that late moment that Walter might be a suspect, Casey added, "These are not dumb guys—I did not suggest that."

Casey outlined the detectives' version of how the statement progressed: they took Walter to the bathroom to wash his face, got him a cup of coffee, and then he started talking about his childhood and said he was going to tell them something he'd never told anyone, not even his shrink. How they stopped him and had him read and sign the rights waiver, and then he talked for two hours and forty-five minutes straight.

"You will see the defendant's signature at the bottom of each of the pages where he admits what he did to Barbara Jean Horn," Casey told the jury. "I ask nothing more than that you give your full attention during the trial, as you have during the entire time I am talking to you."

He thanked the jury and sat. Mark Greenberg stood.

"Ladies and gentlemen, good afternoon," Greenberg said. "There is nothing worse than the death of a child at the hands of a murderer. There is nothing more heart-wrenching than to see the parents of that child and know the pain they feel, have felt, and will always feel for the rest of their lives."

But the jury wasn't there to mourn for Barbara Jean or to comfort the Fahys, he said. They were there to say whether the Commonwealth of Pennsylvania could convince them beyond a reasonable doubt that Walter Ogrod was the murderer. And when they heard all the evidence, they would say Walter Ogrod was not guilty.

Greenberg listed four things that proved Walter's innocence: he was not the man carrying the box; he was a man of good character, a law-abiding citizen; the "confession" was false; and no evidence connected Walter to the crime.

Greenberg described what each witness had told police at the time of the murder and emphasized that one of them, David Schectman, originally said he'd seen and spoken to the man with the box for eleven minutes. Three of the witnesses would testify, Greenberg said, and describe the person carrying the box as five feet six to five feet nine, 160 to 180 pounds. That description did not match Walter Ogrod, who is six feet two, 220 pounds.

Greenberg spent a fair amount of time on Ross Felice, the original suspect, and then explained that because of his job Walter hadn't slept in more than a day when he went in to speak with the detectives.

"I am telling you unequivocally that the defense in this case is that Walter Ogrod did not kill this child and that the confession taken from him is bogus," Greenberg said.

He described how, during the interrogation, the detectives had posed questions to Walter—"Well, could you have done this? Could you have done that?"—until Walter doubted his own memory.

"An important cog in this case will be the testimony of Walter Ogrod," he said. Walter was not articulate but would tell them what happened, Greenberg said. He asked them to follow their oaths, to wait for the case to be over before deciding anything.

"If you do, I am confident you will find Walter Ogrod not guilty."

Joseph Casey's first witness, a detective, put fifteen blown-up pictures on an easel, one at a time, to show the jury the scene where Barbara Jean's body was found. Sharon and John were sitting directly in front of the easel. When Barbara Jean was shown, naked in the box in a fetal position, hair matted in blood, Sharon bowed her head and held a handkerchief to her eyes. John put his arm around her. After a few minutes they went out into the hallway and hugged each other by the marble staircase, crying.[4] Walter sat, his expression blank.

A supervisor of the criminalistics unit for the City of Philadelphia testified that he'd isolated a single sperm cell with no tail in a spot of Barbara Jean's saliva in the box; Greenberg confronted him with the fact that a scientist hired by the defense thought the "sperm" could be many other kinds of debris. This disputed sperm head was the only thing approaching evidence that Casey had to support the idea that Barbara Jean had been sexually assaulted, and it wasn't much. (Later the slide with the alleged sperm head was sent for DNA testing, but no DNA was extractable.)[5]

Casey tried to move quickly through what the witnesses had seen, since they hurt his case. Michael Massi took the stand and explained he was sitting in his cubicle in the car dealership with his feet up when the man with the box walked past him heading north. He said he didn't get a good enough look at the man to identify him but also said he disagreed with the composite sketch—the man's hair, in particular, was longer than depicted in the sketch, he now said. This was what Casey needed from him—doubt about the sketch.

On cross-examination Greenberg pointed out that Massi had told detectives two days after the murder that the sketch was a very good likeness, the hair "almost exact."[6] Massi said he didn't remember that.

Casey was addressing the weakest parts of his case as best he could, tossing out possibilities for the jury—there could've been a sperm head, maybe the sketch wasn't accurate. He then began the work of building a visceral case against Walter based on the horror of the murder and an image of Walter as the kind of demon who would kill a child.

Sharon testified that she'd never met or seen Walter before the murder and told her story of the day of the murder. She described Detective Kelly informing her about the child in the box, how she didn't think it was going to be Barbara Jean and wanted to be out looking for her daughter. She described going to the medical examiner's office to identify Barbara Jean's body.

Mark Greenberg had no questions; nothing Sharon said had much to do with Walter's guilt, and there was no point in looking like he was badgering the victim's mother.

John testified about watching TV with Barbara Jean on the morning of her death, walking to the market with her, doing his chores. When he described how she'd come to ask if she could help clean the refrigerator and he'd sent her outside, he broke down crying.[7] He described his panic as he ran through the neighborhood, unable to find her.

Greenberg asked only a couple questions, nothing confrontational, establishing that Barbara Jean went over to the Greens' house a couple times per week. Had Greenberg known how Devlin and Worrell had interrogated John and Sharon in February 1992 he could have asked about it, showing that Devlin's idea for clearing the case was to interrogate everyone involved until someone cracked.

After their testimony, the Fahys were in court every day, leaving only when pictures of Barbara Jean's body were shown. They watched the jury to see what effect different testimony had; it seemed any time a witness made an important point, no juror was taking notes, or one or another wasn't paying attention.

Sharon stared hard at the back of Walter's head, hoping he could feel how much she hated him. He never looked at her.

Casey chose Paul Worrell to give the detectives' version of Walter's interrogation. Devlin's performance on the stand at the suppression hearing had been problematic. He was a good witness, well-spoken and confident, but his arrogance also came across, both in manner and in thinking he could get away with his "verbatim" claim. Judge Stout had let it go, but a jury might not.

So Worrell told the jury the detectives' version of Walter's statement, the same story Devlin had told using so much of the same language that it's hard to imagine the testimony wasn't rehearsed: Walter called on the Sunday, made the appointment, showed up early; they had no idea he was a suspect until he burst into tears and gave the two hour and forty-five minute uninterrupted confession. He never seemed tired; they never noticed his speech impediment or that he seemed "off."

Worrell offered no explanation for how, if John Fahy knocked on Walter's door on the afternoon of the murder, as Walter had supposedly told them, Walter had managed to come upstairs in the middle of the murder or cleanup to have that conversation or why he hadn't mentioned this terrifying interruption to them in his statement.

As Devlin had, Worrell tried to make the outlandish nature of their version of how the confession happened into a strength.

"You could have knocked me over with a feather [when Walter confessed]," Worrell said. "My partner and my expression was utter disbelief. . . . It was like TV stuff. You just don't bring in a guy to talk about the time of day and he is giving you this four-year-old case."[8]

———————

Mark Greenberg cross-examined Worrell. Unlike Devlin at the suppression hearing, Worrell admitted Walter looked the same now as he had on the night of his statement—that, as far as Worrell knew, Walter hadn't grown five inches and gained fifty pounds since his arrest.

Greenberg highlighted a few of the more difficult-to-believe aspects of the Devlin/Worrell story—that, for example, Walter, who hadn't slept in thirty-six hours, never yawned or looked tired.

"Isn't it true, Detective Worrell, that the reason you give Ogrod coffee . . . is to keep him awake and alert and keep him going?"

"No, I gave him coffee because he was very upset," Worrell said. "It may not have been the first cup of coffee I had given him."

Greenberg took Worrell through the list of the facts of the murder the detectives had known before ever talking to Walter: that Barbara Jean had gone to the Greens' house regularly, that she'd been found naked and barefoot, dead from six or seven blows from a blunt object; that her hair had been wet, so she might have been washed off, and she'd been covered in a blue-green garbage bag. They'd also known the TV box came from 7208 Rutland and about the man seen carrying and dragging that box down St. Vincent Street. Worrell admitted the detectives had known all of that.

"Weren't either you or Detective Devlin, with this information that you had . . . asking Mr. Ogrod, 'Could you have done this? Could you have beat her with the pipe? Could you have got the box and put her body in the box?'" Greenberg asked Worrell.

"No, no, sir," Worrell said.

Greenberg questioned another odd claim: that they never showed Walter a photo of Barbara Jean until the end of the interrogation.

"Was it your concern, detective, that after these hours and hours of interviews that you described, that Mr. Ogrod and you were not on the same wavelength as to the identity of the deceased in this case?"

"I got those photographs and laid them on the desk next to Detective Devlin and he showed them to Mr. Ogrod . . . although we had just went through this whole thing. I wanted, 'Is this the girl and is that the box?' I wanted that in the statement," Worrell answered.

"Didn't you show those photographs to Mr. Ogrod at the beginning of the statement in order to prompt him to remember about what supposedly happened or maybe what he supposedly did to this little child?" Greenberg asked.

"Those photographs, again, were shown at the end of the statement for identification purposes," Worrell said. "I made what I thought would be a 360 degree circle. I didn't want a 340 degree circle. . . . I wanted him to identify [the] two pictures."[9]

When Casey's chance to ask more questions came, he tried to prop up the statement by having Worrell describe what the detectives hadn't known before interviewing Walter: who had been living in the house, that little Charlie Green was nicknamed "Charliebird," that there were two dogs, that Walter had a weight set, that Barbara Jean had knocked on the door and gone inside 7244 that day. They also hadn't known anything about Walter's childhood or about him having a psychiatrist, Dr. Ganime.

None of this background information shed any light on the murder, and the story about Barbara Jean going in his house that day had come from the detectives in the first place.

———————

Casey's next witness was Detective Edward Rocks, Devlin and Worrell's colleague from the SIU who'd worked both Maureen Dunne's murder and Barbara Jean's murder.[10] Rocks had overseen the taking of crime scene photos at the Dunne murder, so he had a particularly good reason to remember that there had been a weight set in the basement and that it was in some of the crime scene photos. Since he'd been working out of the same office as Devlin and Worrell when they took over Barbara Jean's case and were looking for a "trouble house" in the neighborhood, it would've made sense for him to tell them about the Dunne homicide file—but if he'd done that, they would have seen the weight set and the alleged murder weapon before they ever talked to Walter. So Casey needed Rocks to testify that the Dunne homicide had never come up with Devlin and Worrell until after Walter confessed; only then did Rocks have the file retrieved from storage.

Casey stood Rocks next to a large picture of the Dunne murder scene on an easel, a piece of paper covering Maureen's body, and had him describe Walter's basement: the weight set, the big sink in the corner. He asked Rocks if he remembered Devlin and Worrell telling him about Walter's "benign [and] gentle" interrogation, and Rocks said it was only when he heard Walter had confessed to killing Barbara Jean with a pull-down bar that he remembered the weight set at the Dunne crime scene.

On cross-examination, Greenberg established that Rocks, Devlin, and Worrell were colleagues in the SIU and that Rocks knew they were working the unsolved murder of Barbara Jean Horn, beaten with a blunt object. He didn't directly press Rocks on his claim to have forgotten the Dunne murder until after Walter's statement.

———————

Casey next had to establish the pull-down bar from Walter's weight set as the murder weapon. He put the manager of a sporting goods store on the stand to explain what a pull-down bar was and which model of gym set had been in Walter's basement. Then he called Dr. Haresh Mirchandani from the medical examiner's office to testify that Barbara Jean's wounds could be consistent with the pull-down bar. Mirchandani admitted on cross-examination that he couldn't be sure the pull-down bar was the murder weapon, since the wounds could have been inflicted with any other blunt object of the same size.[11] But Casey's use of Mirchandani was a bit of a sleight of hand to begin with: the medical examiner who had actually performed the autopsy, Dr. Hoyer, had suggested in his report that the murder weapon was flat, like a two-by-four, which would rule out the pull-down bar.[12]

Alice Green testified next. She was eighteen now, and her father, probably the closest person in the world to her, had recently died of sepsis at the VA hospital in Philadelphia. Her mother was drinking heavily, so she'd taken care of her father for months, as well as her little brother. Alice was holding up OK, but this trial was hard. She felt terrible about what had happened to Barbara Jean; she'd loved that little girl from the first day they met, when Barbara Jean stood across Rutland Street and yelled, "You wanna be my fwiend?" at her. She'd felt bad for the little girl, too, when she saw John and Sharon fighting.

When she'd first heard that Walter was the killer, it hadn't made much sense to her. She thought he was disgusting and obnoxious but not into kids or violent like that, and not clever enough to get away with if he did do it. Other things about the case bothered her—the pull-down bar as murder weapon didn't make sense. She'd seen the thing and it was too small; she didn't think Walter could have used it to hit the little girl the way they said he did. Also, she had been in that basement after the murder pretty regularly and had never seen any disruption or blood or anything like it. And most of all, no one in her family could figure out how Walter could have killed Barbara Jean in the basement when Sarge and Linda were home that afternoon without them hearing anything. Sarge said he would have heard it, gone down there, and killed Walter himself.

But the detectives insisted—he confessed, he was the killer. And they could make lots of little things look bad.

Alice had come in once to meet with Joseph Casey and be prepped for trial. She thought he was really grasping at straws, pressuring her to make things about Walter sound bad. At one point, referencing a Judge Stout ruling that Alice couldn't mention some of the rumors about Walter that Casey wanted her to, Casey became explicit about what he wanted her to do.

"Alice," he said, "you're sharp." He told her any chance she got to mention the disallowed stories, she should take it; if she didn't get to say it during one answer she should squeeze it in somewhere else.

Casey pushed her so hard during the prep session she broke out in hives.[13]

On the stand Alice said she hadn't gotten home until later in the afternoon on the day of the murder. She said that Walter had lifted weights for hours every night for months prior to Barbara Jean's death but stopped after the murder. Then Casey surprised her by bringing up the fact that she'd lit a candle in Barbara Jean's memory every day and that Walter never paid much attention to it. To Alice, this was classic Casey, making everything Walter said or did seem sinister. Casey asked her if Walter could have seen Barbara Jean's house from the windows in his room, the implication being that Walter could have watched Barbara Jean. She said he could.

On cross-examination, Greenberg had Alice admit she wasn't home all day, every day, so really couldn't know if Walter lifted weights or not.

Charliebird was next. He was twelve now, stocky and blond with a pageboy haircut and a very soft voice.[14] He said he'd been swimming at the rec center the day of the murder. He said Barbara Jean was his best friend and once when she came over two days in a row Walter asked him about it. He'd seen Walter's weight set in the basement, and Walter had been working out before the murder, he said, but he couldn't remember if he ever worked out after. Noticeably absent were some of the creepy stories about Walter he'd allegedly told detectives back in 1992.

Casey's final witnesses were a police officer who photographed 7244 Rutland Street after Walter's arrest, a medical expert who explained the injuries to Barbara Jean's brain, and a detective who had been on the crime scene the night of the murder. Casey also recalled John Fahy to the stand to say he'd been in 7244 Rutland with Sharon and Barbara Jean only once, in June 1988. Then Casey called up a plainclothes cop, a friend of the Greens who'd known Walter well enough before the murder to say hi occasionally when they ran into each other at the AM/PM mini-mart or a local bar, and whom Walter called by his nickname, "Bebop." After the murder, the cop said, he never saw Walter in the bar, and when he did see him at the AM/PM Walter didn't say hi.[15]

With that, the prosecution rested.

Casey had done his best to fill the holes in the evidence against Walter with innuendo and create a simple story: Walter, the weird guy across the street, killed Barbara Jean during a spur-of-the-moment sexual assault and managed to keep the secret for four years until, wracked with guilt and confronted by Detective Devlin, he confessed in a long, painful rush.

Walter's defense would have to convince the jury that though he'd signed every page of the detectives' sixteen-page transcript of that statement, he hadn't committed the crime.

14

REASONABLE DOUBT

WALTER'S TESTIMONY WOULD BE the center of the defense case, but before Mark Greenberg put him on the stand, he wanted the jury to understand how flimsy the case against him was. To reinforce that Walter looked nothing like the man with the TV box, Greenberg would put on the two witnesses whom Joseph Casey had conspicuously *not* wanted to call. Then he would put on witnesses who would make sure the jury understood that for about three years, several of the witnesses and many of the detectives on the case had been sure Ross Felice was the killer.

First, Greenberg wanted the jury to know that plenty of people thought Walter was actually a good person. A woman Walter had worked for, the parents of one of his friends, and a friend of his all testified that he was a good person and a conscientious worker.

Then Greenberg put on Jonathan Jones, the detective who'd become suspicious of Ross Felice on the night of the murder, and other detectives who described the identifications of other suspects—Ross Felice, his brother, Michael, and Raymond Sheehan—that each of the witnesses had made. Greenberg put Detective Joseph Walsh on to confirm that two days after the killing, Michael Massi, the witness Casey had put on the stand to say he didn't agree with the composite sketch, had told him the composite was "almost exact."[1]

Christian Kochan, the paperboy, described squeezing past the man with the box on the sidewalk and said he never got a good look at the man's face but thought he was in his early thirties with dark brown hair.

David Schectman, the fireman who'd told police on the night of the murder that he'd seen and talked to the man with the box for eleven minutes, was the most important witness. (His wife, Lorraine, had passed away due to complications from her MS.) Greenberg led him carefully through a description of the crucial time between 5:12 and 5:23 on the afternoon of the murder, when Schectman had interacted with the man with the box. But Schectman was now vague on many details. He said he'd really only had about fifteen seconds to focus on the man's face and during that brief time had been concentrating on the box anyway. He explained that since his wife died he'd started intensive therapy and learned from it that he fixated more on objects than people and was no good at remembering faces. Guilt about not catching the killer right away, he said, had led him to identify the other suspects.[2]

Greenberg asked if he remembered telling detectives on the night of the murder that he'd spoken to the man with the box for eleven minutes. Schectman said he'd only seen the man off and on. Greenberg asked him about identifying Felice at the basketball court in January 1989 and produced Schectman's interview from the day after, in which he'd said there was "no doubt in my mind whatsoever" about Felice being the man. Schectman said he didn't remember that statement and didn't remember identifying anyone in the gym.[3]

David Schectman's evolving story in Barbara Jean's case demonstrates some of the problems with eyewitness testimony. He was waiting for his kids to come home from camp when a murderer walked up to him carrying a TV box. Schectman couldn't have known that, of course, but when he finds out he can't help but think that if he'd figured it out he would've caught the guy immediately. He calls the police, wanting so much to help, and tells them he saw the man, even talked to him, *for eleven minutes*. He knows this because he was checking his watch the whole time. He could identify the man for sure—he was *right there.*

Schectman and his wife help a police artist make a sketch, it goes up everywhere; the police show him pictures and Schectman picks a guy out. But nothing comes of it. The police come back, they take him to a gym and yes, that's the guy. *That* is the guy. Schectman is trying to help so much he eventually IDs three different people, and each time he's sure. But even the act of working on the composite sketch might have settled certain details in his mind in certain ways, and once the police sketch was up all over town, those details may have been more deeply imprinted on his memory.

These kinds of things happen to eyewitnesses. Because memory isn't a videotape but a narrative we form of our past, it is more susceptible to revision than we realize. Our brains mix events, louden or soften bits of memory based on later impressions, and lock on these later revisions as truth. By the time of the trial, David Schectman had been through several waves of this.

In Walter's case, however, the eyewitness testimony was actually very strong—all five of them describe the man as below-average height, slim, with light brown hair, wearing a T-shirt and shorts. They disagreed on whether he had a light mustache or no mustache or cutoff jeans or hemmed khaki shorts, and whether his T-shirt had a pocket or writing on it.

It's rare to have prosecutors argue that the testimony of eyewitnesses is unreliable, especially when there are five of them. Usually they have to argue the other way, that questionable eyewitness testimony is good enough, and they're often so persuasive that eyewitness misidentification has played a role in about 75 percent of the DNA exonerations since 1989.[4] In this case, Joseph Casey needed to discredit what was, overall, a convincing description, so he did. How many people would have to be freed if the Philadelphia DA's office was as skeptical of eyewitnesses in every case as it was in Walter's?

———————

Since David Schectman was a defense witness, Joseph Casey's questioning of him would technically be a cross-examination. In court, this meant that the prosecutor would have to follow certain rules as he tried to discredit the main witness in his case.

Casey had Schectman explain that, while in therapy, he had realized how much guilt he'd felt about not looking into the box when he might have had a chance to grab the murderer. Guilt, he said, and his desire to be helpful, had led him to identify the wrong men.[5] Then Casey had Schectman, always willing to help, agree that since he had no idea what the man with the TV box looked like, he couldn't be positive it *wasn't* Walter.

With that, the transformation of Schectman's eleven-minute interaction with a man he could identify into a fifteen-second glimpse of a man who might've been Walter was complete.

Greenberg never asked Schectman about the man's voice, which he had described as normal, no speech impediment.

Walter's chance to save his own life came when he took the stand on Friday, October 29, 1993. After a year and a half of insisting he was innocent he now had a chance to tell his story, and if the jury believed him, he'd go home. If not, to prison or death row.

He was twenty-eight but still looked younger, his face still soft, oval. He wore a threadbare tan suit and heavy black shoes.[6] He'd spent much of the trial looking through documents and making notes, trying to hold his face steady. On the stand his expression was blank, limned with fear and defiance.

He raised his right hand and was sworn in, his voice barely audible.

"Please keep your voice up so the jury can hear you," Greenberg said.

Walter nodded. He hunched in his chair. He was scared. He knew his speech impediment made him difficult to understand and that people thought he was strange; he'd heard the names his whole life: "freak," "retard." He wasn't good with expressing emotions and was struggling with so many: fear; anxiety; hope; anger about being in jail for something he didn't do, about Pennsylvania trying to execute him and the lies the detectives told about him; anger at Joseph Casey, who was always bouncing around the courtroom, waving papers, yelling, lying.

Walter focused on following Mark Greenberg's advice: pay attention to whoever is talking to you; don't look at the jury too much, because you never know how they will take it; when you answer a question, get to the point and don't overexplain yourself; and whatever you do, *do not* get angry, Casey will try to make you angry so the jury will think that you might be the kind of man who could kill a little girl if provoked.

Sharon and John were in the front row, as they had been for every court session, surrounded by their families.[7] Listening to Walter was going to be brutal, maybe the worst part of the whole thing.

Greenberg looked pale and tired. At one point he'd found himself in the hallway standing next to Barbara Jean's aunt. He'd tried to tell her he was sorry for her loss, but her eyes flashed hatred and she told him if he was so sure Walter Ogrod was innocent, why not take him home to babysit his kids? Greenberg understood her hatred of him was normal, but it still bothered him.

That the case would come down to Walter's testimony made Greenberg apprehensive. Walter looked and sounded strange and had a very hard time dealing with stress, and what could be more stressful than this? What would happen to Walter on cross-examination? What if Casey got him angry, made him look not just "odd" but like a psychopath, cold blooded enough to sexually assault and kill a little girl?

Greenberg asked Walter how old he was and how old he'd been at the time of the murder (twenty-three), where he'd been living in 1988, how long he'd lived there, how well he'd known the neighborhood. He'd been living at 7244 Rutland Street, he answered; he'd lived there most of his life and knew the neighborhood well.

"And back in 1988, who was living at that address with you?" Greenberg asked, establishing how crowded the house was.

"It was me, Mr. and Mrs. Green, their little son Charlie Jr., their daughter Alice, my friend Hal moved in at the time, and their friend Tom was living in the basement," Walter said.

Greenberg asked Walter his height and weight and what his height and weight had been at the time of the murder (the same). He asked about the Fahys, and Walter explained that John came over sometimes to have a couple of beers with Sarge Green while Barbara Jean played with Charliebird. Walter said Mr. Fahy seemed like a nice guy and that he'd only run into Mrs. Fahy once or twice and had never met her.

"I want to direct your attention to July the 12th, 1988," Greenberg said. "Do you remember hearing about the death of Barbara Jean Horn?"

"Yes."

"Did you kill Barbara Jean Horn?"

"No."

The Fahys held hands, their hatred surging: *Liar. Coward.*

"Do you remember where you were at about 3:00 that day?"

"Yes, I was home," Walter said.

"Can you remember, after you heard the news about Barbara Jean's death, what you did?" Greenberg asked.

"Well, when I heard about it, I was home with the Greens and all, and we heard about some neighbors saying something about it and all, and that wasn't until the next day and all, when the cops came around asking people questions," Walter said.[8]

The jury was getting a chance to hear how Walter spoke when he was nervous. Whether they thought he sounded like the confession would be as important as anything else in the trial.

Greenberg, countering the prosecution claim he knew was coming, that Walter had moved out of his house to avoid the murder investigation, had Walter explain that he'd lived at 7244 Rutland for more than a year after the murder.

He then put into evidence the business card Detective Worrell left with Walter's landlord on April 1, 1992, and asked Walter about Saturday, April 4.

"I woke up [at eight o'clock], maybe got something to eat and all, took the dog for a long walk, came home, watched some TV, got to notice it was time to go to work, showered, changed into work clothes, arrived at the bakery at 1:00," Walter said. "I went to check my load—nothing was ready yet. Got delayed about three hours, waiting for bread from another bakery and all, left about 4:00. I did not return until 4:30 AM the next day."

When he got back to Bake Rite, his supervisor asked if he could do an extra route. He agreed, finished that route at about ten thirty, got home around noon, and called Detective Worrell.

"He wanted to talk about John Fahy, the stepfather of Barbara Jean Horn," Walter said. "He wanted to know some information about it. I said, 'Can I do it over the phone?' He said, 'No, you have to come down here.' [I said] 'I don't have that kind of time.' He said . . . 'We want to solve the case. A little girl was killed. We just want to ask you some questions. We will be in and out quick.'"

Walter said he got to the Roundhouse at about 1:30 PM on Sunday, April 5, and Detective Worrell came downstairs to escort him up to homicide. Worrell told him not to sign in, which Walter thought was strange. Walter asked him about one of the detectives he knew from the Dunne case. Worrell said he remembered the case and the detective was doing fine.

"I must have been there for about an hour or so," Walter said of his wait outside the homicide offices. "After about the first forty-five minutes I asked Detective Worrell, 'Can we do this another time? I am getting tired. I want to go home.'"

"He said, 'Give it a couple of minutes.'"

He described being put in the interview room, giving the detectives his basic information and telling them what little he knew about Barbara Jean's murder.

"And this information that you told the detectives, where did you get that information?" Greenberg asked him.

"I remember reading the papers, *Northeast Times, Daily News, Inquirer,* what I seen on TV," Walter said.

He described Devlin taking a photo of the TV box, empty, out of a folder, asking if it helped Walter remember. More photos:

Barbara Jean in the box with a bag over her, with part of her head showing, and with the bag removed. Walter said Devlin told him he'd seen Barbara Jean that day when she came over for Charlie-bird, that Linda wasn't home so Walter let her in.

"They said, 'Well, you took her downstairs,' and all, you know." Walter's voice faltered again.

"Keep your voice up," Judge Stout told him.

"I am sorry," Walter said.

"The jury must hear you," Judge Stout explained.

"They kept up more and more," Walter said of the detectives pressuring him.

"Tell us about the 'more and more,'" Greenberg said.

"They said, 'Well, you took her downstairs' and all, you know . . . "

Walter's voice trailed off, and Judge Stout asked him again to speak up.

"I said, 'No, I didn't take her downstairs,'" Walter said. "He said, 'Yes you did, man. You took her downstairs to have a little fun. . . . No clothes. She was raped.' I said, 'No, I did not rape her.'"

Devlin, Walter said, told him he was "off" and asked if he'd ever seen a psychiatrist. Walter told him about Dr. Ganime. They gave him half a dozen cups of coffee and woke him repeatedly when he dozed off. "We will be all night, you might as well eat," he remembered one of the detectives telling him when they gave him the cheesesteak. He said the confession wasn't finished until just before he was taken downstairs to be processed and that he never read it over.

Greenberg tried to get Walter, with all his difficulties, to explain how the intensity of the emotions in that interview room that night and his sleep deprivation led him to confess to a crime he didn't commit.

"What was going through your mind during this questioning, this interrogation?" Greenberg asked.

"Horror," Walter said. "They were showing me pictures of Barbara Jean. They set another set of two [pictures on the table] and she was outside the box. . . . I seen the marks on her head, on her body."

Greenberg had him describe how he'd come to sign the waiver of his Miranda rights.

"I said, 'I want a lawyer,'" Walter explained. "[Devlin] said, 'No. You signed it. You didn't have a lawyer here.' I went to the door. He shut the door on me."

The detectives cuffed him into the metal chair that was bolted to the floor and went out of the room. Maybe half an hour later they took him down to booking.

"Now, from the time you got down to the Police Administration Building about 1:45 [PM on Sunday] until everything was completed, did they allow you to sleep at all?"

"No."

"How were you feeling physically?"

"Tired."

"Anything else?"

"Little stressed. You know, physical work from before and all, and I wanted to help out. That is why I came down in the first place for, to answer some questions. And that was about it."

"That is all," Greenberg said.

Joseph Casey's strategy for cross-examining Walter was basic: antagonize him by treating him with scorn and calling him a liar, hoping he'd get angry in front of the jury; confuse him by changing topics suddenly and frequently; and, through it all, drop little questions and asides that would let the jury know what kind of scum Walter truly was.

Casey's first question was one of these.

"Sir," he asked Walter, "From where your bedroom was in the house at 7244 Rutland Street, if you were to look out, you could see 7245 Rutland Street Is that correct?"

Walter agreed.

"And you can look right out and if you were to look right out, you could see this little girl," Casey continued. "Is that correct?"

"Yes, sir."

No one associated with the case had ever suggested Walter watched Barbara Jean, so Greenberg objected, but Judge Stout overruled him. Casey had successfully floated the idea to the jury.

"Now, that day," Casey continued, "you said you were home, is that correct?"

"I got home around 2:00."

"Did you go up to your bedroom?"

"I went in the house. Mrs. Green was there. I went to my room."

"You did go up to your room?"

"Yes, sir," Walter said.

"You looked out the front window?"

"No, sir."

"Today, five years later, you can look that jury in the eye and tell them you specifically remember not looking out the front window?" Casey asked.

"I don't remember anything about looking out the front window as soon as I got home," Walter said.

"I didn't ask you if you remembered it," Casey said. "My question was, 'Did you look out the window?' and you said 'no.' You want to change that answer?"

"Sir, I do not remember looking out that window as soon as I got home."

"I didn't ask you whether you looked out as—" Casey started.

"Let's not argue with him," Judge Stout told Casey.

Casey did. "Is your answer, 'No, I did not,' or, 'I don't remember'?" he demanded. "You tell me which of those two things you want it to be now?"

"I don't remember now, sir," Walter said.

"You are not saying you did not look out the window. You are saying you don't remember?"

"I don't remember looking out the window."

Casey had picked a fight, starting the work of getting Walter mad: showing his scorn for Walter, suggesting that Walter liked to watch Barbara Jean out his bedroom window, and accusing Walter of being a liar.[9]

Next he jumped topics, asking what time Walter went to the Roundhouse for his interview and whether or not he'd told Worrell he was tired. He wanted Walter to admit he'd agreed to go in for the interview, which Walter did.

Casey jumped topics again.

"You said, sir," he started, "that you heard from the neighborhood or read the following: . . . 'That the man with the box tried to dump it in the . . . Dumpster behind where I live.' Did you say that on direct examination?"

"Yes, sir."

"Where did you read that? I want you to be as specific as you can."

"I read it in the *Northeast Times*. As far as I can remember, that is where I read that from."

Casey was suggesting Walter knew that the man with the box tried to put it in a Dumpster before that detail was in the papers. (Later he would put the *Northeast Times* reporter who had covered the case on the stand to testify she had never written about a Dumpster in her articles. But articles in other newspapers had mentioned the Dumpster, and the story had been around the neighborhood before it was in the paper anyway. Walter could have picked it up anywhere.)

Casey jumped topics again and debated Walter on when exactly during his police interview he'd asked for a lawyer. Didn't you say you only asked for a lawyer half an hour before you were taken downstairs, Casey pushed; no, Walter insisted, he'd been asking all night. Casey asked a dozen more questions along this line, his voice stretching toward outrage as he pushed Walter about when he'd asked for a phone call versus when he specifically asked to talk to a lawyer.

"Objection, tell him not to yell at the guy," Mark Greenberg intervened at last.

Casey said he would stop yelling. He asked more questions about when Walter asked for a lawyer but couldn't move Walter on that point.

Then came the most important question of all.

"But you never confessed, you never said you killed Barbara Jean," he said.

"No, sir," Walter said. "They are the ones who wrote the confession, the so-called confession that I signed."

"Sir, that is the alleged confession," Casey said, holding it up. "Whose signature appears at the bottom of that page?"

"Mine, sir," Walter said.

Casey held up every one of the sixteen pages and got the same answer, then did the same with the rights waiver.

Walter said he'd signed what the detectives told him to sign.

"You did everything they told you?" Casey asked.

"Yes, sir," Walter said.

"So if they said, 'You killed Maureen Dunne,' you would have said 'yes'?" Casey asked.

"No, sir," Walter said.

"You wouldn't have signed a confession which contained that? Is that correct?"

"That is right."

"The only confession you would sign is the confession saying you killed Barbara Jean Horn?"

"That's the only one that has my signature, sir."

"That's the only confession you would have signed?"

"Sir, I never killed Barbara Jean Horn."

"That's not my question. You signed a confession admitting you killed Barbara Jean Horn. You would not have signed a confession admitting you killed Maureen Dunne."

"Because that one, when that statement there [was taken]," Walter said, referring to his interview after Maureen's murder, "I was up, I had my sleep prior to that incident, and I didn't have cops coming down on me, throwing photographs of the dead child's body in front of me."

"But had they done that, you would have confessed to that, wouldn't you, if you had been sleep deprived?"

"Who knows what would have happened in the police department," Walter said.

Casey bristled; he'd just lost an exchange with the supposedly low-IQ murderer he was supposed to be breaking down.

He pressed on: Would Walter have confessed to killing his mother? To killing Maureen Dunne?

"As many hours as it was and the time they had me down there and done the same thing they done with this one, probably," Walter said.

Casey switched to Walter's work sheets from Bake Rite Rolls. He asked questions about the dates and times of Walter's shifts, to try to muddle what the time sheets clearly showed and what Walter's supervisor said during his testimony: that Walter had been up all night driving before his interrogation.

Then Casey took on Walter's claim that he'd gotten to the Roundhouse at about 1:30 PM on the day of his interview, pointing out that Walter's name appears in the logbook at 3:45 PM. Walter explained that Worrell had told him not to sign in when he got there. Didn't the officer at the front desk usually sign in visitors, Casey asked. No, Walter said; every time he'd been to the Roundhouse for the Dunne case, he'd signed himself in.

These lines of questioning were meant to establish Walter as a liar, and now Casey started his main assault: going over Walter's statement line by line, derisively asking which things Walter actually said and which the detectives made up.

"Sir," Casey said, "I will go through the document . . . and I will ask you which words are yours and which words are not yours. 'Question: Walter, did you know Barbara Jean Horn?'

"'Answer: Yes, I did, she was the little girl who lived across the street from me when I lived on Rutland Street, the little girl they found dead in the box.' Did you say that?"

"Part," Walter said. "I knew Barbara Jean Horn . . . yes, I did."

"Did you say that?" Casey asked.

"Yes, I know her," Walter said.

"Did you say, 'Yes, I did'?"

"Yes, I did, yes, sir."

"That's a yes. 'She was the little girl who lived across the street from me when I lived on Rutland Street.' Did you say that?"

"Yes, sir."

"'The little girl they found dead in the box.' Did you say that?"

"I didn't say 'in the box,' sir."

"But you knew she was found dead in the box?"

"Yes, sir."

"But today, eighteen months later, you can specifically remember that you did not say 'the little girl they found dead in the box'?"

"To the best of my knowledge, yes, sir."

"You are qualifying it again," Casey said. "Is it that you did, you didn't, or you don't remember?"

"To the best of my knowledge, I did, sir."

"You did?"

"To the best of my knowledge, I did remember saying everything but 'the little girl they found in the box.'"

Casey turned to the weight set, establishing for the jury Walter's ownership of the pull-down bar and repeating Alice Green's story that Walter had lifted weights for two hours each day in the month or so before the murder but stopped after Barbara Jean was killed.

"For approximately a month before Barbara Jean Horn was murdered, were you downstairs working out virtually every day for two hours in the evening?"

"No, sir."

"Did you work out at all in a two-month period before Barbara Jean was killed?"

"No, sir."

"So sitting here today . . . you can tell us you specifically remember going back from July 12, 1988, and telling this jury that you never worked out during that month. Is that correct?"

"Yes, sir."

"Back to the [statement]," Casey said. "Page three, right after the answer that you did not give. 'Question: When was the first time you knew Barbara was missing?'

"'Answer: When her father John came over to my house and asked me if I had seen Barbara because he couldn't find her.' Did you say that?"

"Yes, sir."

"'Question: Did you tell him that Barbara was inside your house that afternoon? Answer: I am pretty sure I must have told him.' Did you say that?"

"No, sir," Walter answered.

Casey pressed Walter on every line, tossing in unrelated questions to keep him off balance. He kept up the innuendo, too; at one point he asked if Walter had ever dated an adult female while Alice Green was living in the house, implying that Walter didn't date adults while underage Alice was occupying his thoughts. Walter denied every petty smear Casey slipped into his questions to make him seem like a pervert and a liar, but any one of them might stick with a juror, or, after so many, the jury might decide some had to be true.

"Did you break down crying, sobbing [in the interview room]?" Casey asked.

"After a while they were throwing pictures of the dead child in my face, sir. Who wouldn't?" Walter answered.

Casey questioned Walter about what he'd told detectives about his mother and childhood and suggested that Walter told the detectives a sob story about his life as an excuse for the murder.

Casey switched back to the statement.

"Did you say, page eight: 'This is going to be hard for me to say. Please be patient and let me take my time.' Did you say that?" Casey asked.

"No, sir," Walter said.

"Did you say, 'I never meant to do anything bad to that little girl'?"

"No, sir."

"The word before 'meant' is crossed out and there are initials, 'WJO.' Whose initials are they, sir?"

"Mine, sir."

Casey was emphasizing that, since Walter had initialed changes to the confession, he must have read, understood, and agreed to it.

"Did you say, 'I feel like killing myself over this'?"

"No, sir, that is not what I said, sir."

"Did you say something like that?"

"They said, 'You are sick.' I said, 'I would not do that. If I did, I would have killed myself.' Not 'feel like killing myself.'"

"So although you were sleep deprived and they were throwing pictures at you, you said, 'I would not do anything like that or I would kill myself'?"

"I would not have done anything like that, sir."

"Give me the exact words you told them?"

"They were saying I was sick and I said I wouldn't do that. I said, 'If I hurt a kid, I would have killed myself.'"

"And you specifically remember saying that, today?"

"Yes, sir. Never hurt little kids, sir."

"The jury will decide that," Casey snapped. "I am getting these speeches and I have to protect myself," he said to Judge Stout.

Casey asked about Barbara Jean knocking on Walter's door on the afternoon she was killed.

"Did you say," Casey asked, "'I got the idea to ask Barbara Jean to come down to the basement with me and she followed me down the basement'?"

"No, Detective Devlin, sir."

"Detective Devlin said what?"

"He was saying, 'She came in your house, we got people [who saw her]. Look, you decided to take her downstairs and have some fun.' That's what Devlin was hitting me with. 'You took her downstairs, you wanted to have some fun . . .' He was telling me what happened. 'Look, you took her down, you wanted to have some fun,' sir."

"Did you agree with Devlin that that is what you did?"

"No, sir. He kept on saying, 'You did it, you had to have done it. We have people who say they seen you take the girl in the house.'"

"Did you believe that, that people saw you take Barbara Jean in the house?"

"He pressured me all night."

Casey asked a series of questions about little Charlie Green, culminating in one about Charlie's claim that one day a few weeks before the murder Walter had asked him if "that little girl"—Barbara Jean—was coming over to play. This was meant to suggest that Walter had had some kind of unnatural interest in Barbara Jean prior to her death.

Walter said he'd never asked Charlie that question.

Casey jumped back to the interrogation.

"After you believed that someone saw you taking Barbara Jean into the house and the detectives started suggesting things as you have said, did you agree with them that that is what happened?" Casey asked.

"No. Not at all. I said 'no,'" Walter answered.

"Not at all?"

"They said, 'Was it this way?' I said, 'No,' and if I look down they take it like, 'All right, you agree.' I just looked at them and all."

"Did you read this document before you signed it?"

"They read it to me as I stated before, sir."

"Did you know the content of the document at the time you signed it?"

"Not that much, sir. I wasn't very awake."

"So for all you know, you could have been signing a document admitting to killing Maureen Dunne, John F. Kennedy, Jimmy Hoffa, Heather Coffin, Olga Terpeluk Ogrod, and Gregory Ogrod. Is that correct?"

"I could have," Walter said.

"And you were so, so tired, you just signed it?"

"I didn't know, they were putting a story in my head, complete with pictures, sir."

"But you were so tired and all these things had been done to you, you just signed it?"

"I don't know what was going on at the time, sir."

"'Play doctor,' did you say that?"

"No, sir. They suggested that, 'You probably took her down to play doctor.'"

"'And she said "yes," so I started to take her clothes off.' Did you tell them that?"

"No, sir. They wanted to know what happened. They said, 'You probably did it because there were no clothes there.' They said this is probably what happened down there. 'Because she had no clothes, nobody was there, so you figured you could have a quick time with her.'"

"'I remember she didn't have nothing on her feet,'" Casey read. "Did you say that?"

"No, sir," Walter said.

"'Anyway, after I got her undressed, I started stroking her shoulders and her back,'" Casey read. "Did you say that?"

"No, sir."

"Had you ever touched her in the past?"

"No, never had."

"Just to pat her on the head?"

"No, sir, not at all."

"Never touched any little kid. Is that correct?"

How sinister it would seem in this context if Casey could get Walter to admit that he'd patted one kid on the head, once. Greenberg objected and Judge Stout sustained the objection.

Casey returned to whether or not Walter had understood what he was signing when he signed his statement. Walter said again that he didn't know what was going on when he signed.

"At the time you signed this document," Casey said, "do you know that it said you killed Barbara Jean Horn"—Greenberg objected that the question was repetitive but Casey ignored him—"by hitting her with this bar? Did you know that?"

"Yes, sir," Walter said. He said the detectives pushed photos of the dead girl at him, telling him he had to have beaten her to death.

"As of the time they were asking you about this, you did not know she was beaten, you said 'yes.' Is that correct or is that not correct?"

"Yes, I did not know she was beaten."

"Didn't the *Northeast Times* you read say she was beaten? Didn't every paper?"

"Not the way they described it, sir. I didn't see the photos [in] the *Northeast Times.*"

"You didn't see the photos," Casey scoffed. "I am not talking about the photos. I am talking about being beaten. You told this jury that at the time you talked to Worrell and Devlin, April 5, 1992, you didn't know she had been beaten. Did you read it in the *Northeast Times* before April 5 she'd been beaten?"

Walter said it was very different to read it in the paper than it was to be sitting across from two detectives showing you pictures of the dead body. Casey pressed him, and he said again that reading was different than seeing photos.

On the subject of the pull-down bar, Walter was clear: the detectives had told him, "That's how you did it, you hit her with the bar. Look at her. You hit her in the head. She was bleeding a lot."

Casey asked which detective asked about the pull-down bar first.

"I don't know which one because I was like this," Walter said, his face in his hands, "and crying and they kept saying I killed a child."

"And at that time you believed you did?" Casey asked.

"Yes, sir," Walter said. After hours in the interrogation room he'd begun to believe that he'd done it, so he either repeated back to the detectives suggestions they made for what happened—that he hit her with the pull-down bar—or didn't answer their questions at all, which Devlin took as a "yes." Sometimes they told him something *must* have happened—someone *must* have washed Barbara Jean after killing her because her hair was wet when she was found—and, getting Walter to agree that it happened, wrote it down as if he'd said it himself.

Walter said the detectives drew a map of the neighborhood and asked him the route he'd taken with the box, correcting him when he got it wrong: *No, people saw you here, you must have gone this way.*

Casey asked him about telling the detectives he put the box down because it was getting heavy. Walter answered that he'd never said that.

"You didn't say anything about it getting heavy?" Casey asked.

"No, sir," Walter said.

"And it wouldn't have been heavy because you worked out with weights. You were a pretty strong guy?" Casey asked.

"I wasn't working out in weights," Walter said. "I didn't touch those weights since before what happened to my brother." With the Greens' friend Tom living in the basement in July 1988, he said, the mess and furniture in the basement made it impossible to use the weight set.

"Sir, you knew you had a little air vent in your garage. Is that correct?" Casey asked.

"No, sir," Walter said. "There was no air vent. They were saying, 'Where did you put the clothes? You had to hide it. Any place you can stuff it?' and all."

Casey pressed but couldn't make any headway.

When Casey finished, Mark Greenberg was relieved: Walter had come through cross-examination well. He'd gotten a little rattled but had not lost his temper and had told a consistent story. The defense rested.

Casey then had a chance to present "surrebuttal evidence," a final round of witnesses to firm up his case. His first was criminalist Louis Brenner, who told his story of locating a single sperm head on a slide of material from Barbara Jean's mouth. Under questioning from Greenberg, Brenner admitted that a defense expert hadn't even been able to locate the sperm on the slide when he examined it and that he himself had no real way to tell a human sperm head from a cat sperm head or from any other random particle that could've been in the little girl's mouth.

Then Casey called the reporter from the *Northeast Times* who'd written about Barbara Jean's murder to say she'd never mentioned a Dumpster in any of her stories. Greenberg objected to her testimony, since Walter could've just been mistaken about where he read or heard that detail. Judge Stout let the reporter testify. She had a folder of all her stories about the case and said none of them mentioned a Dumpster.

Finally, Casey told the jury he had "irrefutable proof" that Walter had lied: the Roundhouse logbook showing Walter signed in at 3:45 PM on April 5, 1992, and a fax machine time stamp on Walter's statement showing it was faxed to the charging DA at 12:04 AM on April 6. Casey put Devlin on to testify about when Walter was signed into the Roundhouse and what time his statement had been faxed to the charging DA. He argued that the fax time stamp proved Walter was lying when he said the interrogation wasn't over until just before he was taken to be booked the next morning.

When it was his turn to ask questions, Greenberg asked Devlin about another time stamp on the cover of Walter's statement —3:38 AM, April 6. What was that fax time?

"We had sent another document to the charging unit," Devlin answered, "that we had to get approved, as we are, as we asked to get a copy of that document back we asked them, requesting to send us a copy of the statement back we had sent them earlier that morning."

This stumbling answer didn't clear up the mystery of the 3:38 AM time stamp, but Greenberg didn't ask what this other document that needed approval may have been. The timeline of that night offers a plausible explanation: at midnight, realizing their time under the six-hour rule was nearly up and that Walter's statement wasn't done yet, the detectives faxed a portion of it to the charging DA. When the statement was actually finished a couple of hours later, Sergeant Nodiff called Casey. This would explain why he got Casey out of bed, something he didn't need to do if the statement had been accepted by the charging DA two hours earlier. Casey arrived at the office at about 2:30 AM and would later testify he spent about an hour looking over documents—which fits with the final statement being faxed to the charging DA at 3:38 AM.

This theory would still mean Walter was wrong about what time he signed the rights statement—at 3:30 AM instead of 6:00 AM—but given that he'd been awake for over forty hours and in a small windowless room for at least ten, it's not clear if that makes him a liar. He has always said he didn't follow time that night, that all he knows is that he signed the rights waiver just before being taken downstairs for processing.

After Devlin's testimony, Judge Stout sent the jury to their lunch break. Closing arguments would be that afternoon.

15

"LOOK AT THE DEVIL"

MARK GREENBERG BEGAN HIS CLOSING argument by reminding the jury
that their job was to be fair to the defendant and not get caught
up in the "heart-wrenching understanding" of what the Fahys had
been through.

"I ask you to listen to me for the next thirty minutes, or for
however long my voice holds out," he said, "while I explain to you
why there is a reasonable doubt in this case as to whether or not
Walter Ogrod is the man who killed this child."

Walter did not look like the man who carried the box, Greenberg said; there was a better suspect, Ross Felice, who did; and
there was no evidence of a sexual assault, which proved Walter's
statement to Devlin and Worrell was false. The eyewitnesses were
well-intentioned, he said; they'd been trying to help the police in
July 1988 and were trying to help the DA today by backtracking
from the certainty of their descriptions of the man with the box
at the time of the murder, but those descriptions were clear.

He pointed at Walter: "This man is not the individual who
killed that child and doesn't fit the description."

Greenberg said he wasn't there to prove anyone guilty of the
crime but that Ross Felice's suspicious behavior on the night of
the murder and the several identifications of him as the man
with the box raised a reasonable doubt about Walter's guilt. He

150

dismissed the possibility of the single sperm head; the criminalist who thought he'd seen it was wrong, Greenberg said, and even after finding it once it had taken him ten minutes to find it again. Other experts never found it at all, Greenberg said, because it wasn't there; this meant there was no sexual assault and the confession was false. He reminded the jury that Walter's time sheets from work proved he hadn't slept in thirty hours when the interview started. And, he asked, if the bad things the Greens now said about Walter were true, why hadn't they said anything at the time of the murder?

Finally, Greenberg took on the statement itself, chipping at the detectives' credibility by pointing out some of their harder-to-believe claims: that they never looked at the Dunne homicide file, that even though they had pictures of Barbara Jean with them at the beginning of the interview they didn't show them to Walter until the end. The detectives, Greenberg explained, had all the information about the crime before they spoke to Walter and used those details to pressure him.[1]

Greenberg acknowledged that Walter's testimony about what time he signed his rights waiver could have been wrong but said it happened *after* the statement, when Walter was too tired and confused to know what time it was.

He finished by acknowledging the horror of the crime.

"A child is dead," he said. "It is a horrible situation. It is the worst possible death imaginable, the death of a child. But we are not here, members of the jury, to bring that child back. We are here . . . to decide whether or not a man who sits at the defense table is the man who killed that child . . .

"I ask you, I implore you, don't . . . be caught up emotionally in this case. . . . When you go back there [to the jury room] . . . just deal with it dispassionately and coolly, and fairly, and I am convinced that when you look at the descriptions of the person carrying the box, and how it is so at odds with Walter Ogrod, you will agree with me there is a reasonable doubt and you will come back with a verdict of not guilty. Thank you."

It was almost 2:45 PM. Judge Stout ordered a five-minute break.

———————

Closing arguments are supposed to be limited to discussing evidence that was put on during the trial, but, lacking hard evidence tying Walter to the murder, Joseph Casey would need to stretch his narrative. His closing argument would focus on making Walter out to be a liar and the kind of "animal" who could commit such a horrible act.

He began by flattering the jury, telling them their service was second in importance to society only to wartime military service. They were the ultimate fact finders in the case, he said, each chosen because he or she understood that "beyond a reasonable doubt" didn't mean "beyond all doubt."

"If you . . . didn't want to use your common sense, you could have doubt about anything," Casey said. Taking on the role of humble scholar, he told the jury, "There is a German philosopher named Immanuel Kant, and he said, 'I doubt I really exist.' He would go outside and bump into a tree and say, 'I didn't really hurt myself—I don't exist.' That is nonsense. He can't get on the jury I pick, because he has no common sense."

Doubt had to come from evidence, Casey said, not from wanting to avoid an unpleasant job, and in this case the evidence established the defendant's guilt beyond a reasonable doubt. Walter had told them two "demonstrable, provable" lies in his testimony, Casey said: what time he'd signed the confession, and, even more damning, that he'd read about the man trying to put the box in a Dumpster in the *Northeast Times*. The fax time stamp on the confession and the testimony of the reporter from the *Northeast Times* proved that these statements were lies.

"The defendant lied to you," Casey said. "There is a Latin expression, I never learned how to pronounce it, '*Falsis in uno, falsis in omnibus*,' becomes literally translated, 'If a person testified falsely about one material fact, he testified falsely about everything.'"

Casey had told the jury he would give them irrefutable proof of guilt. In a strong case that would be eyewitnesses, physical evidence, a provable recovered weapon to support the disputed confession. Instead, he'd offered them two supposed lies told by Walter on the stand that, even if true, didn't prove much. Casey apparently sensed this. He told the jury that if his arguments for Walter's guilt didn't strike them as powerful, they should feel free to pick their own and, likewise, if he hadn't mentioned something in his closing that they thought was important, they should remember he was just giving them the highlights of what he remembered from the trial, that whatever the jurors thought was important was important.

He kept the single sperm argument alive, or tried to, accusing the defense expert who couldn't locate it on the slide of being greedy and incompetent. Then he said that it didn't matter anyway, the Commonwealth didn't need that sperm to prove sexual assault.

"When you find a little girl, naked, without any clothes, naked in a box, it is a sexual assault death," he asserted.

The jurors, he said, were unlikely to ever again witness the kind of lying they'd seen when Walter testified. He ridiculed Walter for saying the pressure of the interrogation had convinced him he'd committed the murder and then pinpointed what he called "two slips" in Walter's testimony that proved him a liar.

The first had come when Walter referred to seeing a red wound on Barbara Jean's head when, in fact, all the pictures the detectives had shown him of her were in black and white. This had been Walter's worst moment on the stand. But the second "slip" Casey offered as proof of Walter's guilt hadn't actually happened. Casey told the jury that when he asked Walter about carrying the box, "[Walter] said, 'When I was carrying the box,' and then he kind of caught that."

But according to the transcript, Walter never said anything like "When I was carrying the box." Casey had read that line to him; it came from the Devlin/Worrell statement.[2]

Casey told the jury the crime had been eating away at Walter for four long years when the detectives showed up at his apartment, that bludgeoning a child to death might be the most heinous act a person could commit.

"Why? Because of the absolute innocence," he said. "There is no four-and-a-half-year-old who is anything but innocent and beautiful and lovely, untarnished by evil, and that is why, when the defendant killed Barbara Jean and put her in the box, there was planted in his stomach the seed of his own destruction and ruin and it sat there and it sat there, waiting to be stimulated, to grow like some horrible malevolent growth and then explode."

The visit from detectives set off the explosion.

"Four years, four years the defendant was free," Casey said. "Shakespeare, in *Julius Caesar*, tells us, 'Cowards die many times before their death. The valiant taste death but once.' A valiant person does not kill a little girl."

Casey argued that Walter wasn't sleep deprived when he gave his statement, arguing first without any supporting evidence that Walter's work records had somehow been falsified, that he hadn't been driving as long as he said. Then, misstating Walter's timeline for April 5–6, Casey argued that Walter had managed to nap for close to eight hours in the thirty-six preceding his interrogation. (This is not possible. The first two of these alleged "napping" hours were supposedly the two hours after Walter woke up on the Saturday morning; for the next four he was actually driving; for the last two he was waiting on the homicide bench, where he admits he dozed, though the detectives swore he didn't.)

Sleep deprivation is one of the better-known ways to get people to talk. As far back as 1930, an American Bar Association report that was later cited by the Supreme Court said that "it has been known since 1500 at least that deprivation of sleep is the most effective torture and certain to produce any confession desired."[3]

Not according to Joseph Casey.

"Do you think that anyone who hasn't slept would walk in and say, 'Yes, I killed the little girl'? That's the way things go?" he asked the jury. "Hardly. Not within your common sense . . . [Walter] was twenty-six [*sic*] then. . . . You know, you get some home fries and eggs and orange juice, you are ready for another twenty-four [hours]. Young people can do that. When you get my age, you can't, but I don't understand the sleep-deprived thing."

Casey came back to the idea of the "evil growth" in Walter that "Boom! . . . exploded into heavy sobs, chest-racking sobs, shoulder-heaving sobs. . . . This demon has been inside of him for years," Casey said. "'Conscience doth make cowards of us all. Cowards die many times before their death.'"

He argued that Walter had described his bad childhood before confessing to the murder in order to "justify" killing the little girl.

"Look at the devil," he said, pointing at Walter. "What is he thinking when Detective Devlin or Worrell say to him, 'You are not telling us the truth'? The million deaths he died come bursting out."

Though even Worrell and Devlin had admitted knowing most of the details of Barbara Jean's murder before talking to Walter, Casey told the jury that "usually, detectives know everything before they begin to interview somebody. Here, they knew nothing."

He insisted that two previously unknown details of the crime—the sexual assault and the murder weapon—had come from Walter. The detectives had no motive, he said, no interest in getting Walter to confess.

Casey warmed up for his finale, banging his fist on the table to emphasize that premeditation could form in a moment.

"Just sufficient to allow your mind to fully form the intent to kill . . . that's all that is necessary to form the intent to kill. It can be that brief."

Brandishing the substitute pull-down bar, he said, "Keep in mind the Commonwealth did not create the injuries on Barbara Jean Horn. The Commonwealth did not create this bar. The Commonwealth did not push Barbara Jean Horn's head down and then when the poor little girl whimpered, decided, 'Oh my God, I might be caught,' hit her"—he smacked the pull-down bar the prosecution table—"one [BANG], two [BANG], three [BANG], four [BANG], five [BANG], six [BANG], seven [BANG], with the perfect murder weapon . . ."[4]

The courtroom was silent.

It was a fitting end to Casey's argument, a dramatic flourish to reinforce a story for which there was no evidence delivered with a pull-down bar that wasn't the actual pull-down bar that wasn't a good fit for the murder weapon.

The jury had been sequestered for the length of the trial at a hotel in Northeast Philadelphia—an odd choice, jury foreman Charles Graham thought, considering the three hours of commuting time it added every day to load the bus and sit in rush hour traffic to and from the courthouse downtown.

The jurors were told not to speak to each other about the case, but on those long commutes they did.

Graham, a high school teacher, thought the prosecutors had no real evidence against Walter. He spoke with a juror named Alfred Szewczak, a sixty-one-year-old former marine and firefighter with a spiky gray crew cut, who told Graham that his son had been shot in a bar a few years earlier and survived to testify against his assailant, who'd been acquitted anyway based on some technicality. Szewczak told Graham he'd been furious and had vowed if he ever got on a jury he would not let the defendant go free. Graham tried to talk Szewczak out of this notion, reminding him that his duty was to decide the case based on the facts and the law, but Szewczak didn't seem persuaded.[5]

On the second day of deliberations, after eight and a half hours of discussion, the jury sent word to Judge Stout that they were unable to reach a verdict. Mark Greenberg, thinking a deadlock in a case with a signed confession probably meant Walter had barely escaped a conviction, asked for a mistrial. Judge Stout refused and sent the jury back to deliberate more.

The next morning at 10:30 AM the jury sent a note to Judge Stout asking her to clarify what "reasonable doubt" meant. She had them brought into court and explained that "beyond a reasonable doubt" did not mean beyond all doubt or proven to a certainty; on the other hand, a strong suspicion of guilt was not enough to convict. A reasonable doubt must be, she said, "the kind of doubt that would restrain a reasonable man or woman from acting in a matter of importance to himself or herself. If you have such a doubt as to the guilt of the defendant or as to any of the factors upon which his guilt may depend, it is your duty to acquit him."

A few hours later the jury sent word that they'd reached a verdict. Judge Stout ordered the parties to assemble in the courtroom.

As the lawyers and family members gathered, local TV news crews set up live shots outside the building. The verdict would speak directly to the competence of a police department that had struggled for so long to solve a case that seemed so solvable in the days right after the murder; to the credibility of two of Philadelphia's most experienced homicide detectives; to the ability of a DA's office that prided itself on toughness to bring a child killer to justice and help a city that had been gripped by each stage of the case regain a sense of security.

The courtroom was standing room only when the jury filed in and took their seats at 2:25 PM. Most of the DA's homicide office had come over to watch.[6]

Sharon Fahy held John's hand and lowered her eyes; she couldn't look. She thought something was wrong, everyone kept saying so, even Devlin and Worrell, because the jury had taken so long to reach a verdict when it should have been simple: Ogrod confessed, end of story. Convict him, sentence him to death, and let people get on with their lives. With her free hand she held the crucifix hanging around her neck.

John radiated tension. He was sure the jury would convict. They had to; no one could be stupid enough to believe any of the half-assed excuses Ogrod offered about being forced into confessing.

Devlin and Worrell sat next to Sharon's sister, Barb, surrounded by other family members.

Walter sat flat-faced at the defense table with Mark Greenberg.

The court crier turned to the jurors and asked, "Ladies and gentlemen of the jury, have you agreed upon a verdict?"

Charles Graham stood up. "Yes, we have," he said.

"Have all twelve agreed?" the crier asked.

"Yes, your honor," Graham answered.

The crier started reading the verdict. "On—"

Alfred Szewczak stood up. "No," he said.

"Wait a minute," someone in the courtroom called out.

"I don't agree with the verdict," Szewczak said, as loud and clear as he could.

A gasp went through the courtroom. Judge Stout slammed her gavel down.

"If you cannot agree on a verdict," she said, "I will have to declare it to be a hung jury, and I will declare a mistrial. Mr. Ogrod, you will be remanded. You will be remanded to prison." She banged her gavel.

Sharon looked at her husband, horrified; she didn't know what a mistrial was—*Ogrod was getting off? That was it?* She turned to her mother.

John knew a mistrial meant they'd have to go through all of this again. But Ogrod was right there, a few feet away, and John wasn't going to miss his chance. He sprang from his chair and, all of five feet seven and maybe 160 pounds, bowled over a six-foot-five deputy in the center aisle and lunged at Walter.

All Sharon knew was that John's hand was suddenly gone from hers and she heard his mother yelling "My John! My John!" and turned toward him, but he was leaping at Walter. Two deputies were trying to tackle him.

Walter and Mark Greenberg jumped away from the table; Judge Stout recoiled in her chair. More deputies rushed to help as John thrashed his body around, trying to get free.

John was *so close.* If he could just get his fingers around Ogrod's Adam's apple, he'd rip it out and this would all be done with. He could see Ogrod standing back, staring at him.

"I'm gonna fucking kill you!" John screamed at him. Walter looked scared.

It took several deputies to finally pin John, chest down, on the defense table.

"Don't hurt John!" someone yelled.

"She's the one who got beat to death by that fucking animal!" Barb yelled. She saw that a TV crew was filming the scene through the open courtroom door. "Shut that door!" she yelled.

The deputies got John cuffed and hustled him past the reporters in the corridor.

"He killed my daughter!" John yelled over his shoulder.[7]

The jury had voted to acquit: Walter had been seconds from going home.

The local TV stations covered the chaos of the mistrial live—John hustled away in handcuffs, then Walter. Judge Stout ordered John released almost immediately, and reporters followed him and Sharon home.

Reporters also followed Alfred Szewczak.

"I wasn't gonna let him go," he said, standing in front of his house, on the verge of tears, his gray crew cut and craggy face lit by TV lights. He'd been exhausted by the trial, by being sequestered for two weeks, by trying to convince the other jurors of what he knew in his gut: that Ogrod was guilty. To get it over with so he could go home he'd gone along with the "not guilty" verdict but on the way into the courtroom decided he just couldn't do it. So he'd done what he had to do to make sure Ogrod didn't get away.

Szewczak was a replacement juror and reporters found the juror he'd replaced, who told them, "There were gaping holes in the prosecution's case. It's pretty ironic that I got pulled off the jury, because it would have been unanimous if I had been there."[8]

A TV reporter, live outside the courtroom, called the mistrial a "crushing disappointment" for the victim's family, the police detectives, and the DA's office. The DA's office had 120 days to file for a new trial and announced that they would.

Similar coverage was on all three local TV networks, upstaging District Attorney Lynne Abraham, who, originally appointed DA in 1991, had on November 2 won her first election to the post.

Abraham was not one to be embarrassed like that: a child killer had almost walked, and that was simply not going to happen.

———————

John Fahy went to court the next day to apologize to Judge Stout and the bailiff. Judge Stout told him she understood: she thought Ogrod was guilty, too.[9] (This feeling didn't prevent Judge Stout from presiding over Walter's retrial.)

Charles Graham, the jury foreman, in a letter to the *Daily News*, wrote that Szewczak had come to the jury with a closed mind and had voted guilty on the first ballot, telling them, "Nothing you people say is going to change my mind." It was ironic, Graham wrote, that Szewczak, so adamant that a man would never sign a confession to something he didn't do, had, in what he himself described as a "moment of weakness," written "not guilty" on the final ballot despite his belief in Ogrod's guilt.[10]

A retrial was scheduled for early 1994, but Mark Greenberg filed an appeal, arguing that since the jury had signed the verdict slip, Walter had actually been found not guilty and couldn't be tried again. Judge Stout canceled the retrial and everyone waited for a superior court ruling on the appeal.

PART III

A CONVOLUTED THING

16

THE MONSIGNOR

ON A SUNNY TUESDAY AFTERNOON at the end of June 1994, a little more than seven months after Walter's mistrial, John Hall was stretched out, head tipped back, eyes closed, in the driver's seat of a new Nissan sports car idling in a mall parking lot outside Philadelphia. He was in his early forties, with a long, oval face and double chin, high forehead, stringy brown hair, and glasses; his white button-down shirt made him look like an accountant. On the passenger seat were a few blank prescription pads and a prescription for Percocet.

A police officer knocked on the window. Hall opened his eyes and buzzed it down.

"What's wrong?" the officer asked, leaning in. "What are you doing?"

Hall didn't answer, his bland face hiding a mind sparking but not turning over: how to talk his way out of this one. His painkiller fog was thick, the car was stolen, the prescription pads and script on the passenger seat were forged, and he was wanted on parole violations and various new charges in several counties.[1]

"What're you doing with those pads?" the officer asked, nodding.

"I'm a printer," Hall said.

"Oh," the officer said. "You got a business card?"

Hall could only think to drive away fast. The officer had the same thought and grabbed for the keys, but Hall yanked the car into drive, catching the officer's arm in the door and forcing him to run alongside for twenty feet before getting free. Hall sped away down crowded, mall-lined streets and through family neighborhoods, passing into the next town, police cruisers pulling in behind him.

Pursued, he felt heroic, and when he felt heroic he usually wrote about himself in the third person. In a letter to his wife, Phyllis, written a few days later, he referred to himself as an American soldier, the police and DAs as Nazis:

He had become overwhelmed by Nazi armored-personnel carriers. They were coming from everywhere. The poor guy knew he could not escape. . . . Soon, he knew, he was going to be a P.O.W. . . . He had to formulate a plan. If he were captured in the out-lying areas he wouldn't be able to effectively put his plan into action. A dilemma—stay in the more rural areas where he had no more than a slim chance to get away, or head for the city of Berlin, where he could begin Plan B. He decided to go down fighting, but nearer to the Nazi High Command. He knew the Nazis had radioed the city and warned of his approach.

"Berlin" was Philadelphia and the "Nazi High Command" was the Philadelphia DA's office, where he had a better chance to snitch his way out from under the charges he knew were coming.

He saw before him so many Nazis . . . but he dodged and missed all of them. . . . But he knew they would defeat him. . . . . He knew he would be tortured. Maybe killed. But he had made it to Berlin. He opened his storage pack and ate pain-killers to ease his anticipated torture.

Hall described his capture to Phyllis vividly: accepting defeat, he slowed down, let a cruiser ram him, and stopped. Police of all kinds fixed their rifles on him, pulled him out, cuffed him, and beat him. As he wondered if he would die that day, he thought of her. A Philadelphia officer who knew he was supposed to be treated with respect stepped in and saved his life.

As usual with Hall's stories, the truth was more mundane: a cruiser forced him to the curb and another blocked him in. Panicking, grinding the stick shift into gear, he rocked his car back and forth, trying to batter his way free, striking the police car in front. More police arrived but Hall wouldn't stop, so they broke the driver's side window, turned the car off, and subdued him.[2] Bleeding from a cut above his right eye, he was arrested and, news photographers snapping, put in the back of a cruiser.[3]

In jail, Hall assessed his situation. The stolen car, fake prescriptions, and even resisting arrest were relatively minor charges. But dragging the first cop and ramming the cruiser at the end were not.

"I had aggravated assault on police which is a felony of the first degree," he explained later. "Because it would have been my third or fourth [felony] conviction I could've been sentenced to twenty-five to fifty years mandatory minimum. I had to get it off me . . ."[4]

That he could do: Hall was a master snitch, so well known for getting confessions from other inmates and turning them over to prosecutors in exchange for leniency in his own cases that local authorities called him "the Monsignor," because he'd heard more confessions than a priest.[5] He was an intelligent fraud, a craftsman who liked to show off his legal mind and insisted on being the smartest in the room, even in cell blocks full of people who didn't care; a bland everyman with thirteen aliases, four Social Security numbers, and seven birthdays,[6] all of them, he swore, obtained not to commit crimes but to stay safe ahead of all the snitching—crime fighting, in his eyes—he'd done over the years.[7]

Prosecutors in Walter's case had just gotten their big break.

John Hall was born in Philadelphia in 1952, and his father left the family in 1958. A few years later his mother, a sometime nightclub singer, married William Martino, a low-level mobster involved in gambling and loan-sharking. In the late '60s, Martino was paying protection money to a police captain named Hearn, who'd come by the house to collect his payments and who fixed Hall's first criminal charge, a 1971 marijuana bust.

Hall was a runner for his stepfather and then joined Martino's crew in 1978. He worked out a system for stealing cars and forging VIN numbers and another for filling forged prescriptions. Hall's regular pharmacy didn't hassle him about his forgeries, and when passing fake scripts at other pharmacies, he put down the number of a nearby phone booth where he'd wait in case the pharmacist called.[8]

Hall's jail snitching career started in the early 1980s in Northampton County when he said he witnessed an inmate rape and felt so disgusted he had to turn the rapist in. This sense of personal disgust became the founding myth of all the cases he snitched in, always the reason he informed against other inmates— always because of his personal disgust, never in hope of gaining anything for himself. In the early 1980s, he expanded his snitching into more serious crimes and later claimed to have provided the Philadelphia Police Department's organized crime division with statements that led to seven murder convictions.[9] That may be a typical Hall exaggeration, or not: he snitched in that many murder cases in the early '90s, by which time his rap sheet was a thick tangle of charges, snitchings, plea deals, paroles, and probations spanning twenty years and sixty-odd arrests in four counties.[10]

One key to Hall's success as a snitch was that he looked and talked like a lawyer, not the car thief, drug addict, and forger he actually was. He used legal terms and got the inmates he targeted to tell him details of their cases by offering legal advice. Occasionally, inmates thought he was a doctor because of his knowledge of prescription drugs, especially tranquilizers and painkillers. In one letter, he told Phyllis he'd just run into an inmate who kept calling him "doctor" and he couldn't figure out why until he remembered he'd conned the guy into thinking he was a doctor years before, in another jail.[11]

Hall never stayed in jail long; once in, he'd snitch against a fellow inmate, giving the story to authorities in exchange for perks in jail, letters of support, or even personal appearances in court from cops and prosecutors attesting to his cooperation. All of this translated into leniency from judges and early release for Hall.

But he never stayed out of jail long, either; it was as if once he was out, the reality of being a middle-aged drug addict and criminal who'd squandered his significant intelligence would set in, and within days or weeks he'd forge a prescription or steal another car. Sometimes it didn't take that long: he once stole a used car while walking home from jail.[12]

So he'd be back in jail, despondent that he was finally going to get a long sentence, which was worse than death, writing about hoarding pills for the day he would kill himself. His depression would lift when he began his next snitch, at which point he would usually become almost manic with power. It was in the glorious days of snitching, the adrenaline rush of being a big shot in jail, writing briefs better than lawyers could, telling DAs how things were going to go, that Hall lived up to his own image of himself.

Hall was at his confident, incarcerated best when he met his wife. In January 1990 he saved an inmate named Herbie Haak from an assault, and a grateful Herbie put him on the phone with his mother—Phyllis.[13] Soon she came to visit, sitting with Hall in the visiting room, petite, with brown hair and big eyes. Hall couldn't stop thinking about her eyes, he told her, the most beautiful he'd seen; she looked like Betty Boop.[14] When he got out that time they dated, and when he went back in she became his research assistant for snitching. She took his calls from jail, jotted down the locations of crimes, names of victims and lawyers, sent him newspaper clippings from the library. She even went to victims' homes, gathering bits of information for Hall to use in his stories.[15]

With Phyllis's help, Hall's file of letters of support from law enforcement grew. He carried them around jail in an accordion file—another perk that demonstrated his importance.

A January 1990 letter from Montgomery County ADA David Keightly to ADA C. Theodore Fritsch in Bucks County explained that Hall had been a particularly "fine witness" in the prosecution and conviction of Ernest Priovolos and "at least" three other Montgomery County cases, though since Hall's cooperation in those other cases wasn't a matter of public record, he preferred not to give any more details.[16] Keightly stated that he'd agreed to write the letter in exchange for Hall's testimony and was willing to appear in person for Hall if any judge, prosecutor, or Hall's defense lawyer wanted him to.[17]

The Priovolos case was a Hall special—old, high profile, and lacking evidence. Hall testified that Priovolos admitted to killing the victim with a karate chop that sent her over a bridge. He swore he was testifying not in hope of any benefit for himself but out of "human outrage" over the crime.[18] Priovolos was convicted. Two weeks later Keightly sent Hall a personal note: "At the risk of swelling your head," he wrote, "I told the jury you are a man of astonishing brilliance, of keen intellect, and of tragic sickness. . . . Thanks again, John." He signed the letter "Dave."[19]

In August 1991, Keightly wrote another letter for Hall, this one to new Philadelphia district attorney Lynne Abraham, explaining that Hall had been helpful in many cases and deserved a break on his current sentencing.[20] That same month ADA Fritsch wrote a letter of his own to Abraham about another Hall special: Hall had come forward "unexpectedly" a few days before the murder trial of a certain Michael Dirago with "unsolicited cooperation" that changed the six-year-old case from one with a "rather slim" chance of conviction to a "strong one from the prosecution standpoint."[21]

At Dirago's trial Hall gave the jury a horrifying, invented account of the victim gurgling as she died in a car on a bridge. He wasn't getting anything for his cooperation, he swore, and had only come forward because the murder was "revolting."[22] Dirago was convicted. Fritsch's letter explained that Hall had provided important information in other cases, too, "without which major convictions would not have been obtained."[23]

Both Fritsch and Keightly went on to become judges.

The Dirago case also earned Hall letters of support from Howard Barman, a deputy attorney general in New Jersey (where Dirago was eventually convicted because Hall's testimony put the murder on the New Jersey side of the bridge, though the body had been dumped in Pennsylvania), and from Sergeant Thomas Mills of the Bristol Township Police, where the body was found.

Barman wrote that Hall was a remarkable person who, but for an alcohol problem, would probably be a significant member of society.[24] He'd made Hall no promises about writing a letter of support, he explained, but had decided to do so on his own. Sergeant Mills wrote to DA Lynne Abraham that Hall had been of "substantial help" in convicting Dirago and that he was aware of Hall's extensive criminal history but believed that serious consideration of leniency would be appropriate.[25]

Another Hall snitch hadn't gone quite as smoothly but still earned him letters of support. Bruce Castor, chief of the trials division for the Montgomery County DA's office, wrote in May 1993 that Hall had testified at a pretrial hearing against Thomas DeBlase, who was charged with a 1982 murder—another old, high-profile case the prosecutor might well lose.

"Not only did John Hall cooperate fully," Castor wrote, "he testified in a straight-forward, clear, and convincing manner."[26]

Despite Hall's effort, DeBlase's trial was held up by appeals. Castor would write to Hall again in December 1995, repeating his support and informing him that his testimony would be needed when the trial finally started the following month, January 1996.[27] But by then Hall was in the middle of snitching four other homicides in Philadelphia and needed a lower profile, not the press attention that would come from being brought out to Montgomery for a case as high profile as DeBlase's. Castor either decided at the last moment not to use Hall or was told by Philadelphia that he couldn't.[28]

Hall's legend as a snitch grew because of his specialty for these kinds of situations: old, high-profile cases with shaky evidence that prosecutors were in danger of losing. In each case he swore he was testifying out of disgust, without any promise of benefit for himself, but it just so happened that every time he did this the detectives and prosecutors involved in the case followed his court appearances closely enough to know where to send their letters of support and when and where to show up to support him. If the prosecutors in four different counties who used Hall as a snitch are telling the truth that they didn't give him deals for his snitch work and never placed him in jail so as to target a particular inmate, the recurrent coincidences in Hall's life were staggering.

Hall had his own explanation for these coincidences: karma.

"Too many coincidences spaced too close together. It can't be random. It just can't!" he wrote Phyllis. "How do these coincidences occur for him?" he asked about himself. Slipping in and out of the third person, he went on: "[He] gives justice to so many. How do I come into contact with so many that are involved in the most heinous crimes? And that the overwhelming majority are against women. And the helpless. Is this mere coincidence? Contrary to popular perception, I do not seek out these creeps. They fall into my lap. They come to me. And they are scum. Vermin. They deserve what they get from the courts."[29]

With his skills of manipulation, he explained, came the responsibility to use them in a forthright manner.

"Never construe targeting with snitching," he wrote. "They are separate and independent actions. They never merge. . . . I am extremely selective in who I attack. Only scumbags need fear."[30]

In another letter on this topic he veered from something approaching introspection to bragging sociopathy.

"It is hard for me to know what's right always," he admitted. "For so long I've lived in a brutal environment where power and prowess is so necessary for survival. . . . I prevail because of my manipulative skills. If I were to apply them in business (a la Donald Trump), I would be hailed as a legend and hero. . . . There is little doubt that I will stop at nothing to get what I want."[31]

Prosecutors use jailhouse informants all the time, real ones who have real information and help put away actual criminals. The problem is it's very hard to build an honest system by creating an incentive for criminals to lie, and the confluence of a snitch's motive to lie with a prosecutor's need for a conviction can lead prosecutors to ignore obvious signs that a snitch is lying and make them accessories to a snitch's perjury. As a result, false snitch testimony infects our justice system. As of 2015, false informant or snitch testimony played a role in 15 percent of the 325 DNA exonerations to that point.[32]

In the late 1980s the "system" of jailhouse snitching came under scrutiny when Leslie Vernon White, a convicted kidnapper, robber, and car thief who had snitched in as many as forty cases in California, used a jail telephone to demonstrate his snitching technique to a newspaper reporter. Posing as a police officer, prosecutor, and bail bondsman, White called various law enforcement authorities and gathered enough information to snitch out a fellow inmate whom he'd never actually met.[33] In all, White admitted that he had lied for prosecutors in a dozen cases. A grand jury investigating White and the use of snitches in Los Angeles noted that snitch fabrications were a systemic problem. As Robert Bloom summarized the grand jury's findings, "informants often used elaborate strategies to access information about a crime in order to enhance the substance of confessions they fabricated."[34]

The grand jury report estimated that as many as 250 cases over the course of ten years could be affected,[35] and its conclusions about prosecutors were sobering. The grand jury cited one case in which an ADA had actually helped White by providing him information and found, in general, that "very little effort was expended by the prosecutor's office to investigate the background and motivation of informants or to test the veracity of their information and its sources. The prosecutor was primarily concerned with the informant's effectiveness on the stand rather than the authenticity of the testimony."[36]

What one expert on snitch testimony referred to as the "entrenched" nature of the problem became clear in 2014, when it was revealed that authorities in nearby Orange County, California, had been running an inmate snitch factory for years.[37] In May 2015, Radley Balko, a conservative criminal justice reform expert, explained that snitch testimony has become a critical tool for prosecutors because it permits them to put on testimony that is damning and easy to manufacture, and allows them plausible deniability.

"Most jailhouse snitches are lying," he wrote. "This isn't to say that all prosecutors manufacture evidence by using jailhouse informants. It is to say the way informants are treated by the courts makes it very easy to do so."[38]

———————————

Recuperating from minor injuries in the prison hospital in late June 1994 after his high-speed chase, John Hall was anxious: he was looking at twenty-five to fifty years in prison, which absolutely could not happen. He needed to snitch, and soon had an idea:[39] the murder conviction of a prominent Philadelphia mob figure, Ray Martorano, had recently been overturned, and the DA, furious, embarrassed, and worried about losing the retrial, was trying to keep the case from falling apart.

Hall knew an opportunity when he saw it. He described the situation to Phyllis in a letter [emphasis all his]: "The <u>City Nazis</u> were in <u>serious trouble</u>. <u>Very</u> high ranking Nazi officers had lost face, <u>and position</u>, because of certain failures in the past." He then switched into the heroic third person to write about himself:

> He knew of these things from his intelligence work and knew he could give <u>much needed</u> aid to some <u>very</u> influential Gestapo officials in the High Command. In order to get out he knew that he would have to become a Nazi in full uniform. But you can't just call Hitler and say you want to be a Nazi. No, he needed a 'go-between.' Someone who was a Nazi sympathizer, but with allegiance to the American

*who can reward him. Carefully, he came to select Herr Frumer, a
former Gestapo officer with very good connections.*[40]

In other words, Hall needed a lawyer and had chosen Marc
Frumer, a former Philadelphia ADA ("Gestapo officer") who'd
recently gone into private practice. Hall hired him that July, writing to Phyllis that Frumer was a very special attorney, referred by
a very trusted friend, who had a lot of experience as a prosecutor,
knew what needed to be done to get Hall a deal, and knew how
to go about doing it.

The next day, Hall wrote Phyllis praising Frumer again. He was
"a special man with excellent credentials, associations, and insights.
He can get the job done. . . . We have some very high cards in our
hand. Very, very high cards. . . . We want certain things. Basically,
we want spoons. Complete resolution and spoons."[41]

"High cards" meant information on the Martorano case and
"spoons" meant hugging his wife: he wanted all his pending cases
completely resolved, and he wanted to go home. But, he explained,
if you just handed information to the DA's office, they'd take it
and give you nothing. You needed a good lawyer to dangle the
information and make them pay for it.

"Herr Frumer, formerly of the Gestapo High Command," Hall
wrote, "immediately recognized the value [of Hall's information]
to his old colleagues. And HE would make them pay," he just
needed time to "play politics. Make friends. Influence people.
Open doors."[42]

Frumer's $10,000 fee was cheap, Hall wrote. And Frumer
couldn't believe his good fortune that Hall had hired him, that
"he would be paid and do big, big, big favors for the Gestapo,
who would be grateful to him. He would make his name known
to some very powerful people."

Hall, someone again, surged with manic confidence. A super-
hero was needed to get out of the trouble he was in, he explained
to Phyllis. He was that superhero, and every superhero needed
help from someone who could operate in the respectable world.

"Superman had Clark Kent," he wrote. "Incredible Hulk had Dr. David Banner. Underdog had Shoe-shine Boy. Your super-hero needs one too."[43]

His faithful sidekick would be Frumer, putting together the deals for Hall's information.

"What I possess," Hall wrote, "is, as [Frumer] put it, 'Like heroin to junkies.'"

He'd be famous; the tabloid shows would call—*Hard Copy, A Current Affair, Donahue, Geraldo.* There'd be a movie about him. Once he was out and they were rich and famous, he asked Phyllis, how about a trip to Paris?

A week later he updated Phyllis on Frumer's progress, referring to himself as the "expert."

"Marc [Frumer] is going into this meeting [tomorrow] at two in the afternoon with some very important people. Three of them. . . . Guess what <u>they</u> want to discuss? Employing this expert they've heard about who can do amazing things. This guy is really something. He can make all of them famous. Really help their careers. This can have its price, of course."[44]

This meant Frumer was meeting with officials from the Philadelphia DA's office to negotiate the terms of Hall's deal for his Martorano information.

One of the ADAs who worked with Hall and Frumer on the Martorano snitch was none other than Joseph Casey, the prosecutor from Walter's first trial. Frumer's meeting with Casey went well.

"Yes, my salesman came back from the meeting and they are extremely interested in coming to terms with my company," Hall wrote. "While the price was only touched upon so that they had a ballpark figure, they don't see any problems. What we have is a tentative agreement. They want to meet the expert who brings all the technical knowledge [i.e., meet with Hall to hear his stories in person]. . . . As for the buyers, they can't wait to talk turkey . . . They need my [informant] machinery. And at any price, I'll bet. . . . This is in no small part due to Marc. He is very, very good! And, through his friends and contacts, this sale may now proceed from dream stage to reality."[45]

On August 2, Hall and Frumer signed a Proffer of Cooperation agreement with Joseph Casey to share Hall's information about Martorano with the DA's office.[46] Hall carried the proffer with him into his interview with detectives Dennis Dusak and Patricia Brennan the next day—and proceeded to tell them a Martorano story so far-fetched it's a wonder they kept from laughing. If they did.

He started by describing his background, his stepfather, his contacts with the mob going back to the 1970s. He said he'd once helped smuggle a hundred automatic rifles and two antitank weapons to the Irish Republican Army. Later, in jail, he'd befriended Ray Martorano himself and Martorano had come to trust him so much because of his mob background that he'd officially given Hall the title "consigliere."[47] When Hall got out that time, he was to be a hit man for Martorano but wouldn't carry out any of the killings—here, again, we have John Hall's favorite image of himself, the good man trying to do the right thing. Eventually Martorano came after him. Hall said that in November 1993 he was kidnapped, taken to a basement in New Jersey, and tied to a chair; one of his captors started drilling holes in his leg but left the room to get something. When the second captor made a phone call, Hall grabbed a hammer, hit him on the head, escaped, and hitchhiked back to Philadelphia.[48]

If the detectives asked to see the scar on Hall's leg, it isn't reflected on his written statement. Hall knew which mob murders the DAs needed information about, two from 1981 and two from 1993,[49] so he told mob stories peppered with the names of infamous mob bosses, notoriously corrupt judges, and high-profile murder victims.

A letter he wrote to Phyllis at the time shows where the information actually came from.

"I do require those [newspaper] clippings for conclusion," he reminded her. "I know you will do your work as always. With Marc [Frumer], we get gifts, swift and sure."[50]

"Gifts" meant meetings with DAs, detectives, and FBI agents, and offers of plea deals in exchange for his information.

"Nothing can stop him," he wrote of himself. "He does come through. He has never failed."[51]

In early October, Hall wrote out an affidavit describing his Mafia stories. It began, as all his snitch stories did, with the insistence—clearly an outright lie in this instance—that he was snitching not in exchange for a deal but because of his conscience.

Hall wrote Phyllis that he was pleased with how Frumer had been handling the "salesman and public relations" responsibilities "without letting on" what Hall was actually doing: Frumer made the connections, Hall told the stories, Frumer put together the deals with the DA. Hall wrote that Frumer admitted Hall was teaching him things—"Not about law, but about procedures outside the system."[52]

Hall wrote to Frumer that when the Mafia stories made him famous and the tabloids paid for his story he'd give Frumer a percentage, of course, and Frumer's fees would skyrocket, too, as he gained prominence.

"These are mafia matters," Frumer wrote back. "You should look the part, so I'll get you a double-breasted suit, like John Gotti wears."[53]

As Hall proceeded with his Mafia snitching in mid-1994 he was briefly transferred to Bucks County to resolve some outstanding parole violations, which he did by snitching. This time he created one of his more incredible documents: a signed, notarized affidavit that spells out how Hall read the defendant his Miranda rights and amounts to a description of the kinds of mental contortion Hall's prosecutor allies went through in order to accept his stories.

Prosecutors were not allowed to move Hall or any other informant to target certain inmates. If a prosecutor did, Hall (or any other informant) would be considered an "agent of the state"—law enforcement—when he heard those confessions and would be required to read inmates their Miranda rights before talking to them, just as any other law enforcement officer would. Without a Miranda warning, those confessions would be worthless. The problem was, by that summer Hall's pattern of showing up in the same cell block as high-profile defendants against whom prosecutors had weak cases and then miraculously producing "confessions" from those men was widely known among judges, prosecutors, and defense lawyers. Within a few years even newspaper columnists would speculate about Hall's jail placements.

"I don't want to go out on a limb here," reporter Elmer Smith would write in the *Philadelphia Daily News* in 1997. "But I can't help wondering how it is that Hall keeps turning up in the right cell at the right time. Because if he is being planted in these cells, it raises serious ethical questions."

Smith quoted an unnamed prosecutor who agreed that if someone in authority placed Hall in position to get information from another inmate, Hall was arguably acting as an agent of police.[54]

On this issue, Hall's 1994 snitch in Bucks County looked bad even by his standards. In Bucks, Hall was housed with an accused child molester named Raymond Lamoureaux. A few days later, Hall met with a prosecutor to tell her Lamoureaux would confess to him. The prosecutor put him back with Lamoureaux and soon enough Hall had the man's confession—a confession Hall wrote out and attached to a signed document of Lamoureaux waiving his Miranda rights.

But it was so clear from the timing that Hall had been put back in the cell to get information from Lamoureaux that Hall knew he had to address the issue somehow. So he wrote an extraordinary affidavit and attached it to the Lamoureaux confession.

Hall opened it by acknowledging that if he had been put back in Lamoureaux's cell to get information about Lamoureaux's crime, the confession could be considered a state action. And, he wrote, he understood that his meeting with the DA just before being put back in with Lamoureaux might make it *look* like he'd been put there to get that confession. It wasn't true, he insisted; his placement with Lamoureaux had been "by happenstance and chance and not design"; no agent of the state of Pennsylvania nor any of its agents or police nor any prosecutorial authority of Pennsylvania or elsewhere had "intentionally created any situation likely to induce any persons named herein to be together for any purpose of deliberate solicitation of any statement to or from any of the men named in this affidavit."[55]

But, Hall went on, understanding that the "happenstance" in this case might *seem* too convenient for the authorities, he would read Lamoureaux his Miranda rights. Just in case.

And so John Hall, who often considered his "selective targeting" a form of police work, actually Mirandized another inmate. A third inmate witnessed the whole thing.

This information for the DA took care of Hall's parole issues in Bucks County, and he was moved back to Philadelphia to continue his work with Joseph Casey.

―――――――――

As Hall worked on his Martorano stories with Joseph Casey that fall, Marc Frumer gathered fresh letters of support for him from the prosecutors in some of his prior snitchings. Frumer called in a favor from Casey for Hall's information about the Martorano case, which prosecutors were still considering using, writing to Casey that his attendance and testimony were required at a violation of probation/parole hearing for Hall. Frumer enclosed a subpoena but explained that a letter from Casey summarizing the value of Hall's cooperation would suffice.

"Unfortunately, John is facing a potential State sentence," Frumer explained. "Your insight and request for leniency on John's behalf may sway the judge towards a County sentence. Obviously, John's life and well-being is at great risk in state prison due to his cooperation."[56]

Frumer was negotiating the price for Hall's information, and this letter shows another way a prosecutor could pay: help Hall get county jail time instead of state prison time.

"These buyers have very deep pockets and will pay dearly for my product," Hall wrote after one of Frumer's meetings with the DA's office.[57]

17

"THE DEADLIEST DA"

In the Philadelphia Detention Center that fall, Walter waited for the Pennsylvania Superior Court to rule on his double jeopardy argument, that the "not guilty" verdict at the first trial had been signed by the jury and should therefore stand. If they agreed, he'd go home; if not, he'd be tried again. He spent most of his time in his cell. Some inmates had been convinced by following his trial that he actually hadn't killed Barbara Jean, and they left him alone. Others beat him if he showed his face.[1]

Walter became friends with David Dickson, a thirty-four-year-old army veteran and former Wells Fargo security guard. Dickson was charged with the 1984 murder of Deborah Wilson, a Drexel University student. Walter and he had met that spring in the infirmary, where Walter was being kept separate from the other inmates for his own safety and Dickson was under observation after being discovered twisting his sheets into a noose. Dickson found Walter to be not as sharp as an average person and child-like, more a twelve-year-old than a grown-up. They played chess and talked. Dickson never heard him say anything about his case except that he was innocent.[2]

As Philadelphia district attorney Lynne Abraham waited for the superior court's ruling on Walter's appeal that fall, the distorting effect of politics on our justice system was on display in the Pennsylvania governor's race between Republican congressman and former prosecutor Tom Ridge and Democratic Lieutenant Governor Mark Singel. The race focused on crime—"our only issue," a Ridge spokesman said[3]—and reinforced an important lesson for the politically ambitious Abraham: show no mercy or be prepared to lose.

Singel's staff searched through cases from Ridge's time as a prosecutor, hoping to embarrass him with any case in which he'd taken less than the toughest stance possible. Ridge's team likewise searched for something to damage Singel, who, as lieutenant governor, was chairman of the Pennsylvania Board of Pardons, overseeing recommendations that the governor commute the sentences of a few inmates per year for good behavior.

Or, as a Ridge TV ad put it, "Mark Singel met with convicted murderers and rapists to promise understanding and mercy. Then, incredibly, Singel voted to release forty-eight criminals serving life sentences."[4]

Singel was ahead by four points when, a month before the election, one of the inmates the Board of Pardons had recommended for release was arrested for kidnapping, rape, and robbery in New York and was also suspected of murder. The tragedy was a political gift for Ridge, who used it to attack Singel, pulled ahead by twelve points, and won the election by five.[5]

"When it comes to the death penalty," Lynne Abraham told Tina Rosenberg, a writer for the *New York Times Magazine*, in 1995, "I am passionate. I truly believe it is manifestly correct." It wasn't a deterrent, Abraham said, but it gave the people of the city the feeling of control. "We are so overwhelmed by cruelty and barbarism, and most people feel the legal system doesn't work," she said. "We feel our lives are not in our own hands. . . . I represent the victim and the family. I don't care about killers."[6]

John, Sharon, and Barbara Jean. (Courtesy of John and Sharon Fahy)

Sharon and Barbara Jean about a week before the murder. (Courtesy of John and Sharon Fahy)

Rutland Street, looking north from the corner of St. Vincent Street. The Fahys' house is about halfway up the block on the right; Ogrod's house is across the street. (Thomas Lowenstein)

LEFT: The Fahys' house, 7245 Rutland Street. At the time of Barbara Jean's murder there was a hedge at the edge of the lawn. (Thomas Lowenstein)

RIGHT: Ogrod's house, 7244 Rutland. The house was owned by his aunt, who evicted him and his tenants in the fall of 1989. (Thomas Lowenstein)

7244 Rutland Street, rear view. Note the back door and the garage door. (Thomas Lowenstein)

The alley behind 7244 Rutland Street, looking south toward St. Vincent Street. The TV box was taken from the rear of 7208 Rutland Street, almost at the corner of St. Vincent, and according to the police statement Ogrod walked down this alley with the box. (Thomas Lowenstein)

The corner of Castor Avenue and St. Vincent Street, looking west. Michael Massi, sitting in one of the cubicles in the dealership on the left of the picture, saw the man with the box walk past him, heading north on Castor Avenue, though according to the police statement, Ogrod only ever walked directly west on St. Vincent. (Thomas Lowenstein)

St. Vincent Street, corner of Castor Avenue, looking west. The man with the box paused here to rest before walking west. David Schectman, the witness who interacted with him for eleven minutes, was leaning on the tailgate of his car just past the church. After leaving the box on the street, the man continued west. (Thomas Lowenstein)

The police composite sketch of the suspect. More than a thousand flyers with this picture were put up all over Northeast Philadelphia in the days after the murder, bringing in many leads but ultimately no arrests. (Author's collection)

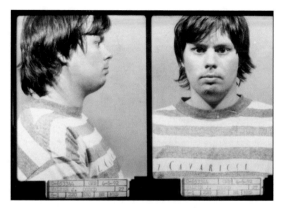

Walter Ogrod's mugshot, April 6, 1992. (Author's collection)

A courtroom artist's sketch of Walter Ogrod testifying at the first trial. (Susan Schary)

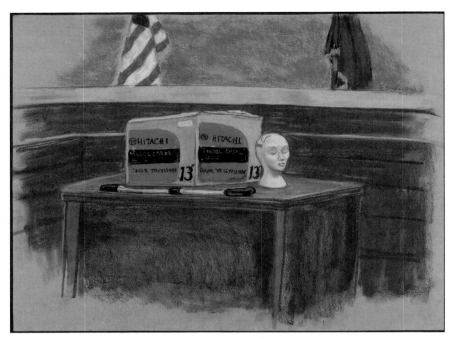

A sketch from the first trial of the TV box, a Styrofoam head showing the injuries to Barbara Jean, and the disputed murder weapon. (Susan Schary)

John Fahy lunges at Walter after the mistrial is declared. (Susan Schary)

John Hall, the infamous jailhouse snitch known as "the Monsignor," because he'd heard more confessions than a priest. (Author's collection)

Front page: Will Bunch's February 1997 article about Hall, which laid out the lies he'd told in cases going back fifteen years. (Used with permission of *Philadelphia Daily News*. Copyright © 2016. All rights reserved)

A page of Hall's notes from his conversations with Walter Ogrod. He would refine these notes in further drafts into a fantastical story of Barbara Jean's murder that did not fit any of the evidence in the case. (Author's collection)

Abraham's willingness to admit that the death penalty isn't a deterrent but offers a sense of control to a scared populace is startling for its honesty: prosecutors don't usually admit they do things for appearances, especially in death penalty cases; it sounds better and is more in keeping with their job descriptions to say they follow the facts and pursue justice. Because if their goal is to make society feel safe or in control, as opposed to finding the truth, a conviction helps whether the defendant is guilty or not.

Philadelphia County had 105 people on death row in 1995, third most of any county in the country behind Harris County (Houston), Texas, and Los Angeles County—both of which had many times more people and more murders than Philadelphia. No prosecutor in the country used the death penalty more than Abraham, who sought it in nearly every case the law allowed.[7]

Asked if she'd ever seen a death sentence given to someone who didn't deserve it, Abraham said "no"; asked specifically about the case of an innocent Philadelphia man who'd spent four years on death row because, a court ruled, Philadelphia police lied on the stand at his trial, Abraham said, "He wasn't executed. The system worked." She was arguing that what mattered wasn't that police lied to put an innocent man on death row but that the lies eventually came out—despite, it should be said, the best efforts of her office, which had fought the exoneration. She didn't address the larger implication of her own argument, that if the system catches some of its mistakes it must miss others, which means innocent people spend their lives in prison and are executed. Only since the Innocence Project and other groups started using DNA to prove wrongful convictions in droves have a sizable number of DAs and law enforcement leaders been willing to admit this.

Lynne Abraham was fiercely political, but her toughness was not just posture. She'd grown up, in Tina Rosenberg's memorable phrase, a "tomboy and alley-prowler"[8] in West Philadelphia; her father was a butcher, a nightclub owner, and a bookie, who took his daughter along on money collection runs. She put herself through Temple University and Law School and, in 1967, took a job in the DA's office under future US Senator Arlen Specter.

She earned a reputation for toughness even in that cutthroat, male-dominated world, investigating cases in high-crime neighborhoods with a .38 on her waist. She was willing to do "whatever she had to do to win," as a police officer who worked with her at the time put it.[9]

In 1971 Mayor Frank Rizzo, a former police commissioner, appointed Abraham head of the Redevelopment Authority in Philadelphia, only to fire her thirteen months later when she wouldn't hire clerks he sent her as part of his patronage machine. Standing up to Rizzo made Abraham famous, and she was elected a municipal court judge in 1975. In 1979 she moved to the Court of Common Pleas, and in 1983 became one of the select judges in Philadelphia who heard only homicide cases.

To admirers, Abraham was knowledgeable, firm, courteous, and extremely tough; to some defense lawyers she was more like a prosecutor than a judge.[10] That was made official in 1991 when DA Ed Rendell quit to run for mayor and a panel of common pleas court judges appointed Abraham to replace him. She became the latest in a line of politically ambitious Philadelphia DAs that included Specter, Rendell (mayor of Philadelphia, governor of Pennsylvania), and Ron Castille (later chief justice of the Pennsylvania Supreme Court). Abraham didn't create the win-at-all-costs philosophy that dominated the Philadelphia DA's office, but she was trained in it, and, as DA, with an eye on higher office, openly considering runs for mayor and attorney general, perpetuated it.[11]

The Philadelphia DA's office was well known for this philosophy. In 1992, a Pennsylvania superior court judge, throwing out a Philadelphia murder conviction, wrote that prosecutorial misconduct happened in Philadelphia County more than in any other county in Pennsylvania and reminded prosecutors that the Commonwealth's client was justice.[12] In response Abraham, stung and politically sensitive to public outrage, demoted the head of her homicide office because of systemic cheating in that office—hiding evidence from defense lawyers, striking African Americans from juries because of their race. Abraham needed to hold someone responsible, but it's hard to imagine how such organized cheating could have happened without her knowing about it.

In fact, as far as striking African Americans from juries went, she did know; her office used a 1986 videotape made by ADA Jack McMahon to train young prosecutors in jury selection, including how to remove blacks from juries.

On the tape McMahon explained that jury selection was the most important part of a criminal case: preparation, evidence, and witness statements didn't make a damn bit of difference without a good jury, he said.[13]

"The case law says that the object of getting a jury is to get—I had to look this up because I didn't know this was the purpose of a jury—a 'competent, fair, and impartial jury,'" McMahon said. "Well, that's ridiculous. You're not trying to get that. . . . And if any one of you think you're going to be some noble civil libertarian and try to get [fair] jurors, that's ridiculous. You'll lose and you'll be out of office. . . . The only way you're going to do your best is to get jurors that are as unfair and more likely to convict than anyone in that room."

The ideal juror from the Commonwealth's standpoint, McMahon went on, would be willing to hang his own mother. Young prosecutors should remember, he said, that the key to getting that best juror is, like in blackjack, to stay within your own rules: take solid, well-dressed citizens from strong families, people who read simple books instead of Karl Marx. Never take a lawyer or a law student, never take a social worker, don't take a teacher, they're too liberal, unless maybe it's a white teacher from a mostly black school who's fed up with black teenagers. Never take Quakers, they need too much evidence. Blacks from low-income areas are less likely to convict, so you don't want "those people" on your jury; it may look like you're being racist, but you're just being realistic. If you are going to take blacks, you want older black men.

"Black women, young black women, are very bad," he said.

But he wasn't arguing for all-white juries, he said, because an all-white jury might not even care about the case if the defendant and victim were both black. An ideal jury is eight whites and four blacks, or nine and three. To get around the then-recent Supreme Court ruling in *Batson v. Kennedy* (1986) that declared striking black people from juries for their race alone unconstitutional, McMahon said they should interview the black potential jurors at great length and make sure to jot down things they could excuse them for without mentioning race as an issue. Death penalty cases offer a chance for this, McMahon explained, because the lawyers get to interview, or voir dire, the potential jurors one at a time, so they can be more confrontational without the risk of alienating the rest of the jurors.

Most of all, McMahon explained, keep smart people off the jury.

"Smart people will analyze the hell out of your case," he said. "They hold you to a higher standard. . . . They take those words 'reasonable doubt' and they actually try to think about them. You want people to come in there and say, 'Yep, she said he did it, he did it.'"

Abraham herself would make the tape public when, in 1997, McMahon ran against her for DA. She used the tape to damage him; it was also a "surprise gift" for hundreds of convicted felons whose cases would all be subject to greater review because of it.[14]

Abraham won the election.

18

A BIG, GOOFY GUY

CRUSHING NEWS CAME FOR WALTER on December 7, 1994, when the Pennsylvania Superior Court ruled two to one that he could be retried for Barbara Jean's murder. Once more, he had come within one vote of going home; once more, he would go on trial for his life.

The ruling was a great relief for DA Abraham. Now she had a chance to bring this case, a six year, front-page embarrassment—four years without an arrest followed by the near-acquittal and mistrial—to a positive conclusion: Walter Ogrod on death row.

In mid-December, a week after the superior court ruling that Walter could be tried again, John Hall was moved into his cell block. Another coincidence, according to the DA's office, that led Hall to an inmate accused of an old, high-profile murder case that prosecutors were worried about losing. Hall would, as usual, deny he'd been moved to target anyone in particular, but in this instance he did tell an investigator later that Joseph Casey, in a phone call, originally brought up the idea of him talking to Walter. At first, Hall claimed, he didn't want to go near the Ogrod case.[1] This sounds like an extension of the standard Hall story, that he didn't like snitching and only did it out of a sense of duty. On the other hand, it's hard to figure out how lying about Casey suggesting a case to him could help him; he wouldn't have wanted anyone to know that.

Casey denies ever mentioning Walter to Hall, and Hall certainly could've come up with the idea himself. Maybe no one had to suggest it directly; maybe Hall was transferred into Walter's orbit and just spotted the opportunity: Walter struck him as a "big, goofy guy; some kind of mental deficient."[2] And a mental deficient facing a murder charge in an old, high-profile case was a godsend for Hall. He wouldn't have had to ask the DAs what to do.

Hall approached Walter.

"Are you Walter Ogrod?" he asked. "I'm John Hall. Marc Frumer sent me to check up on you."

Hall was presenting himself to Walter as a kind of family acquaintance. Frumer had been Walter's brother's lawyer on a case, and his father, Marshall Frumer, had helped the Ogrod boys with some inheritance issues after their father died.

Isolated and depressed in the wake the denial of his appeal, Walter fell into the classic snitch trap, which Professor Barry Tarlow described this way: a defendant charged with murder, worried about his future and needing a friend to confide in, gets a cellmate who has appeared at the key moment purely by happenstance. The cellmate offers a shoulder to lean on, earns the defendant's trust, gets him to talk, and manufactures a "confession." It turns out the new cellmate is a jailhouse snitch, who offers the manufactured confession to authorities in exchange for leniency.[3]

Walter's version of what happened with Hall matches this prototypical jailhouse snitch scenario exactly. Walter took Hall for a friend, a good friend with obvious clout—the accordion file of legal papers, the flip-up TV in his cell, the regular visits from important officials.[4] Lacking the good sense to not talk to anyone in jail about his case, Walter talked to Hall about his late father, jobs he'd had, his apartment in Glenside, his mother's death, the mistrial, his plans to sue the detectives and prosecutors who had put him away. He discussed his case and his legal strategies in great detail.

Hall, despite his close ties to Joseph Casey, including visits, phone calls, a signed cooperation agreement on the mob case, and possibly Casey's suggestion that he talk to Walter, never read

Walter his Miranda rights. He talked to Walter about his truck-driving route, the superior court ruling, the other suspects, the case in general.

Hall tried to put together a story of Barbara Jean's murder but was dissatisfied with Walter's level of knowledge about the case.

"There were gaps in Ogrod's story," Hall explained later. "I had enough to proceed against him but I needed more. Ogrod didn't know about particulars, and [I am] a stickler for details."[5]

The "gaps" in Walter's story, the particulars he didn't know, were details of the murder itself. Hall spoke to Phyllis and she sent him newspaper clippings about the murder, but they were too general, lacking the specific detail that he wanted.[6] With his research failing, Hall obscured the lack of specifics about the murder in his story with overwhelming detail about Walter's life.

"I got mostly everything I needed from [Ogrod]," he explained. "Then I kept notes. Eventually I assembled those notes into a composite summary and then an elongated account and history of the events leading up to the incident, the incident itself, and the aftermath."[7]

Hall sent his "composite summary" and "elongated account" to Marc Frumer. Both letters, headlined ATTORNEY-CLIENT PRIVILEGED COMMUNICATION, JOHN HALL TO MARC FRUMER, are full of Walter's background, his complaints about the police setting him up, and his determination to sue the DA's office when he got out, but lack any specific information about the murder. Out of the several thousand words crammed into five pages, two written lines to a ruled line, that make up the "composite summary," the murder itself gets thirteen words: "Walt said he fucked her and beat her and smashed her skull in."[8] This is no more than a poor summary of the state's case, complete with the inaccuracy about Barbara Jean being raped. Neither of the descriptions of the murder that Hall sent to Frumer has any details about the murder that hadn't been in the papers or discussed at Walter's trial.

Hall even created a new and twisted motive for the crime: according to Hall, Walter said Sharon was nice to him, he fell in love with her, and he killed Barbara Jean so he could pin the crime on John Fahy and, with him out of the way, marry Sharon.[9] According to Hall, Walter thought John was related to Henry Fahy, a man on death row for strangling a young girl with an extension cord years before, so if he killed Barbara Jean the same way, John would be arrested for it.[10] (According to John Fahy, he and Henry are probably not related and did not know each other, though it's possible they are distant cousins. In the papers at the time of Barbara Jean's murder they were variously described as brothers or distant cousins.)[11]

Once John was arrested, according to Hall's version of what Walter had told him:

Sharon's love for John would turn to hate for raping and killing her daughter, the police would put him away for life or give him a death sentence so he could be with his brother [Henry Fahy]. Sharon would then be grieving for the loss of her daughter and the betrayal and loss of her creep husband, and because she'd be in that house alone and upset, and because she already knew and liked him, Walt said [she] could turn to him for comfort and support and then love him."[12]

Walter, Hall wrote, was excited to move in with Sharon without even leaving the street he'd grown up on, and planned to tell her Barbara Jean would want them to have another baby.

This story is pure Hall—dramatic, outlandish, featuring a villain who is a master of evil and disgusts him. It would make the murder clearly premeditated, which would help prosecutors get a death sentence.

It also has no basis in fact. Hall claimed Walter told him he fell in love with Sharon because she was nice to him; in reality, Sharon and Walter agree they never met and didn't know who each other were until after the murder. According to Hall, Walter said he befriended Barbara Jean over the course of the spring of 1988, getting her used to being around him; in reality, no one ever saw Walter speak to or interact with her.

According to Hall, to prepare for the murder Walter stashed gloves, an extension cord, garbage bags, and rubber bands in his basement. The extension cord was the key, the link to the Henry Fahy murder that would get police to arrest John Fahy.

Hall said Walter tried twice that spring to abduct Barbara Jean but was thwarted once by a car driving by and once by a passerby on foot.[13] On the afternoon of the murder, according to Hall, Walter said he saw Barbara Jean outside, playing by herself, and lured her across the street to his door by blowing her kisses. She came happily and Walter took her to the basement, but the extension cord was missing so he raped her and then killed her with the pull-down bar from his weight set. (In later versions, having learned that there was no evidence of a sexual assault, Hall would write that Walter had tried to penetrate the little girl but couldn't. There was no evidence of that, either.)

Hall's story fundamentally changed the nature of the murder from a spur-of-the-moment sexual assault that turned into a panicked homicide with the nearest weapon at hand when Barbara Jean screamed to a calculated murder carried out by a manipulative psychopath who beat a little girl to death and then sat in the living room talking with the Greens and, later, a detective who came by, without betraying any nerves, and who got away with it for years. Walter only cracked, Hall explained, when he thought his mother had told the police he did it.

Hall's writings to Frumer about Barbara Jean's murder offer scant information about the actual killing, and his descriptions of Walter's motive and plan and cool demeanor in the aftermath of the murder are fantastical. But his description of how Walter got rid of the body is merely impossible. According to Hall, Walter originally wrapped the body in a garbage bag and carried it around the neighborhood looking for a place to ditch it before getting nervous and leaving it in some bushes. He went home but started feeling nervous that there were fingerprints on the bag, so he went back out, found the TV box, and carried it, empty, to St. Vincent Street.

"Walt said . . . he didn't go past [the car dealership window] carrying the box in his arms," Hall wrote. "Walt said he had the box in his hand and at his side because there was nothing in it and he didn't use his arms or [walk down] St. Vincent Street."[14]

After leaving the empty box on St. Vincent, Hall wrote, Walter retrieved the body and carried it, wrapped in the garbage bag, to the box by a back route—not down St. Vincent Street from Castor Avenue, where the man with the box had actually walked. Walter dumped the body in the box, took the garbage bag with him (though Barbara Jean had actually been found wrapped in it), and walked down to Castor and Magee, a fifteen-minute walk each way,[15] to toss the garbage bag in a Dumpster. This trip would've meant Walter was gone from his house from at least 5:00 PM until at least 6:00 PM, though all of the Greens and Walter's friend Hal Vahey say he was home during that time.

"People said they saw a man other than Walt, with lighter hair, carrying a box and he didn't know what that was but it wasn't him," Hall wrote, brushing aside the four witnesses on St. Vincent Street who'd all seen the man with the box.

Unlike the detectives' statement, which just ignored the existence of witnesses by saying that Walter didn't talk to anyone while carrying the box down St. Vincent Street, Hall's story at least tried to address why Walter didn't talk to anyone or even resemble the man who'd carried the box: he said Walter's guess was that around the time he was carrying his empty box through the neighborhood the man with the heavy TV box came up the street, too, and the witnesses mistook *that* box for the box Walter was carrying.

Another fantastic coincidence for Hall, but also not possible, as four witnesses saw one man carrying and dragging a heavy box west on St. Vincent Street from Castor Avenue, and the box was opened, revealing Barbara Jean's body, within three minutes of being placed on the curb.

According to Hall's story, Walter was happy when he got Detective Worrell's card in April 1992, thinking John Fahy was finally going to be arrested for the murder, and rushed downtown to talk to the detectives. When the questioning started, "Walt said he was

scared and [the detectives] told him he'd be in a lot less trouble if
he told the truth," Hall wrote. "Walt said that he was told that he
could get help instead of rotting in prison or the death penalty,
so he let them hand write . . . a confession that he signed. . . .
He said he couldn't think straight and he was scared and he just
let them write it all out and he wanted to get out of there because
he was embarrassed and scared."[16]

This description of the interrogation sounds like it did come
from Walter, since it's the same story he's been telling since his
arrest.

Hall sent Frumer the "elongated account" of his Ogrod story, a
smoother version created from his two earlier summaries and written in block letters for easy reading, on January 5, 1995. For this
version he wrote that Walter "fucked [Barbara Jean] by sodomy"—
his updated version of the assault, given that there was no evidence
of even attempted vaginal rape. As in Hall's earlier drafts, details
about Walter's life overwhelm nearly nonexistent details of Barbara
Jean's death, and the description of Walter's walk through the
neighborhood and his handling of Barbara Jean's body is impossible. In this last draft Hall emphasized the powerful but false story
that Walter had admitted the murder to his mother and confessed
to Devlin and Worrell because he thought she'd turned him in.
Or, as the jury would hear it from the prosecutor: even Walter's
mother thought he was a killer.

Hall met with detectives about Walter on January 6. Given his
history as a snitch, that the DA knew he'd lied in other cases,
and that much of what he said about Walter did not fit the evidence in Walter's case, the detectives ought to have been skeptical. They weren't. Hall said he'd come forward because he could
not in good conscience remain silent and see the murderer of
an innocent girl go free, and he told his impossible story as two
experienced detectives, trained to break down every lie a suspect
told, transcribed it without asking anything substantive and had
him sign it.[17]

"The District Attorney was salivating at the account given to
them," Hall explained later. "They had previously proceeded

on a simple statement by Ogrod of admission. . . . My account was replete with details and chronology. He would burn on my recounting of the facts."[18]

———————

That Hall was a liar was well documented by the time I heard of him. In 1997 the *Philadelphia Daily News* ran a front-page story by reporter Will Bunch laying out Hall's snitching career, piecing together the repeated coincidences of Hall being moved near high-profile inmates as well as the several times when even prosecutors had decided Hall was lying—which is what happened eventually in the Martorano case. The question was, how to prove it.

After I'd been working on the case for a year or so a source claimed to have proof that Hall lied about Walter and agreed to send it to me. Nothing came. I followed up with the source few times over the course of a year, but when I never heard back, I decided the person probably didn't want to be involved after all. Then a legal-size manila envelope, thickly taped shut, arrived in the mail. It was a lesson in investigating old murders: people tell you things when they're ready. Police and DAs have legal means to pressure people to talk, and police can even lie to make it happen. Journalists just have to wait.

I cut the tape, opened the envelope, and spread the contents out on my desk: John Hall's private notes and papers. His letters of support from law enforcement; fake IDs, one of them in the name of his wife's ex-husband; letters to his lawyers and his wife; handwritten transcripts of court hearings; enigmatic postcards that seemed written in code. I could follow Hall's snitching process from the quick notes he jotted on the back of an envelope to the fruits of Phyllis's research for him—pictures of a murder victim's house, newspaper articles printed out from library microfilm—to affidavits he'd sworn out against other inmates and warm letters of thanks from prosecutors.

John could be very creative when he needed to be, my source explained. He could make a great novel out of a few details.

The papers included a copy of Will Bunch's 1997 *Daily News* article "The Snitch," with its photos of seven of the men Hall had snitched out. The biggest picture was of Walter, handcuffed, being led from the courtroom.

Many of the documents related directly to the Ogrod case. There was a draft of the cooperation agreement Hall and Joseph Casey had made in the summer of 1994, and a library microfilm printout of a 1988 article about Barbara Jean's murder. Then a few pages of blue-lined, college-ruled paper with ATTORNEY-CLIENT PRIVILEGED written in block letters across the top of the first page and, in handwriting small enough to fit two lines of print between each line on the page and fill the margins with notes, the first draft of Hall's Walter Ogrod story. There was a second draft, also headlined ATTORNEY-CLIENT PRIVILEGED, with fewer additions and cross-outs, written a few days after the first draft.

There was a transcript of Hall's interview with detectives about his Ogrod story, though it wasn't much of an interview, because the detective didn't ask any follow-up questions. The whole conversation took less than half an hour.

Once I'd read John Hall's papers and understood the development of his story about Walter, I decided it was time to call Phyllis, his wife. I didn't expect her to talk to me, a random stranger calling up and asking about her infamous husband.

She answered, her voice soft. I told her I was a writer, looking into an old John Hall case. She didn't hang up, but she didn't say anything. Did she know where John was now, I asked? Back in jail, she said. Yes, she said, she knew about some of his cases. She'd researched some of them for him by going to the scene of the crime or, in one instance, to a victim's house to gather details that Hall then presented to authorities as things only the killer could have known.

She paused and said, "I'm not sure I should tell you any of this."[19]

I didn't say anything. I'd been told that it's important some-times to shut up and let awkward silences sit so that the person you're interviewing is more likely to keep talking.

"I know John lied in twenty or thirty cases," Phyllis said after another pause.

"Do you think he lied in the Ogrod case?" I asked.

The pause was long this time.

"Off the record, I know he did," she said. (She later agreed to put all of this on the record.)

"How do you know?" I asked.

"Because I helped him do it," she said.

Phyllis lived in a nice house in the country and worked as an accoun-tant in an office. She was small and quiet, her eyes bright as we talked at her kitchen table. Her daughter and grandchildren lived with her, and occasionally one of the kids would run through. She seemed nervous and wondered out loud sometimes why she was talking to me. But she talked for a long time about herself and John and her involvement in his snitch work. She took me through the papers I already had, explaining what everything was. She pointed out one of John's little jokes—the fake ID in the name of her sec-ond husband.

I didn't know how much of what she was saying to believe, but she had various documents of Hall's to back up her stories. She also had dozens of his letters going back to the early 1990s, some from around the time Hall was snitching on Walter, in which he bragged about making up stories and selling them to the DA's office for leniency.

As we were talking, Phyllis said, "Oh, I remember one thing John had me do to get information from Walter. He had me pose as a stripper and write him letters."

I hadn't thought to ask her about Walter's story about Autumn, the stripper who'd written to him in jail four years after they met. But now it made sense: there was no stripper. John Hall had been the "friend" of Walter's who'd been on the jail phone, supposedly with a friend at the strip club, and he had called Walter over to tell him how excited Autumn was to hear from him. John Hall had told Walter she was too excited to speak to him but would write to him. John Hall had had Phyllis write the phony letters.

Later I found one of Walter's letters to the stripper in John Hall's papers, proof that Phyllis's story was true. Walter was thirty and had been in prison for close to three years when he wrote it, but it still reads like a seventh grader's:

"I must be dreaming about this letter from you," he wrote. "But it's real and I remember you weren't just better than the others you were <u>great</u>. . . . If you were to asked [*sic*] if I would take you out for some coffee, I would have and <u>maybe</u> <u>dinner</u> if you wanted to go with me."[20]

Walter exchanged a few letters with this person he thought was Autumn but never wrote anything about the murder other than that he was innocent, so Hall stopped the ruse.

Walter had told me he never understood why the stripper stopped writing to him.[21] The next time I talked to him I told him the stripper letters really came from John Hall. There was silence on the line for a few seconds.

"Really?" he said. "Aw, come on. Really?"

19

THE MONSIGNOR'S
APPRENTICE

HALL, FOR ALL THE RIGHTEOUS INDIGNATION he employed to explain his snitchings, was a practical man, and knew his credibility with prosecutors wasn't very good. For Walter's case he decided, either on his own or at the urging of the DA's office, to add a backup snitch. He chose Jay Wolchansky, a thirty-two-year-old with a criminal record, including twelve convictions for burglary, theft, forgery, and escape. Wolchansky had arrived at the detention center on three new burglary charges on December 20, 1994, and Hall befriended him in January 1995.

Jay was the youngest of Geraldine and Michael Wolchansky's five children and grew up in a small row house on North Twenty-Second Street in Philadelphia, across the street from the infamous Eastern State Penitentiary, the oldest jail in the United States. His father abandoned the family when Jay was two and never sent any money, leaving Geraldine to work as a domestic and waitress to support her family. One son, Michael Jr., died at ten in a truck accident; another, George, was shot to death walking home from a concert in 1980 at age twenty.[1]

Jay was in constant trouble from an early age. He dropped out of high school after ninth grade, started using drugs—pot, alcohol, speed, Valium, cocaine, and various combinations—and was arrested eighteen times as a juvenile. He earned a GED but by twenty-eight had been arrested seventeen more times, resulting in seven convictions and eight probation and parole violations, three of which had landed him in jail. In 1987 he made it through three months of a court-ordered six-month rehab; at another point he showed a "chronic pattern of non-compliance."[2]

On the night of August 1, 1994, Wolchansky, a few months out of jail after serving time for burglary and parole violations, and drunk, threw a brick through the window of a restaurant. The alarm went off and an employee called the police. Out on bail from that, after midnight on November 14 he tried to break into a house by shattering a basement window. That effort put him in jail until December 5, when he was released again, this time staying free for two weeks until, on December 19, he broke into a house through a bedroom window.[3] The next day he was in the detention center, charged with all three crimes and facing, because of his lengthy record, up to ten years on each and a $75,000 fine. He was going through alcohol withdrawal and not getting enough of his schizophrenia and depression medications; in fact, throughout that winter and spring, all during the time of his supposed dealings with Walter, he was filing requests to the prison medical authorities for more medication.[4]

Why John Hall decided to protect Wolchansky and help him get home by teaching him to snitch isn't clear. He told Phyllis he felt bad for Wolchansky, who had a young daughter and said his criminal troubles were caused by drinking and drugging after a bad divorce; maybe he reminded Hall of his image of himself, a decent man who, through bad luck and addiction, ended up in jail time and time again. Or maybe prosecutors were concerned enough about Hall's credibility that they told him to find someone to corroborate the story he'd supposedly gotten from Walter.

Hall and Wolchansky were put in cells next to each other and kept away from the other inmates, who were locked down when they came out.[5] Hall would put Wolchansky on the phone with

Phyllis when he called home, and Wolchansky, lucky to have Hall for a protector and teacher, followed him around like a puppy.[6]

The official story would be that Walter confessed to Hall and Wolchansky at the same time. The timeline for this version of events is not impossible but nearly so: Hall started talking to Walter (and making notes) on December 22, Wolchansky's second day at the detention center. Hall probably hadn't even met Wolchansky, and they certainly weren't friends yet on the morning of the twenty-sixth when Wolchansky, not yet under Hall's protection, was kicked in the face badly enough by other inmates that he couldn't see out of either eye.[7] Hall, according to his notes at the time, then finished his conversations with Walter on December 29, and his snitch on Walter was completed when he met with detectives on January 6, 1995. This timeline leaves no room for Wolchansky's later claim that he had a month of lengthy conversations with Walter before Walter would open up about his own case. It fits with Hall's later admission that he made up the Ogrod story first and gave it to Wolchansky.[8]

Hall's friendship with Wolchansky probably dates from the middle of January, when he first mentioned Wolchansky to Phyllis, telling her he felt bad for Wolchansky and was going to give him a chance at freedom by giving him the Ogrod story. He taught Wolchansky about Barbara Jean's murder, Walter's background, and Walter's disputed statement,[9] and around this time he got his lawyer, Marc Frumer, to take on Wolchansky as a client as well.

On January 23, Wolchansky, with Hall's help, wrote to Joseph Casey, the DA from the first trial who was now Hall's patron in the DA's office. The one-page letter had no details of the crime; it was pure hook and taunt, pure Hall.

"Mr. Ogrod won't shut up about [the murder] and he is making me sick," Wolchansky wrote. "He continually talks about what he has done to this child, and about how he is going to get away with it, and sue you, the city, the newspapers, and TV news.

"If what Mr. Ogrod says is true," he went on, "then you need to speak with me. He cannot be allowed to go free, and get away with the horrible and disgusting things he says he did to that poor little girl."[10]

Casey didn't reply.

Walter played cards and checkers with Hall and Wolchansky. Hall thought Walter didn't like Wolchansky, since Wolchansky only ever insulted him, calling him "baby in the box" or "whackem-and-sackem."[11] Walter, used to being the butt of jokes, thought Wolchansky was all right but never had an actual conversation with him and never talked to him about his case other than to say he was innocent.

In March 1995, Hall helped Wolchansky write another letter about Walter, this one to Lynne Abraham. This was the first time Wolchansky mentioned any details of the case, and they are the same details described in almost the same terms as Hall used in his letter. Wolchansky's letter even looks like a Hall snitch letter, with a quasi-legal heading ("In RE: Comm. Vs. Walter Ogrod, Murder of 4 Year Old Barbara Jean Horn") and two lines of writing pinched between every ruled line on the page.[12]

"I am writing in regard to Mr. Walter Ogrod, and his admitted murder of Barbara Jean Horn," it began.

All the Hall information is there, the details of Walter's life, the new motive, the impossibilities from the day of the murder: Walter killed Barbara Jean to pin the crime on John Fahy; on the day of the murder he saw her outside her house and lured her across the street by making kissing noises and dangling a Hershey's Kiss; he took her downstairs, hit her, and tried to force her to perform oral sex on him but she screamed so he put his hand over her mouth and tried to penetrate her vaginally but she was too small. He reached for the extension cord, gloves, and trash bags he'd stashed, but the extension cord was gone. He became enraged, grabbed the pull-down bar from his weight set, and killed her. Then he got nervous that someone would come home.

Hall: "Walter said he took Barbara out of the back of his house down the driveway and then down the next driveway for the next set of homes to Friendship Street. Walter went to the spot he'd picked out but there were people there. Walter said he put the child in some bushes. He said that there was a dog barking."[13]

Wolchansky: "He then took Barbara Jean out his backdoor, down a driveway/alley he had behind his house, across St. Vincent Street to the next street, over this street, across Castor Ave to Friendship Street where he seen neighbors outside, so he sat in some grass behind some bushes. . . . A dog started to bark. . . . He became scared and left her body near the bushes. . . . He then went home the same way."[14]

Hall: "Walt went back down St. Vincent Street to Rutland Street and grabbed a neighbor's TV box and carried it up to Loretta [sic] Ave from Friendship street and then put it at St. Vincent Street and Loretta Avenue. He said he got the trash bag [with the body] and sat down on the opposite corner and waited for it to be all clear of cars and dumped Barbara Jean into the TV box."

Wolchansky: "He went back to the bushes where he left the body, this time with a TV box he found on his street . . . left the TV box near the curb at St. Vincent and Loretta [sic] Streets, got the body in the trashbags, and dumped her body naked into the TV box. He said she was lying on her side in a fetal position."

Wolchansky's letter even included Hall's misspelling of "Loretto Avenue." Both stories ended with Walter making the half-hour round-trip walk to Castor and Magee to throw the garbage bag in a Dumpster.

That Wolchansky's story matched John Hall's exactly and neither story matched the evidence should have made the DA suspect that they either invented it together or one of them made the story up and taught it to the other. But when Wolchansky met with Detective Michael Gross on March 20, 1995, Gross didn't even ask him to tell the story through, let alone ask him any substantive follow-up questions about it. The entire interview took twenty-five minutes.

"Did anyone help you or advise you to write these letters?" Gross asked.[15]

"No," Wolchansky said.

Gross didn't know or didn't care that Hall had told the exact same story two months earlier. He never asked about Hall. He did ask if there was anything Wolchansky wanted to add, and Wolchansky said Walter had just told him the week before that when he got home after leaving Barbara Jean's body on St. Vincent Street he masturbated, showered, and then cleaned up the basement. Gross didn't ask if anyone was home or why Walter left the crime scene untouched for an hour while he went on his long walk with the body and then to dispose of the garbage bag, or how Walter managed to arrive home sweaty from the long walk and go upstairs and shower, which anyone in the house would've heard but no one did, before finally going down to the basement to clean up the bloody crime scene, all of this happening with other people in the living room, with whom Walter at times hung out, acting normally.

Gross did ask the setup question Wolchansky needed to give the response Hall had taught him: "Why did you write these letters?"

"The way he talks about it . . . it's like he's proud of it," Wolchansky said.

"What do you expect to get out of this?" Gross asked.

"Nothing," Wolchansky said.

Two days later, on March 22, Wolchansky got a Marc Frumer–negotiated deal, what Hall called the "minimum possible sentence": eleven and a half to twenty-three months for each charge he was facing, to run concurrently. This was instead of the up to thirty years and fines of up to $75,000 he'd been facing. The deal was signed by Frumer, Wolchansky, a judge, and an assistant DA.[16]

Hall was pleased.

"I didn't just give [the Ogrod story] to [Wolchansky]," he explained later. "I used it first. . . . In exchange for my Ogrod cooperation [my sentence] was reduced to nine to eighteen months! (And other stuff, too.) Jay got eleven and a half to twenty-three months. Everybody made out."[17]

Marc Frumer, who negotiated the deals for both men, confirmed that both of his clients benefited from snitching on Walter.[18]

David Dickson, the inmate who'd befriended Walter in the infirmary, met Hall and Wolchansky because he was the coordinator of the inmate law library, where they spent a lot of time. Dickson asked them what they needed, gave them forms to fill out, helped them with their legal research.

He never talked to Hall or Wolchansky about his own case, but it was well known. On the night of November 29, 1984, Dickson was working an overnight shift as a Wells Fargo security officer in Randell Hall at Drexel University. Deborah Wilson, a twenty-year-old math major who wanted to be an engineer, was in a basement computer room working on a project due for a class at 10:00 the next morning.[19]

Deborah, who still lived at home, called her mother at 1:30 AM to let her know she'd be another hour. At 1:38 she stopped typing in the middle of a sentence—the last word on her computer was "the." Half an hour later the computer shut down automatically. At 8:50 the next morning Deborah's body was found at the bottom of an outside stairwell that led to a door down the hall from the computer room. She'd been beaten with a blunt object and strangled with an electric cord; two bricks and a piece of lumber with blood on them were found near her body[20] and an extension cord found in the room where she was working matched the marks on her neck.[21] She had all her clothes on except her white sneakers and socks.

Dickson and the rest of the security staff were all interviewed. Dickson told detectives he was at the front desk, on the phone, at 1:38 AM, when detectives figured Deborah's attacker got her, given that she stopped typing so abruptly. He said his supervisor came by a little before two o'clock and they talked for fifteen minutes, so he left on his 2:00 AM rounds late and never saw Deborah.

The murder wasn't solved, and Dickson wouldn't talk to detectives again. In early 1993, almost nine years later, police found out he'd been arrested in 1979 while in the army for breaking into a woman's apartment and stealing her white sneakers. They searched his apartment and found seventeen pairs of white women's sneakers and seventy-seven videotapes, from workout videos to porn, of women in sneakers.[22] They didn't find Deborah Wilson's sneakers, but they did find a pornographic love letter on Dickson's computer addressed to a woman named "Rochelle" and titled "Fantasy." The letter, allegedly written on the seventh anniversary of the murder, fixated on Rochelle's white sneakers.[23] Detectives found a former coworker of Dickson's who said he'd written her lewd letters that mentioned her sneakers.[24]

Dickson was arrested for Wilson's murder in June 1993. The *Daily News* ran a full-page, front-page headline: JUSTICE DELAYED.[25]

ADA Roger King, who prosecuted the Dickson case, had been an ADA since 1973, in the homicide unit since 1976, and over the course of his career put more than two dozen men on death row.[26] In 1995 Lynne Abraham described him as "simply the best . . . the Hank Aaron and Babe Ruth of homicide prosecutors, responsible for sending more killers to death row than any prosecutor in the history of Pennsylvania."[27]

King had a good circumstantial case against Dickson, built on what appeared to be Dickson's sneaker fetish. But he had nothing to directly tie Dickson to the murder—no witnesses, no physical evidence. In fact, blood from the scene didn't match his or the victim's.[28]

Dickson's case was another Hall special—an old, high-profile murder with only thin evidence against the defendant—and soon Hall got in touch with King. He'd started talking to Dickson in early January 1995, he said, and Dickson had confessed the murder to him. To explain the coincidence of Dickson and Ogrod confessing to him at the same time, Hall now claimed that he, Wolchansky, Ogrod, and Dickson had all became friends, and Ogrod and Dickson confessed their crimes to Hall and Wolchansky.

For his part, Dickson says that he knew better than to talk to other inmates about his case and never did, and that Wolchansky and Hall only ever harassed Walter. Walter remembers it the same way: "Dickson never talked to those idiots. They tried to get people to throw sneakers at him."[29] Walter says Wolchansky and Hall didn't like black people (Hall's letters make liberal use of the *n*-word) and threw sneakers at Dickson, who is African American.

In the spring of 1995 Marc Frumer told Hall's sentencing judge that Hall was helping authorities with four murder prosecutions: Walter, Raymond Martorano, David Dickson, and a new one, Tremayne Smith, a young man charged with beating his one-year-old son to death, whom Hall snitched out in March of that year. Hall's snitching against Smith didn't get much attention, but it fit Hall's pattern: the case was circumstantial and the detectives working it didn't have much evidence until Hall snitched, after which Smith confessed and pled guilty.[30]

Hall was released from the detention center on April 27. He left Wolchansky with the Ogrod story and the Dickson story, and with Marc Frumer to parlay those stories into deals. Frumer continued to visit Wolchansky after Hall got out. Walter would see them talking in the library when he went by on his way to get his medicine, and Frumer would wave to him through the glass.[31]

David Dickson's murder trial opened in May 1995 in front of Judge Stout, the same judge who'd overseen Walter's trial. During his opening statement, ADA Roger King held a white sneaker up to the jury and told them the whole case revolved around Dickson's fetish for white sneakers. Dickson, King said, came upon Wilson during his rounds and hit her in the head with his security guard clock before strangling her with an extension cord. He took her shoes and socks and dragged her body to the stairwell outside.

In his opening statement Dickson's lawyer, Harry Seay, allowed that his client had a foot fetish but argued that didn't make him a killer. He scoffed at the prosecution's evidence, including the "funky" sneakers and the videotapes found in Dickson's home, and accused King of preparing to "repulse" the jury with testimony about Dickson's sexual tastes.[32]

Which King then did: he spent the first four days of the trial showing the jury white sneakers taken from Dickson's apartment and snippets of the videotapes featuring women in white sneakers.[33] In all, King called thirty-five witnesses and entered into evidence nearly one hundred exhibits, mostly the videotapes and sneakers taken from Dickson's apartment.

It wasn't until the seventh day of the trial that prosecutors presented anything that actually linked Dickson to the murder—and that "link" was Jay Wolchansky.[34] On the stand, his hands fidgeting in his lap, Wolchansky followed the Hall formula, saying he'd come forward because Dickson had disgusted him by bragging all the time that he'd get away with the killing.[35] Wolchansky then told the story he said Dickson had told him: that after Wilson's boyfriend left at about 1:30 AM the night of the murder, Dickson strolled into the computer room and talked to her for a while before going back up front to the guard desk to take a telephone call. When his call ended he went back to the computer room, walked up behind Wilson, grabbed her hair, and punched her in the left temple. She fell, and he kept hitting her until she passed out, at which point he grabbed her sneakers and smelled them.

"Then Miss Wilson groaned," Wolchansky testified. "[Dickson] said he choked her again until she expired. At that point, he said he only had five to ten minutes to work with. He rubbed her feet on his face. He said he picked up a book and her papers. He straightened up in the bathroom; then he went out to the street to cool himself off."

Dickson killed Wilson because she was a "white bitch" who blew him off when he hit on her, Wolchansky said. He'd kept her sneakers in a plastic bag for a year afterward, taking them out sometimes to smell them and masturbate. He added that Dickson was called "Dr. Scholl" in jail.

"I didn't make this up or dream this up," Wolchansky told the jury as Dickson stared at him, shaking his head.[36]

But Wolchansky had made two big mistakes: first, Wilson had been strangled with an extension cord, not hands, as he'd said; also, he'd forgotten to say she'd been beaten with a heavy object— the prosecution's theory was that it was Dickson's guard clock, though it could have been the bloody bricks and lumber found next to her body.

Under cross-examination Wolchansky kept to the Hall script.

"It bugs me that people do that [sniff sneakers]," Wolchansky said when asked why he was snitching. "I'm not a violent man. . . . To know how that lady was killed, Miss Wilson, disturbs me. I pray for her every night."[37] He denied expecting to receive any reduction in the thirty-year prison term he was looking at for his string of burglaries in exchange for his testimony.

Seay pointed out to reporters that Wolchansky's testimony was totally inconsistent with the medical examiner's report that Wilson was strangled with a cord or wire. He suggested, accurately, as it turns out, where Wolchansky learned details of the crime.

"They get newspapers in jail just like we do," Seay said.

"If there's a smell emanating from that side of the courtroom, it's not dirty sneakers; it's his story," Roger King said, gesturing at Dickson as he built his closing argument.[38] "There's something wrong about somebody who's into worshipping feet." In a stage whisper he narrated for the jurors what, based on nothing other than his own imagination, he claimed Dickson thought when he saw Wilson that night: "I gotta have the sneakers. I gotta sniff 'em."

King's voice rose and he indicated Dickson: "You kind of lost it, and you hit her again and again," he said.

Harry Seay, in his closing argument, derided King's case.

"Sneakers, sneakers, sneakers. . . . Because he's different from you and me, he's a murderer. Because of his proclivity for sneakers and his desire to do whatever he does with them, he's a murderer," Seay said. "He's a sneak[er] freak, so he's a killer."[39]

The jury deliberated for days but, locked on a ten to two "guilty" vote, couldn't reach a verdict.

"So the man liked sneakers," one of the holdout jurors told the *Daily News*. "There was no proof of murder, no fingerprints, no blood, no semen, no nothing for us to work with."

The jurors didn't think much of Wolchansky.

"I don't think anyone found him credible," the foreman said—even the jurors who thought Dickson was guilty.[40]

For his part, John Hall enjoyed a little more than a summer vacation's worth of freedom before being arrested again on October 7 on drug possession charges and multiple parole violations.[41] Three days later, in jail, he ran into Wolchansky and asked what happened with the Dickson case. Wolchansky told him about the hung jury. Hall couldn't believe his luck. On October 12 he wrote to ADA King, telling his story about Dickson. On the nineteenth he spoke with two detectives. In less than two weeks he'd cut a deal to get out again. He would testify against Dickson at the retrial in November.

This moment may seem like the bottom of the wormhole that was John Hall's 1994–1996 snitching spree, but even before he testified at Dickson's he snitched again. But this time, with a chance to settle an old score and help himself at the same time, Hall got sloppy.

Maybe it was too personal.

20

UP TO SOMETHING

SOMETIME BETWEEN 6:00 AND 7:00 AM on November 2, 1995, a young paralegal named Kimberly Ernest, out for her morning jog, was raped and murdered in an upscale Center City neighborhood known as Fitler Square. Her body was found in a stairwell at Twenty-First and Pine Streets at 7:45 AM by a man out walking his dog.

The murder of a professional young woman in a nice part of town, dubbed "the Jogger Murder," was front-page news, the most talked-about murder in years; the city was shocked by the brutality and randomness of it, and there was an outpouring of support for the victim's family.[1] Mayor Rendell, reelected on the day of Kim's wake, spoke at her memorial service and wept.[2]

Kim Ernest's murder, one of more than four hundred in the city that year,[3] was exactly the kind of random killing by a stranger that made people feel unsafe. Worse for District Attorney Lynne Abraham, it happened just as she was up for reelection.[4] The pressure on police to clear the case was enormous, but the very randomness of the murder made it hard to solve.

High-profile murder, no good suspects: enter John Hall, on his own initiative for sure this time, seeking revenge against his stepson, Herbert Haak.

Hall and Haak had originally been friends; it was Haak who introduced Hall to his mother, Phyllis. But once Hall and Phyllis got together, it hadn't taken long for Hall to decide that Phyllis's children, Haak and his sister, Robyn, were against him. And anyone who was against him deserved to be crushed.

"Your kids are pigs," he wrote to Phyllis at one point. "I love you very much, but it is hardly me who ranks in your life. When it comes to the list of cared about people, it always seems that I'm not even on it. . . . Where do I come in? Definitely after Robyn [and] Herb. . . . How about just in front of the parakeets?"[5]

He told her he knew Haak had stolen things from them but would let it go for her sake.

"I do nothing because of you," he wrote. "And it is seething inside of me like a bomb about to explode!!! That piece of shit [Haak] laughs while you cry over your loss. . . . He should be beaten to <u>never walk again</u> for what he has done to you. . . .

"I'll love you forever. But don't shit on me. Don't betray me. It doesn't work. I would be far more destructive than you could ever imagine. That is why Herb better stay miles from me. He is going to learn a hard, hard lesson."[6]

In February 1994, Hall got home from a stint in jail and convinced Phyllis to move from their house to an apartment in the city to stay ahead of various charges he faced. Robyn, twelve, said she wouldn't go, so Hall and Phyllis decided to leave her by herself. Phyllis promised to visit at least a few times a week to bring supplies.

Haak went by to see his sister a couple of weeks later and found her living alone with little food and no heat in the middle of winter. He called the police. Phyllis was arrested, and because the movie *Home Alone* had just come out, the case caught the tabloid eye and became a national story. Invitations came for Phyllis to appear on TV programs—*Hard Copy, Geraldo, Inside Edition.* One rag goosed the story with an old photo of her on vacation in Hawaii, suggesting that's where she'd been while her daughter froze. She served four months in jail for child abandonment in the spring of 1994.

Ironically, Hall considered calling the police to be the ultimate betrayal.

"He makes me sick," he wrote to Phyllis of Haak. "He makes everyone sick who comes to know him. He *is* scum. Immoral jackal! . . . The biggest rat bastard alive, who would (literally) turn in his own mother."[7]

Phyllis had to choose between him and her kids, he wrote. No compromise was possible; his decision was carved in stone.[8] Haak was a hyena who'd done nothing but lie, a plague on her life, a cancer that had spread from Phyllis to Hall and needed to be eradicated.[9] Robyn was an ally of the hyena and a miserable wretch in need of institutionalization; there would be nothing but trouble with her sexually, socially, and academically.

Hall's hatred for his stepson grew to homicidal proportions. In another letter he wrote that he wanted Haak dead, that it wasn't in his nature to kill but he wasn't adverse to letting the state do it.[10]

Now Kimberly Ernest's murder gave him his chance.

In the fall of 1995 Herbie Haak and his friend Richie Wise were small-time criminals. In fact, at 8:00 AM on the day of Kim Ernest's murder, they'd been in a Bucks County courtroom, forty-five minutes from where the body was found, for a preliminary hearing on a theft charge they'd picked up two weeks earlier. Court workers and police who were there would remember Haak, congenial and wearing a three-piece suit, joking with them.[11] After the hearing Haak was held in Bucks County Jail. Wise was released and went back to Philadelphia, where he stayed in Haak's apartment with Haak's fiancée.

In jail in Bucks County, Haak ran into John Hall. When Haak's fiancée told him Wise was threatening her and stealing things from their apartment, Haak could only think of one way to get Wise out of the apartment—get him arrested. He went to Hall for advice and on November 8, at Hall's suggestion, called Philadelphia homicide and told them he thought Wise had something to do with the Ernest murder.[12] Detectives went to interview Haak and then picked Wise up for questioning that same day but didn't have enough evidence to hold him.

Hall gave Haak more advice: talk to Wise more, get more details, don't hurry.

"Take weeks or months, like I do," Hall told his stepson. "I know what it takes to build a case. And you can't just say, 'He told me he did it.'"[13]

Hall was springing a trap, and he went about fabricating a story against Haak. The next time Haak ran into him in jail, Hall couldn't resist hinting at what he was doing.

"John and my mom are up to something," Haak told an acquaintance during a phone call. "John keeps saying I'm going down big time, and I don't know what he is talking about."[14]

On November 8, Hall met with ADA Roger King about his upcoming testimony at David Dickson's retrial. He may have snitched out Haak at that meeting, though he later insisted all he did was tell King that Haak wanted to talk to him about Ernest.[15] Hall had Phyllis tell police that sometime after the Ernest murder, Haak showed up at her house and threatened to hurt her if she didn't keep quiet about what he'd "done to that girl."

Meanwhile, Hall had to finish the Dickson business. He was also still scheduled to testify against Walter.

The witnesses at David Dickson's retrial later that month were largely the same as at the first trial. The medical examiner adjusted his testimony to accommodate the snitch story by allowing that Wilson could have been strangled by hand before the killer used the extension cord.[16] The psychologist with an expertise in sexual violence gave the same testimony as at the first trial but went further, at one point stating that the "fantasy" letter from Dickson's computer came from Dickson's sense of triumph after the murder and later referring to the "aggressive components" of Dickson's foot fetish.[17]

Dickson's lawyer, Harry Seay, objected to both statements as speculative and inflammatory and requested mistrials both times. Judge Stout considered declaring a mistrial, given that the remarks had come from an expert and so might have an effect on the jurors, but decided instead to tell the jurors to disregard the comments.[18]

Roger King's most important new witness was Hall. Legally and ethically, King was required to let Dickson's defense lawyer know he was going to use Hall, but he did so only a few minutes before Hall took the stand on November 15. This left Seay no time to investigate Hall or prepare questions. Judge Stout wasn't pleased but let Hall testify anyway. He went through his Dickson story in his practiced fashion, avoiding Wolchansky's mistakes, and gave another version of his usual "disgust" answer when King asked why he was testifying.

"Mr. King, I'm a human being, like everyone else here," he said. "I know Mr. Dickson to be an admitted, vicious killer."[19]

Seay objected and asked for a mistrial.

"Listen, I really think it almost is worth a mistrial," Judge Stout said, "but we have invested too much in this case to have a mistrial now, but I'm afraid you're going to have another one of those prosecutorial misconducts. I am shocked. I am absolutely shocked. I will deny the mistrial, even though I think one is due. It is."[20]

Maybe Judge Stout thought Dickson would be acquitted and that, given this was the second trial, she should just let the verdict play out. Maybe she was sure he was guilty and couldn't bring herself to declare another mistrial.

Whatever it was, she let the trial continue.

For the defense case, Harry Seay called just one witness, thinking, as he had at the first trial, the case was so circumstantial and the snitch so patently incredible that the jury had to find a reasonable doubt. Dickson didn't testify.

On November 28, though ten detectives working the case had checked out more than two hundred tips, Kim Ernest's murder was still unsolved. Detectives contacted Hall to see if he'd heard anything about it, and at this point Hall officially snitched on Haak. He told the detectives Haak and Wise said they got up at 3:00 AM on the day of the murder so they could go out stealing cars and still get to Bucks County in time for their 8:00 AM hearing. Ernest confronted them as they were breaking into a car, so they pulled her into the backseat, raped her, killed her, dumped her body in the stairwell, and drove forty-five minutes to their hearing and arrived on time.[21]

The story was incredible, and unsupported by evidence: one witness had seen Ernest jogging a few blocks from where Haak and Wise supposedly attacked her a few minutes after the attack had supposedly happened. Also, there were no reports of stolen cars or car break-ins in that neighborhood that morning.[22]

After getting Hall's story, Philadelphia homicide detectives brought Haak in at 7:30 PM on November 28 and interrogated him. When he emerged from the room at 1:07 AM with bruises on his arms, neck, and face, they had his confession. He said the detectives made him sign blank interview forms and then filled them in with a confession they beat out of him. A court later agreed that he'd been beaten.[23]

With Haak's confession in hand, detectives brought Wise in and interrogated him all night until he signed a confession to the Ernest murder at around dawn. He said later he was beaten with fists and telephone books, was stripped, had a cord tied around his neck, and was psychologically abused.[24]

The solving of the "Jogger Murder" was big news; Philadelphia breathed a "sigh of relief."[25] That the solution involved John Hall, the well-known snitch who was also the stepfather from the *Home Alone* situation, was news, too, featured in both the *Inquirer* and the *Daily News* on November 30—which was the very day the Dickson case went to the jury.[26] Dickson's lawyer again asked for a mistrial, this time out of concern that jurors who saw in the newspaper that Hall had helped solve such an important murder might think more of his credibility.

Judge Stout, again citing the amount of time and effort that had already gone into the case, denied the motion.[27] But she was upset.

"I'm inclined not to grant the motion for a mistrial," she said. "However, as I've said before, there is no doubt in my mind that if there is a conviction, it will certainly be overturned. There is no way, with all of this, that it can stand. But I think, with all the time and money and effort which has gone to bring it this far, I think we ought to go on to the end, and then we'll see what happens. I don't know whether that's a legal decision or not, but to me, that's common sense."[28]

The jury deliberated all day and into the late afternoon the next day, when they informed Stout they were deadlocked and unable to reach a verdict. Stout polled them to determine if continued deliberations would be helpful—something she had not done at Walter's first trial—and eleven of the twelve jurors said they wanted to continue to talk.

"You've only deliberated nine hours and you heard testimony over eleven and a half days," Stout told the jury. "Eleven [of you] feel further deliberations will be helpful."

The next morning the jury reconvened and after four more hours of discussion found Dickson guilty of second-degree murder and robbery. He was sentenced to life in prison.

"I told you," Roger King said to Deborah Wilson's father, shaking hands after the verdict. "Trust the system. Good things happen to good people."[29]

Dickson's appeals lawyer thought Stout was going to grant Dickson a new trial, but Stout died in 1998 before signing an opinion to that effect.

In March 1996, John Hall went in front of Judge Kenneth Biehn in Bucks County to deal with outstanding possession of stolen property and narcotics charges. In the two years since his arrest after the high-speed chase in June 1994, he'd been on one of the most prolific snitching sprees documented, which included at least six murder defendants—Martorano, Dickson, Ogrod, Tremayne Smith, Haak, and Wise. It was time to get paid back.

Biehn had presided over Hall hearings before and knew what to expect, but even he was surprised by the extent of law enforcement support for Hall this time.

Marc Frumer opened the hearing by explaining that, while no promises had been made to Hall about his sentencing, four Philadelphia homicide detectives had shown up on their own initiative to support him: Frank Miller (Dickson and Ogrod cases); Dennis Dusak (Ernest); Joseph Walsh (Dickson and Ernest); and Patricia Brennan (Ernest and Smith).[30]

Officially, these detectives showing up for Hall was a coincidence, the result of each of them deciding on his or her own to do so, making the effort because a detective showing up in court carried more weight than writing a letter. But even if each of the four really had followed Hall's legal journey carefully enough to mark his or her calendar to appear on Hall's behalf, their boss would've needed to sign off on all four of them taking the time to go to Bucks County to plead for leniency for a snitch.[31]

Each detective took the stand and vouched for Hall, a greatest-hits review of his recent snitch career and a reminder of how important his testimony had been.

Frumer also produced letters of support for Hall from several people, including one from Charles Joey Grant, former head of the homicide office in the Philadelphia DA's office, and another from a higher source:

"You're not going to believe this," Frumer told Judge Biehn. "I also have a letter from His Eminence Cardinal Bevilacqua advising my client, signed by the Reverend John Bonavitacola."

Frumer explained to Judge Biehn that Hall was willing to accept responsibility and punishment for his actions and was helping the court save time by accepting one charge and agreeing to waive all issues in order to proceed. Frumer said he could talk for hours on end about Hall's cooperation, but Biehn cut him off.

"I don't think anyone can argue that Mr. Hall has been of value to a number of different law enforcement people," Biehn said. "On the other hand, and I don't mean to be sarcastic, but it seems to me that perhaps the best thing I could do would be to put him in jail for the rest of his life so he wouldn't commit crimes against others and he would be able to ferret out crime within the state correctional facility. I mean, this is a joke, is what this has become. How many convictions does your client have? Twenty? Twenty-five?"

"Let me address his cooperation," Frumer said. "He tries to make the best of the situation where he is. . . . When he does testify and assists and gets first-degree convictions in cases, some of them are retrials, where he now testifies and a jury comes back with a verdict of guilty, he is cross-examined for hours on his prior record, and it doesn't matter—"

"No," Biehn interrupted, "because people believe him. Because his blessing and his curse is that he is such a con, the first time, or second time, or the third time, and sometimes a fourth time, you believe him."

Frumer said Hall was at great personal risk for testifying in these cases and reminded Biehn that countless prosecutors had vouched for him simply by putting him on the stand.

"It's not like they do not want to call him," Frumer said. "But as you heard from the detectives, without him they would not have a case. Someone, a wrongdoer, would go unpunished."

Biehn looked over Hall's record again.

"You have written down that there are twenty-seven misdemeanors, eight felony-three, one aggravated assault, and four burglaries. Is that [right]?"

Frumer said it was.

When Hall stood to address the court, he stressed that his snitching had prevented criminals from getting out and hurting other people, mostly women.

"These have all been women that they've attacked," he said, "and I have a personal problem with that."

He said he'd been very conflicted about snitching against his wife's son and mentioned again the letter from Father John Bonavitacola helping him with his moral quandary.

"I have a tremendous problem with this case," he said. "Obviously, this is my wife's son—"

"Yes, but it's your wife's son who turned your wife in on another occasion," Biehn said, unfooled, referring to the *Home Alone* case.

"So people could at least look and probably cross-examine you on some of your motives with respect to this."

"I understand that," Hall said.

"I recognize," Biehn continued, "and will accept . . . that you have provided tremendous help to law enforcement which resulted in convictions. The dilemma I have is that . . . your record and your risk to the community is [sic] such that would justify maximum sentence in all these cases. That's the dilemma I have. . . . Anything else you want to say?"

Hall was nervous. Biehn was talking about giving him the maximum, and in state prison, which was harder time. He told Biehn there are many ways to do penance for a crime, that his career as a snitch was like community service and that he was at great risk from having given the DA all the mob information.[32] He told the leg-drilling story again, this time coincidentally remembering that John Veasy, a mob hit man who was just then in the news, had been one of the men attacking him.

Biehn said he understood Hall could be in jeopardy from all his snitching and softened Hall's punishment by running the sentences he handed down concurrently instead of back-to-back, but gave him one and a half to four years in a state facility.

Frumer asked the judge to reconsider the state time. Biehn said no.

Hall was angry after the hearing and blamed the failure on Frumer, whom he no longer trusted. He was in a bad situation, he felt: no lawyer, no money to hire a new one. But not without assets.

"So, what do we have going for us?" he wrote Phyllis. "There is, of course, the People of Philadelphia. The Fat Lady and the Colored Kid [Judi Rubino and Roger King]. They are forces to be reckoned with. They only have one clear shot at a win with Jogger and Ogrod, and that is with Dadees." This was the pet name Phyllis had for him. "No Dadees and no cases. Dadees is their only path. Those two cases are priority-one. If they lose them, Lynn [sic] Abraham is going to look really bad to the voters. . . . The country will be watching on these two matters. Lynn [sic] can always blame someone else for Ogrod, but not Jogger. She inherited Ogrod, but Jogger is hers."

His position was firm: he would not testify in either case if he was still in prison.[33]

––––––––––

That Hall had produced a letter of support from Cardinal Bevilacqua at the hearing before Judge Biehn surprised no one more than Cardinal Bevilacqua. The next day he contacted Father John Bonavitacola, the director of chaplaincy for the Philadelphia prison system, the same priest who'd visited Walter after his arrest and whose job included responding to all inmate mail, to ask what had happened.

Hall had, in fact, written to the cardinal, expressing concern about testifying against his stepson. The letter had gone to Father John, who, knowing Hall's reputation, had not given him any advice specifically about snitching but had said he should always tell the truth. This was the letter Frumer had tried to pass off as a letter of support from the Cardinal himself, as if Hall somehow had Bevilacqua's blessing.

Father John contacted Frumer and asked that Hall recant his statements implying that Cardinal Bevilacqua somehow approved of what he was doing, and Hall did so. But Father John was fed up. He had been visiting Walter regularly since his arrest, knew the case against him was weak, and knew John Hall was a liar and that Walter's case was the kind of case prosecutors used Hall for. To Father John, you could understand how prosecutors worked by looking at the housing assignments in jail and tracking where the jailhouse snitches were put. How else did snitches housed in one place suddenly turn up as cellmates to high-profile murder defendants in another? Father John thought this was clear evidence that prison officials and police conspired to produce phony jailhouse confessions that led to convictions in otherwise weak cases. He'd seen it several times himself with John Hall.

It made him angry to see that authorities manipulate the justice system to get convictions against people with so little power, and that everyone was supposed to accept that this was justified so long as the right people ended up in jail. Eventually he came to feel he couldn't work in so corrupt a system, gave up his job, and moved away.[34]

John Hall was supposed to testify at the Ogrod retrial scheduled for September 1996 and the Ernest trial in early 1997, and Judi Rubino, the prosecutor in charge of both trials, was in regular contact with him through the spring of 1996, speaking with him half a dozen times. As late as August 14 Rubino wrote to Mark Greenberg that Hall and Wolchansky would both testify against Walter.[35] At some point between then and Walter's trial—the end of August, according to Hall—Rubino informed Hall she would not be using him against Ogrod because she wanted to use him for the Ernest case.[36] Apparently two John Hall trials, back-to-back, was too much for her.

For Ogrod, Rubino would use Jay Wolchansky, despite the rough time he'd had at the first Dickson trial. Though he would later swear, as Hall had taught him, that he came forward against Ogrod only out of a sense of moral outrage, he recorded his real motives in a letter he wrote to Hall in August 1996—probably just after being told he would be the only witness against Ogrod.

"I will not do anything for the Ogrod trial unless I am free first," he wrote. "And then I will only think about doing it, since I don't enjoy the publicity. I guess this will be all over the news and I want to avoid this aspect of this."

That he and Hall were working together on Walter's case is evident in his closing: "Keep me posted on Ogrod."[37]

Rubino took Hall off the Ogrod case but still planned to use him for the Jogger case despite many reasons to be skeptical of his Ernest story. First, Haak's and Wise's confessions didn't match each other, and the physical evidence in the case didn't implicate either of them: DNA from semen and hairs taken from Ernest's body didn't match either of them, and the car Hall said they'd raped and beaten her to death in showed no evidence of a physical struggle, no blood.[38]

Also, by July 1996 concern about Hall's role in solving the Kimberly Ernest case was widespread. Will Bunch published an article in the *Daily News* titled "Cops Try to Plug Holes in Jogger Murder," which pointed out that the "break in the case seemed to come from left field . . . when John Hall . . . entered." Bunch laid out Hall's long, checkered history as a snitch.[39] In another article, Bunch questioned why Haak would've confided anything to his stepfather, given their well-known antipathy after the very public *Home Alone* situation.[40]

All of this doubt pushed Hall to another level of lying. He decided to strengthen his story and the prosecution's case by telling them Haak had kept a necklace of Kimberly Ernest's after the murder. He told Phyllis to go to a jeweler well out of town and have a necklace made with the inscription "Kim I love you Ernie Burt" on it.[41] He would then claim to have found it by accident in the front casing of a radio he retrieved from Haak's cell.[42] It would be the first definitive evidence linking Haak to the murder.[43]

But Hall's hatred for his stepson had swamped his caution and he made mistakes. First, the story he'd told about Ernest's murder had left him open to an accomplice to murder charge, because of his link to the car he'd claimed Haak had used in the murder. He wrote to Phyllis that he would fix this by arranging for "immunities" with "Lynne [Abraham], Judy [Judi Rubino], Roger [King],"[44] and on August 10 he wrote a petition for immunity to Rubino. With so many people suspicious of his involvement with the necklace, he added to the petition that, for the record, he hadn't known about it until he heard about it from Herb.

But Hall had another problem: Phyllis didn't want any part of fabricating a necklace. She was angry enough at her son that she'd started to listen to Hall's relentless attacks against him; she'd even gone along with telling the police Haak had threatened her. But she wasn't going to help forge evidence that would stick her son with a death sentence.

Hall wrote to her, employing his full palette of manipulation: accusation, flattery, sentimentality, threat, condescension.

"Maybe you secretly want to sabotage this case," he started, then switched tones: he loved her, they didn't fight, they were in it all together, he could protect her, but she had to stop telling people things they didn't need to know. He then touched a menacing chord: her son was finished, and if she changed her story now about Haak threatening her, she would alienate the DA and no one would be able to protect her. But, he went on, she was smart, she was capable, she could do this. He explained how to testify at Haak's trial when the time came.

"Answer 'yes,' 'no,' or 'I don't know,'" he advised. "Do <u>not</u> volunteer anything. Let them ask and you answer with the facts as you know them. Remember that <u>you</u> control the attorneys. They must respond to <u>your</u> rhythm. You can slow them down by answering at <u>your</u> pace."[45]

Personally, Hall wanted Phyllis to know, he was eager for the combat of trial. Her son's lawyer was going to wish he'd never seen the Ernest case.

"I'm going to kick his fucking teeth in at trial, and you tell him I said so, too," Hall wrote.

But Phyllis struggled with what would happen to her son, and Hall intensified his attack.

"He is scum," he wrote in his anger and impotence at trying to convince her to hate her own son enough to stick him with a death sentence, digging the tip of his Bic pen into the paper: "Faggot . . . rapist . . . woman beater . . . fucking sludge . . . demented faggot who hates his mother and needs to injure her . . . if they gave him the death injection I sure as hell wouldn't lose any sleep."[46]

The case against Haak and Wise for murdering Kimberly Ernest would collapse early in 1997 when the truth about the "Kim" necklace forgery leaked. This proof that Hall was a liar finally made him too toxic for a courtroom; he invoked his Fifth Amendment rights and refused to testify at the Ernest trial. Rubino pressed on, arguing that Hall wasn't central to proving her case but was only a "straw man" defense lawyers wanted to use to distract the jury from the real issues.[47] She went to trial with only Haak's and Wise's disputed confessions and on March 14, 1997, after less than three hours of deliberation, the two men were acquitted. The jury believed their confessions had been coerced.[48]

The embarrassment Hall caused the Philadelphia DA's office with his necklace stunt permanently damaged his brand and ended his most prolific two-plus year run of snitching. He would never again have the same kind of access to power that he had enjoyed so much.

For what it's worth, Hall later said he thought Rubino didn't know he was lying about the case until she found out about the necklace. Marc Frumer, Hall said, knew all along.[49]

As for the Ogrod case, Hall's letters to Phyllis at the time suggest Frumer knew generally what Hall was doing (*Marc tells me I am teaching him things outside the system*), but he never wrote or said that Frumer specifically knew the Ogrod story was a lie.

After the Biehn hearing in 1996, Hall's relationship with Frumer deteriorated. He wrote to Phyllis that Frumer was incompetent and had betrayed him. This was Hall's pattern with his lawyers—even if he liked them at first, at some point they would prove unable to completely rescue him from his own pathology, and he'd turn on them.

21

A NEW VERSION
OF EVENTS

WALTER'S RETRIAL BEGAN ON SEPTEMBER 30, 1996. He sat at the defense table, his face a studied blank, pancake makeup around his eye to cover a bruise he'd gotten when, left in a holding cell with his hands cuffed behind him, he'd been attacked by several other inmates. Mark Greenberg had rushed out to buy the makeup so Walter wouldn't look bad in court.

The courtroom was crowded, the seats behind the prosecution table filled again with John and Sharon Fahy and their families. The jury was sworn in and Walter pled "not guilty."[1]

Judi Rubino, the prosecutor, was one of Lynne Abraham's stars. The two women had known each other for twenty-five years, and Rubino's toughness and courtroom abilities were nearly as legendary as Abraham's: to that point, she'd sent more than twenty men to death row without losing a murder trial.

Rubino was every bit the street fighter Abraham was, though from a more comfortable background. She was born Judith Frankel in Philadelphia; her father was an OB-GYN, and her mother had started law school during World War II but quit with a year left because she wanted to marry before Judi's father was sent overseas. Later she chose to stay home with the kids, a decision

Judi thought she always regretted because if she'd finished she would've been one of the first women to graduate from the University of Pennsylvania Law School.[2]

Education was important in the Frankel family. Judi's brother earned a PhD, and her sister became a high school English teacher whose moot court team once placed ninth in the country. Judi attended an all-girls high school in Philadelphia and then the University of Pennsylvania; she wanted to help people, wanted to get into court, and loved detective stuff, so she enrolled in Temple Law School. After law school she took a job in New York with the Securities and Exchange Commission, doing "blue sky" work, but it wasn't for her. She moved back to Philadelphia in 1969 and took a job at a big law firm but figured out quickly that she'd never make partner because she was a woman (the firm didn't end up having a female partner until 1988), so she left in 1971 to join the DA's office. There, in Arlen Specter's office, she learned the prosecutorial craft under Ed Rendell and Lynne Abraham. Her reputation as an extremely smart and tough prosecutor grew quickly, and she was soon promoted to the homicide office. She found the work very exciting, very "real life"; the cases that stuck with her the most were the murders of children and police.[3]

By 1996 Rubino was highly respected, the longest consecutively serving ADA in Philadelphia. Married to a police officer, she had strong connections with the police department and had many friends and former colleagues rising through the ranks of political office.[4] She had a particularly close relationship with Judge Stout, whom she said "was brilliant and wonderful and sweet and . . . ran a great courtroom. Of all the judges I've ever met, she was my absolute favorite, the finest judge on the bench."[5]

To convict Walter, Rubino was planning a simple, powerful case. If the narrative of Walter's guilt *felt* right, the jury would convict him. The basics of the story, however, had changed from the first trial. Instead of the spur-of-the-moment sexual assault/panic murder described in the Devlin statement and presented to the first jury, Rubino would describe a murder hatched carefully over the course of months by a devious master manipulator who'd been able to lie to Devlin and Worrell about what really happened but later told the truth to another inmate. To smooth over the differences between the two stories, Rubino would tell the jury the snitch story was the more complete truth but that it didn't matter which particulars they believed, since both stories came from Walter and both said he killed Barbara Jean.

Rubino simplified the prosecution's case by dropping the question of whether or not a single sperm head had been found in Barbara Jean's saliva. While it offered the only possible evidence that Barbara Jean had been sexually assaulted, only one criminalist thought it existed and the medical examiner did not, so it just confused jurors. Rubino also wanted to adjust Walter himself: she thought his lawyer had him overmedicated at the first trial so the jury would think he was a "moron" who couldn't have given the Devlin/Worrell statement. She contacted the detention center and asked them to review Walter's medications, and though she insisted later she couldn't tell the jail to change them, she wanted them reduced, asked for a review, and they were reduced.[6] If Walter testified again, and she thought he would, this time the jury would get a better sense of who he really was.

Rubino also decided to handle the witnesses in the case differently than Casey had. In a pretrial meeting in Judge Stout's chambers, Rubino asked Stout to throw out the police sketch of the man with the box on the grounds that it was "hearsay from a dead witness."[7] Lorraine Schectman, Rubino argued, was the only witness who'd actually helped with the sketch, and since she was dead she couldn't come to court to "adopt" the sketch in front of the jury. Therefore the jury shouldn't see it.

This was a switch: at Walter's first trial, Joseph Casey had argued that *David* Schectman was the only person who'd helped with the sketch.[8] In fact, as an affidavit signed by one of the detectives involved in making the sketch attests, both Schectmans helped the sketch artist.[9]

Despite this, Rubino argued to Judge Stout that David Schectman had just been walking "in and out of the room" while his wife gave the description for the sketch.[10] Mark Greenberg reminded Judge Stout that at the first trial she had allowed him to hold up the sketch and a picture of Ross Felice, "an exact match," as Greenberg put it, for the jury to compare.

Stout ruled that Greenberg could use the sketch.[11]

Rubino next argued she should be able to tell the jury that Walter loved child pornography and had a pile of it in his room. But she had no evidence of this. (Walter has always denied it utterly and no one has ever claimed to have seen him with such material, nor has any ever been found in his house or apartment. Even Linda Green, who lived with him and hated him, told detectives she'd seen his magazines and there was no child porn.)[12]

Judge Stout ruled that Rubino could not bring up the child pornography claim. But that didn't mean she wouldn't.

Mark Greenberg was once more representing Walter alone. He got a small amount of money to hire an investigator again and had the investigator pull Hall's and Wolchansky's criminal records. When he found out Wolchansky would be the one testifying against Walter, he tried to get Wolchansky's psychiatric records, but on September 19, 1996, eleven days before the trial, a judge denied Greenberg's request for an order for the prison to release the records, pending conversation with the trial judge (Judge Stout). Greenberg never saw the records, so he didn't know that Wolchansky was schizophrenic and undermedicated during the time he was supposedly speaking to Walter.[13]

Greenberg's strategy would be to emphasize reasonable doubt. Walter looked nothing like that man carrying the TV box: reasonable doubt. Three of the witnesses identified other people as that man: reasonable doubt. The statements Walter had supposedly given to detectives and to the snitch didn't match each other and, worse, got important facts of the case wrong: reasonable doubt. The jury, he would argue, couldn't pick and choose the pieces of

each story that made sense without admitting that they couldn't
know for sure what happened: reasonable doubt.

———————

The jurors for Walter's second trial were sequestered; those picked
to serve were taken directly home from the courtroom by bailiffs
who waited while they packed and then took them to the hotel
where they would live during the trial. They were told it would
probably take a week or ten days.

When Thomas James, a thirty-seven-year-old computer engineer
with a master's degree, was chosen as a juror, he was allowed to
call his employer to say he would be out for a while. He also
snuck a call to his family so they would know he wasn't dead. He
couldn't call his friends, though, and some of them did wonder
if he'd died.[14]

Another juror, David Miller, had a master's degree in library
science and had moved to Philadelphia in 1994 to work in the
city's records department. Miller was selected as an alternate juror,
meaning he would listen to all the testimony but wouldn't vote
on the verdict unless another juror had to leave for some reason.
He was an unusual juror on a death penalty case, because he
opposed the death penalty. Jurors on capital cases are supposed
to be "death qualified," meaning they are willing to impose the
death penalty if the law requires it, and Miller knew during jury
selection that saying he disagreed would get him dismissed. But
he thought it was his duty to stay on the jury—if he were ever
up on such charges he would want a jury of people with varied
opinions on the death penalty. So he said "yes," he could impose
the death penalty if needed.

Neither James nor Miller had heard of the Barbara Jean Horn
case before.

At the jurors' hotel, the airport Hilton, the TVs, telephones, and
radios had been removed from their rooms. Jurors were allowed
supervised phone calls if they could convince the judge they needed

them. Miller didn't have children and wasn't married—the usual reasons a judge granted calls—so he didn't get any.

———————

On the first morning of the trial, as Miller watched the proceedings begin, he felt a greater sense of responsibility than he had ever felt. A man's life was at stake; justice was at stake, and Miller felt the weight of it. He almost hyperventilated during opening statements.[15]

The prosecutor went first. Judi Rubino, sitting at the prosecution table, greeted the jury. She didn't stand much during trials, conducting her case from her seat.

Rubino's first task in her opening was to lower the jury's expectations about the evidence.

"In this case," she said, "as in any case like this, you will not hear from anybody who can come in here and say, 'I saw Walter Ogrod kill Barbara Jean Horn.' Those people who actually saw the man carrying a box are not going to be able to tell you that Walter Ogrod is the person they saw carrying the box. They're going to tell you they can't say it is but they can't say it isn't Mr. Ogrod."[16]

It was true no one had seen Walter kill Barbara Jean, and Rubino knew what the witnesses who'd seen the man with the box were going say when they testified. In this way she dismissed a huge flaw in her case—that none of the witnesses could identify the defendant—as a regular occurrence, even adding "as in any case like this" to underline how common it was.

Rubino's next task in her opening was to build up the two main characters in her story, Detective Devlin and Jay Wolchansky. Since both men's honesty would be challenged by the defense, Rubino set out to make them appear not just honest but beyond reproach, brave, ethical in a world of criminals and liars.

She began with Devlin, describing him standing on the steps of Barbara Jean's house in early 1992 with Detective Worrell, looking around the neighborhood for somewhere Barbara Jean might've gone that day, seeing Walter's old house across the street, abandoned and boarded up, an eyesore in the family neighbor-hood, and deciding, "Let's start there."

This emphasized Devlin's instincts and his claim that neither he nor Worrell knew anything about Walter before interviewing him. Nothing in particular had led them to 7244 Rutland, just two detectives with good instincts.

Rubino then described for the jury the version of Barbara Jean's murder in the Devlin/Worrell statement. She told them an officer from the city of Philadelphia clean and seal unit who cleaned out 7244 Rutland Street in 1990 would testify she'd found bloody clothes in the basement. (The officer would also tell the jury it wasn't unusual to find bloody clothes in an abandoned drug house and that she hadn't found anything that could've been Barbara Jean's.)

"It wasn't just to the detectives that the defendant told what he had done," Rubino said. "He told other inmates about what he had done in much greater detail than what he had told the police."[17]

Rubino now told the snitch version of the murder, explaining that Walter had actually planned the murder for months in order to pin it on John Fahy so John would be arrested and Walter could marry Sharon.

"It sounds like a convoluted thing," she told the jury. "It all sounds very distorted, but that's what [Walter] said."[18]

For John and Sharon, sitting in the second row of the court-room holding hands, hearing this was horrible. They walked out.[19] It made them furious and fed Sharon's guilt—it was her fault somehow that this weirdo she'd never met had fixated on her.[20] They believed the snitch story. John remembered a time a few weeks before the murder when he'd been over at 7244 Rutland and some guy who lived there had given him a hard time about being from Kensington, a bad part of the city. John hadn't known who the guy was or what he was talking about, but now that he'd heard the snitch story it made sense: the guy was Walter Ogrod, and Henry Fahy, the guy whose crime Walter was copying, was from Kensington. That's why Walter had been him asking him about that.

Rubino finished her opening statement by explaining away, again, the witnesses.

"You will hear all this evidence," she said. "You will also hear, probably, that many of these people testified at a court proceeding back in 1993, and many of them may be asked about things that they testified to in 1993. . . . This is now 1996, the killing of Barbara Jean Horn occurred in 1988, some eight years ago. Imagine yourself trying to recall details of what you might have done eight years ago on a particular day, trying to remember exactly what you might have said when you testified three years ago. So when you hear the witnesses, try to put yourself in their positions and realize that they're trying to do the best they can remembering something that happened so long ago."[21]

This was actually a good argument for taking the statements the witnesses gave within hours of the crime as the closest possible version of the truth, but those were the statements Rubino wanted to discredit. Her message was simpler and applied to her whole case: everything won't add up precisely and some things will seem outlandish, but that's just the nature of these things and didn't change the most important fact:

"Walter Ogrod is guilty of murder in the first degree," she said. "A premeditated, willful, and deliberate killing with malice. . . . He's also guilty of rape, in that he attempted to rape Barbara Jean, and . . . of involuntary deviate sexual intercourse."

When Rubino finished, Mark Greenberg jumped up, speaking right away, so intent on making his point while Rubino's admissions of the weaknesses in her case were fresh in jurors' minds that he forgot the usual "Good afternoon, ladies and gentlemen" for the jury.

"The reason why no Commonwealth witness or any witness will identify Walter Ogrod as the man carrying the box on July the 12th, 1988, is because Walter Ogrod was not carrying the television box on July the 12th, 1988," he said.

Walter had lived in the neighborhood for years, Greenberg went on; if he'd been carrying that box, someone would have recognized him and said so.

"[No one identified him] because he is not the man, members of the jury."

"Objection, Your Honor," Rubino said. "This is not an opening."

Judge Stout sustained Rubino's objection and told Greenberg to say what he intended to prove—the proper language for an opening statement.

Greenberg went on. His story needed a real killer, so he offered the original suspect, Ross Felice, explaining that Felice had come to detectives' attention the night of the murder for hanging around the scene for too long. And he told the jury, "When you have evidence that someone else was identified as the person carrying the box, that is going to be relevant to your determination."

He moved to the two disputed statements.

"The details of those two confessions are totally, absolutely different," he said, "and when Ms. Rubino characterizes it as 'it sounds distorted,' this so-called jailhouse confession, the reason why it sounds distorted is because it's bogus, it's false."

"Objection, your honor," Rubino said. "This is a closing, not an opening."

Stout agreed and Greenberg corrected his form.

"The evidence will show, members of the jury, that this so-called jailhouse confession is bogus," he said, "and the evidence will show that the so-called confession to the police is also bogus—not that this is a technicality to get Mr. Ogrod off but that the so-called confessions are false."

The lack of physical evidence also proved Walter was not the man, Greenberg said: no one ever saw blood in his basement or on him, and the fingerprint taken from the TV box didn't match his.

No one was minimizing how horrible the murder was, Greenberg said. But it would be more horrible if the jury didn't put aside the sympathy they would naturally feel for the child and her parents to focus on the sole issue in the case: was Walter Ogrod the man who carried the TV box with Barbara Jean's body in it?

Greenberg emphasized that he wasn't arguing for an acquittal on a technicality: Walter was innocent.

"And after listening to all the evidence, members of the jury," he said, "I believe sincerely that you will conclude that there is a reasonable doubt in this case and will find Mr. Ogrod not guilty."

Greenberg's opening touched on the key points of the defense but lacked any mention of how false confessions can happen and why Walter would have been at high risk for giving one that night in Interview Room D. He hadn't even mentioned Walter's lack of sleep prior to his interrogation. He also could have described more clearly why it was impossible for Walter to have killed Barbara Jean: the tiny house with two or three adults home and two large, protective dogs; the fact that Walter was in his living room all afternoon with the Greens, watching the commotion out on the street when it started, talking about the missing child, without any sign of nervousness.

22

BUILDING IN ERROR

THE PROSECUTION'S FIRST WITNESS was Joan Zablocky, in front of whose house the box had been left, who described her call to 911. She was followed by Michael Massi, the car salesman witness, who identified the TV box and said the man carried it "like it was pretty heavy."[1] Rubino led Massi carefully through an explanation of why he hadn't gotten a good look at the man and why he'd been wrong on the day of the murder when he'd described the man to detectives as between five feet six and five feet eight: the man had been hunched over, dragging the box, so, Massi now said, he hadn't had any way to gauge how tall he was.

"Are you able to tell us whether or not you see, in this courtroom today, the person who was carrying the TV box on July 12th of 1988?" Rubino asked.

"No," Massi said.

On cross-examination, Greenberg produced the statement Massi had given police at 7:50 PM on the night of the murder, a little more than two hours after the event, when Massi said that after putting the box down on the sidewalk across St. Vincent Street, the man had stood up to catch his breath for about twenty seconds, giving Massi a sense of how tall he was: five feet six to five feet eight.

"Mr. Massi, were you shown this sketch on July the 13th or 14th, 1988, two days after your observations?" Greenberg asked, showing Massi the police sketch.

"Yes, I was," Massi said.

"Do you remember telling those two detectives . . . that the composite was a very good likeness to the male, and that the hair-style depicted in the composite was almost exact?" Greenberg asked.

"No, I do not," Massi said.

Greenberg had made his points, but Rubino had gotten what she needed—a witness muddling the clear statements he'd given to police around the time of the killing.

At a meeting in Judge Stout's chambers before the second day of the trial, Rubino and Greenberg argued about whether Rubino could show a picture of Barbara Jean, dead, to the jury. Judge Stout worried that a gruesome picture might prejudice the jury, and since the fact that Barbara Jean was the victim in this case had been established in other ways, told Rubino to use a photo of Barbara Jean alive.

"I don't see anything wrong with that," Stout said. "That is certainly not gruesome. . . . It's a picture of the child."[2]

"Right, with a [teddy] bear," Greenberg said.

"They get to see him march in here every day with his suit," Rubino said, referring to Walter.

"Yeah, Walter with the black eye, with the lousy makeup job," Greenberg said.

"You should blame him for being smart with the prisoners," Rubino said.

"Now, I'm going to tell you all in front, don't start the fussing," Stout said.

Rubino opened the second day of the trial with eyewitness David Schectman, guiding him through his story: leaning against the station wagon, waiting for his kids, a man coming toward him on St. Vincent Street carrying and dragging a TV box by a garbage bag inside.

Schectman knew to be as vague as possible and, by this point, probably didn't have to pretend: he'd been trying to help detectives for so long, identifying people whenever they asked him to, reconsidering height, weight, and hair color so many times, he may easily have been confused. But on some things Schectman wasn't confused at all. The TV box was heavy and the man carrying it had been panting and sweating and at one point had dragged it by the garbage bag inside—a key point, since the snitch was going to say Walter never actually carried Barbara Jean in the box. And Schectman could remember times: he first saw the man with the box at 5:12, last saw him at 5:23 when the camp van arrived with his kids, and last saw the box at 5:26 as he and his wife drove west on St. Vincent, the same direction the man with the box had been walking.

Rubino had him describe how terrible he'd felt when he'd found out there was a body in the box: if he'd only stopped to look in the box, he could've helped catch the murderer.

Schectman testified that the man had been "somewhere about 5'8", 5'10", maybe 165 pounds and . . . sandy-colored hair" and lowered his estimation of the man's age to between twenty and twenty-five. He tried to explain that after his wife died he'd gone to therapy and had learned in therapy that he wasn't good at recognizing faces.[3]

Greenberg objected; he didn't want the jury listening to some supposedly therapeutic reason why Schectman's detailed statement from the night of the murder was inaccurate.

"Do you recall what hairstyle he had?" Rubino pressed on.

"Shortish," Schectman said. He repeated his story from the first trial, how he'd really only seen the man for a few seconds, not eleven minutes as he'd told detectives that night. And he now said that he couldn't be sure of the man's height because the man had been bending over much of the time or had been elevated on the steps to the backyard.

"Do you see the person in court today who was carrying the box?" Rubino asked.

"I couldn't really tell you," Schectman said. "I did not get a good enough look at the person to tell you whether that person is here or not here."

This was a win for Rubino: she would make "couldn't be sure" into "could be Walter."

"As a result of the counseling you've gone through," Rubino asked, "have you learned anything about yourself that explains to you why you were not able to get a better impression?"

Greenberg objected. Stout upheld the objection. Rubino wasn't deterred.

"Are you good at remembering faces?" she asked Schectman.

"Objection," said Greenberg.

"Overruled," said Stout, allowing Rubino to get her dubious point across to the jury.

"No, I'm not particularly good at remembering faces," Schectman said. He added the psychological cover for his drastic change of story: "For 31 years [as a fireman] I dealt with buildings and objects and I was very good at sizing up on fires [sic] and the situation developing on a fire ground, I discovered that I was more object- and building-oriented than people-oriented, you know. . . . I generally need to meet someone and shake their hands and repeat their names three or four or five times."

On cross-examination Greenberg read Schectman his statement to police on the night of the murder.

"He was a white male, about 25 to 30 years of age, dark blond hair or dirty blond hair, it was short. . . . He was tanned slightly. He was sweating heavily. He was 5'8" to 5'9", 160 to 165 pounds. He was wearing a white crew neck T-shirt with some printing on the front . . . but no pocket."

"Now," Greenberg continued, "is that the description that you gave police, Mr. Schectman, on July the 12th, 1988, at approximately 8:20 PM?"

"Yes."

"And the question that was posed to you by the officer who took this statement was: 'Would you be able to identify him again?' Do you see that question?" he asked, referring to the copy Schectman was using to follow along.

"Yes, I do."

"And what did you tell the officer?"

"According to this, [I] said, 'Yes, I would.'"

Did he remember telling a detective the composite sketch was a "good likeness" of the man carrying the box? Schectman didn't. Greenberg had him describe the time detectives took him to the gym to look at Ross Felice and read from Schectman's statement that day:

"I, at once, recognized this male as the male I had seen carrying the TV box west on St. Vincent Street on July 12, 1988, the box Barbara Jean Horn's body was found in. . . . This male stood up, turned his head away from me, and walked away from me out of the gym."

"Are you positive it is the same man?" one of the detectives had asked.

"Very positive," Schectman had answered. "No doubt in my mind whatsoever."

Greenberg took Schectman through his July 12 story again, got him to admit that he did remember plenty of specifics—when he had looked at his watch, his interactions with the man with the box. Once again, Greenberg never asked Schectman what the man's voice had sounded like, though Schectman had told police the man's voice was normal, which Walter's was not.

Rubino next called Christian Kochan, the newspaper boy, leading him carefully through his testimony about riding down the St. Vincent Street sidewalk on his bike and squeezing past the man with the box. Because he was only fourteen at the time, Kochan now said, his estimates about the man's height and age had been wrong.

For her last question, Rubino asked if he'd ever identified anyone as the man he'd seen carrying the box, and Kochan said "no."

On cross-examination, Mark Greenberg held up the photograph of Ross Felice, whom Kochan had identified as the man carrying the box five weeks after the murder.

"In fact, [this] is a photograph that you identified on August the 18th, 1988, which you signed your signature to, is that right?" Greenberg asked.

"Objection to the term 'identified,'" Rubino said.

It's not clear by what technicality Rubino argued that that wasn't an identification—witnesses only sign photos to establish that they've identified the person. But Judge Stout upheld the objection.

"It's a picture that you selected that you put your name to on August the 18th, 1988?" Greenberg asked.

Kochan admitted he'd signed the back of the photo to indicate it looked like the man carrying the TV box.

During her follow-up questions Rubino got Kochan to say that he'd only identified the picture that looked most like the composite sketch. Even if true, that was very different from the claim that he'd never identified anyone.

By the time Kochan left the stand, Rubino, with helpful rulings from Judge Stout, had succeeded in muddling the eyewitness testimony. And the pattern for the trial was set: Rubino would say whatever she thought could help her case, overstating some things, denying others, the only limitation being her old friend Judge Stout's willingness to uphold Greenberg's objections against her.

———————

After the eyewitnesses, Rubino put on the medical experts. As at the first trial, the jury wouldn't hear from Dr. P. J. Hoyer, who'd actually performed the autopsy, but from one of his assistants, Dr. Haresh Mirchandani, who hadn't been present.

John and Sharon left the courtroom, and Mirchandani described the autopsy results: the wounds, that there was no evidence of sexual assault, that Barbara Jean had probably been alive for several of the wounds she suffered.

On the key question of the murder weapon, Mirchandani said, in response to a question from Greenberg, "I can't say if this [pull-down bar] was the object, no way."[4]

Greenberg hadn't hired an independent forensics expert to review the autopsy photos. It's not surprising, given his lack of resources, but an expert could have helped a lot. Dr. Hoyer had written in his notes the day after the murder that the weapon was probably a "2 × 2 or 2 × 4"—in other words, flat, unlike the pull-down bar from the weight set[5]—and years later, when Walter's lawyers did have the resources to hire an expert to examine the autopsy report, Dr. Marcella Fierro, the retired chief medical examiner for the Commonwealth of Virginia and onetime head of the National Association of Medical Examiners, would confirm this. She discredited the idea of the pull-down bar as murder weapon once and for all, finding that the wounds on Barbara Jean's back showed a distinctive pattern of two central parallel lines and two oblique parallel lines, meaning the murder was caused by a "blunt, flat object with a distinctive pattern on its surface, such as a golf club." The lacerations on Barbara Jean's head were also characteristic of a flat object, certainly not a pipe or anything round. She found to a reasonable degree of medical certainty that the pull-down bar (which she also reviewed) was *not* the murder weapon. She consulted with Dr. Hoyer, who had performed the original autopsy, and he agreed that the pull-down bar could not be the murder weapon.[6]

The jury never heard any of this.

Rubino's next witness, Dr. Lucy Rorke, described the injuries to Barbara Jean's brain. Dr. Rorke also said there was no evidence in the brain of suffocation, potentially another problem with the snitch's story, since Walter was supposed to have said he covered her nose and mouth with his hand as he killed her. Rubino tried to mitigate this problem by getting Rorke's opinion about whether Barbara Jean's brain would show signs of suffocation if the suffocation hadn't been prolonged.

The suffocation issue may be the best example of Stout's deference to Rubino.

When Greenberg objected to Rubino's question about suffocation Judge Stout upheld him, but that didn't stop Rubino from asking again anyway.

"Assume, if you would, hypothetically, that this child was being held by someone," Rubino said, "that she began to scream when someone was sexually assaulting her, and that her mouth was covered."

"Objection," Greenberg said: the trial was supposed to determine whether those things happened, not the prosecutor.

"I don't think those facts have been brought out," Judge Stout said, sustaining Greenberg's objection.

"Well, they will be," said Rubino. "So I think I can ask a hypothetical."

"All right, then I'll allow it."

Stout had just told the jury to assume the prosecution would present facts to back up their version of the murder because Rubino said they would.

"Assume hypothetically, Doctor," Rubino said to Dr. Rorke, "that the child was being held and that a hand was placed over her mouth to stop her from screaming. What changes, if any, would you expect to see [in her brain tissue] if it were a short period of time, not a prolonged suffocation?"

"None."[7]

Dr. Rorke agreed with the medical examiner that Barbara Jean's injuries were caused by a blunt object and said the pull-down bar could have caused the injuries. On cross-examination, Greenberg got Rorke to agree that any kind of blunt object would be consistent with the injuries—a broom handle, mop handle, tire iron.

———————

John Fahy took the stand to tell the story of Barbara Jean's last day. He broke down weeping twice during his testimony. On the important question of whether he'd knocked on the door of 7244 during his search for Barbara Jean, he said he couldn't remember for sure but thought he'd yelled across the street to Linda Green between 5:00 and 5:20 and she'd come to her door to answer him. Whether he crossed the street or not, if this conversation occurred then it occurred at a time when several witnesses, including the Greens, all put Walter in the living room—at the exact time the man with the box was dragging it down St. Vincent Street.[8]

———————

At the airport Hilton that night, Thomas James, juror number ten, started a journal, which I later discussed with him. He remembered the witness David Schectman as having been unreliable and antagonistic to the defense.[9]

Schectman's determination to help the prosecution had come through, then, but the "unreliable" part was all Rubino needed.

David Miller, the alternate juror, had been confused by the witness testimony too: people saw a guy carrying a box, he was tall, he was short, he was medium, none of it was definitive, he felt none of it told him much about the case.

Rubino had succeeded in her first task—undermining the witnesses.

James also remembered that the Fahys had left the courtroom for the forensic testimony and that John broke down twice on the stand and clearly felt guilty about what had happened to his daughter. He didn't remember or note in his journal that both forensic experts had said they couldn't be sure the pull-down bar was the murder weapon.[10]

———————

The next morning Sharon Fahy took the stand and told her story of the day of the murder. Greenberg asked a few questions, clarifying that she'd never met Walter and didn't know who he was until the November night four months after the murder when she'd watched Sarge Green beat him down Rutland Street and asked John who he was.

Greenberg needed this so he could later put the lie to the snitch story that Walter had fallen in love with her because she was nice to him.

After Sharon, Rubino came back to the murder weapon. Whereas with the eyewitnesses she'd needed to create a muddle out of clear testimony, now she needed to create clarity out of a muddle. Fortunately for her, Stout allowed, as she had at the first trial, a salesman from a sporting goods store to testify about which pull-down bar would have been on the weight set Walter had. She then let Rubino introduce one of those pull-down bars into evidence and wave it around, as Joseph Casey had at the first trial, a vivid image for the jury.

In order for Rubino to push the idea of the pull-down bar as the murder weapon she also needed to convince the jury that neither Devlin nor Worrell knew of the weight set and pull-down bar in Walter's basement before talking to him. If it came out that the detectives had heard of the weight set first, the last thing "only the killer would know" was gone from Walter's statement and Rubino's case might collapse.

Rubino put on Detective Edward Rocks, Devlin and Worrell's colleague on the SIU, to claim, as he had at the first trial, that he'd never mentioned the weight set or the pull-down bar to Devlin or Worrell before Walter's interrogation.

On cross-examination, Greenberg asked Rocks about his work on the Maureen Dunne murder and about Maureen's father being a Philadelphia detective. He wanted the jury to understand that the detectives had known each other and that the murder of a detective's daughter was a very big deal—that there was no way Devlin and Worrell didn't go over the Dunne murder when they were looking into the trouble house at 7244 Rutland as part of the Barbara Jean Horn investigation.

Rocks stuck to his story, and Greenberg didn't debate his claim that he'd never shown the Dunne murder file to his colleagues. Stout allowed Rubino to show the jury a photo of Maureen Dunne's murder scene, the weight set near her bed, her body covered by a piece of paper. Rocks said clearly that Walter had not been involved in her murder, but showing the jury a picture of a murder scene in his house with his alleged murder weapon in it helped cast an aura of violence and murder around him for the jury.

And this time the jury never even heard the argument about whether Devlin and Worrell had asked Walter's landlord about the weight set four days before Walter's interview.[11]

———————

Rubino put on a fingerprint technician to explain that the fact that the one fingerprint on the garbage bag didn't match Walter's didn't mean much. The technician explained how the fingerprinting process works and that the fingerprint on the bag could have come from anybody who'd handled the garbage bag at any time. He also told the jury that no usable fingerprints were lifted from the cardboard box.[12]

Rubino's next witness was Marty Devlin, and to aid his testimony her office had created a timeline graphic that used the word "confession" to describe Walter's statement to police.

Greenberg objected to this, and the lawyers met in Judge Stout's chambers to argue the topic. Greenberg argued that the entire trial was about whether or not Walter had confessed; it was for the jury to decide if that had happened or not, but if Stout let the DA label the interrogation a "confession" on a poster she would be essentially settling that question.

Stout deferred to Rubino, ruling the DA's office could use the word.

Greenberg couldn't believe it.

"It is for the jury to decide [if it was a confession]," he said. "That's why [putting that word on the sign] is prejudicial."

"It isn't prejudicial," Rubino said.

"I am a lawyer, not a doctor," Judge Stout said, "and I don't want you having a heart attack back here. I have ruled. If I am wrong, then the appellate court will correct me."[13]

"Judge . . . this is plain error," Greenberg said, meaning a mistake that could force a higher court to throw out the trial. "I don't understand why you will allow this document."

"She doesn't think it is error," Rubino said.

"You show me a case which says so, if you think it is error," Stout said. "Do you have a case?"

"I only saw [the DA's graphic] five minutes ago," Greenberg said. "She never even told me about it. It is a classic sandbag."[14]

Greenberg suggested a compromise: put quotation marks around the word *confession* on the graphic.

Judge Stout liked the idea. "There wouldn't be anything wrong with that, really," she said.

"Why do I have to?" Rubino asked. She said the graphic had already been typewritten.

"I know. . . . That is his suggestion," Stout said weakly.

"I don't accept it as a suggestion," Rubino said.

"All right, let it go just as it is," Stout agreed.

Greenberg asked for an eight-by-eleven photo of the timeline to be taken for use on appeal, but Rubino wouldn't allow it and Stout didn't push her.

"You are building in error," Greenberg said.

"Once we get a conviction, I will worry about error," Rubino answered.[15]

That night, Thomas James remembered, he was impressed by Sharon. He'd worried that Greenberg would badger her and was relieved that Greenberg knew better. Though Greenberg had tried to make the point that the house was too small for Walter to commit the murder there with other people home, all that had come across to James was Greenberg asking a lot of weird questions on dimensions and distances and trying hard to throw Ross Felice's name to the jury as much as he could. The fact that there'd been a murder in that same basement two years before had made an impression on James, as had the pictures of the Dunne murder scene showing the gym set and pull-down bar.

23

MAYBE I CRY
EVERY TIME

THE COURTROOM WAS CROWDED the next day for Marty Devlin's testimony. Rubino took care of a small bit of business first, calling the clean and seal officer who'd cleaned out 7244 Rutland to describe finding bloody clothes and a bloody rug remnant in the basement of the house. The officer admitted when Greenberg asked that it wasn't unusual to find bloody clothes in abandoned houses that had become drug dens and that she hadn't found anything of Barbara Jean's.

Then Devlin took the stand, serious in a dark suit. His testimony had the potential to be awkward, since his version of events, in which his keen ability to know he was being lied to cracked Walter's four-year silence about the murder, had been replaced by Rubino telling the jury that Walter had actually successfully lied to him and the true story of the murder would come from the snitch.

Devlin had retired from the Philadelphia Police Department in December 1994 after twenty-eight years on the force. He joked to the jury that he'd taken a whole weekend off before starting his new job the following Monday at the Camden (New Jersey) County prosecutor's office. He testified about being assigned the Barbara Jean Horn case and reviewing some of the files.

"We went and talked to the Fahys and we decided that we were going to start an investigation right there on Rutland Street," he said of himself and Detective Worrell.

This mild description hardly fit the six-hour-plus interrogations he'd subjected John and Sharon to in February 1992, but it did fit the version of events painted in Rubino's opening statement—Devlin and Worrell, after consulting the Fahys, looking across the street at Walter's abandoned house, deciding to focus there. Greenberg, unaware that Devlin had actually accused John of the murder for several hours, wasn't able to debunk this story.

Devlin told the detectives' version of Walter's interrogation again. This time he left out his original claim that he'd written Walter's statement down verbatim, so the jury never heard that he'd changed this central aspect of his story only after Greenberg forced him to.

Rubino walked Devlin through his story, the unexpected confession.

"Could you tell us at approximately what time it was you were giving [Ogrod] his constitutional rights as it appears on the [timeline]?" Rubino asked, referring to the graphic she and Greenberg had argued about in chambers.

"Seven thirty PM," Devlin read. "Constitutional rights given."

Whether this had happened was actually intensely disputed, but the timeline announced it to the jury as a fact.

Devlin then read the statement he'd taken from Walter into the record. At the most horrifying moments he wept, pausing dramatically to regain his composure.[1] The courtroom was spellbound and completely silent except for Devlin's voice and the stenographer typing.[2]

Devlin remembered Sergeant Nodiff calling Joseph Casey to come in and look over the confession at around 2:30 or 3:00 AM, and Rubino had him reiterate that no pressure had ever been put on Walter.

"Was Mr. Ogrod handcuffed at any point?" she asked.

"He was not handcuffed during the interview or even after the interview," Devlin said.

"Did he make any requests of you or of Detective Worrell in your presence that were not satisfied?"

"He did not."

"Did he seem to you to be tired or emotional after the statement was concluded?" Rubino asked.

"No, he didn't seem tired when he walked in the door and after the statement. As a matter of fact, he was full of life, if I could use that term—he was revived from the time he started convulsively crying," Devlin said.

It's hard to imagine someone who already hadn't slept in thirty hours not yawning or seeming tired over the course of the fourteen hours or more Walter spent in the homicide offices. It's hard to imagine anyone, least of all Walter, with his history of reacting poorly to stress, acting "full of life" in a homicide interview room at 3:00 AM if he understood he'd confessed to a murder and was going to prison for the rest of his life. But it makes sense if Walter, as he told his brother a few hours later, thought he'd told detectives what they wanted and was going home.

On cross-examination, Greenberg pressed Devlin about implausible details in his story. Devlin, in return, provided evasive answers without being openly confrontational.

Greenberg, wanting to establish how different Walter looked from the man the witnesses had seen, asked Devlin Walter's height and weight as recorded on the questionnaire Devlin had filled out as part of their initial conversation on the night of Walter's interrogation. Six feet two, 220 pounds. But Devlin maintained through several questions that he couldn't tell if Walter looked the same now. Greenberg had Walter stand up; Devlin said his hair had been a little longer in 1992. Greenberg asked if Walter didn't look pretty much the same. Devlin said he wasn't saying he didn't but couldn't be sure if Walter had told the truth about his weight in 1992.

Greenberg's exasperation at Devlin's unwillingness to agree to even the obvious grew.

"Obviously, Mr. Ogrod, who was nothing more than an information witness who will help you in the investigation, would have no reason to lie about his height or weight?" he demanded.

On the subject of when he showed Walter pictures of Barbara Jean dead, Devlin said, "Let me be explicitly clear about this: no photographs were shown to this defendant until the very end of the statement. That was the only time any photograph was ever shown to this defendant."

He admitted he'd looked through the pictures in the hallway just before going in to interview Walter but claimed he couldn't remember if he brought the pictures in with him or not. Either way, he hadn't shown them to Walter.

Greenberg couldn't believe this: Why have pictures of the victim in hand in the hallway outside the interview room but decide not to show them to the suspect until after he'd confessed?

Devlin was not going to change his story and seems to have enjoyed getting to Greenberg, who became more and more sarcastic about Devlin's claims. But Devlin had taken many confessions, had been cross-examined many times, and knew how to make sure the jury heard his story and never saw him get mad. He explained to the jury that he and Worrell didn't close the door of the interrogation room or put Walter in the iron chair with the handcuffs attached; in fact, he said, Walter was free to go anytime. Even when Walter burst into sobs, Devlin said, he and Worrell still had no idea what was going on. They gave him his Miranda rights at 7:30 PM. No, they didn't write that time on the rights waiver form or on Walter's interview form, nor did they note on the interview form that rights had been given at all. But that was how it happened, Devlin insisted.

Devlin's demeanor was key to the prosecution: he was a professional, just doing his job by the rules.

Greenberg persisted in trying to crack him.

"You testified that [Walter] was crying and the confession was labored?" Greenberg asked.

"Yes," Devlin said.

"And I think I noticed you were crying this morning when you were reading the confession. Is that right?"

"Maybe I cry every time I read about a brutal murder about a little baby," Devlin said.

"And you were probably crying when he was confessing to the murder of the little baby?"

"Nope."

"Detective, let me ask you this question," Greenberg went on. "Any part of the sobs, any part of the labored confession, the head in the hands, anything like that, was that ever videotaped?"

"Of course not."

That there was no proof of what Devlin said was another important point for Greenberg.

"The interrogation proceeds from 7:30 until 10:15 PM. Is that right?" he asked.

"That is correct."

"From the time you say the constitutional rights were given, that is a period of time of two hours and forty-five minutes. Right?"

"That is correct."

"Now, I think Ms. Rubino asked you as you read that portion—that would be from page six to page sixteen. Right?"

"Yes."

"Those ten pages certainly didn't take you two hours and forty-five minutes to read in this courtroom?"

"They did not."

"Detective . . . during the two hours and forty-five minutes that you say Mr. Ogrod confessed, was there anything that was said by him, by you or Worrell that is not contained in this statement?"

"Anything that was said concerning the murder of Barbara Jean Horn?"

"Concerning anything."

"There was still him crying, and I might have said, 'Take it easy, Walter, just take it easy.'"

"Let me ask you this question, Detective Devlin. You testified that at about 6:50 PM you put a notation that Mr. Ogrod was crying and putting his head in his hands. Right?"

"Yes, I handled that very fairly, I thought."

Greenberg jumped at Devlin's word choice.

"Did you handle it equally fairly, Detective, from [pages] six to sixteen when Mr. Ogrod was also crying or being labored in his statement? Is that reflected at all in this so-called confession?"

Devlin was getting annoyed.

"You mean is there, 'Sob, sob, cry, cry, cry, teardrops falling'?" he asked. "Is that in the statement? No, sir."

"What I mean is, is there a notation at all about Mr. Ogrod sobbing or crying or doing anything?"

"Yes, right in the beginning."

"Whatever he did," Greenberg pushed, increasingly frustrated, "that would be redundant as far as crying or sobbing, is not reflected in that [document]. Nor would it be reflected that you wanted to be as accurate as possible?"

"I was."

"You weren't accurate and precise with respect to the portion where he cried."

Rubino jumped in. "Objective. Argumentative."

"Sustained," Stout ruled.

"Out of the two hours and forty-five minutes, how much crying time was there?"

"There was a lot of quiet time," Devlin answered.

"Is that quiet time reflected on these ten pages, from six to sixteen?"

"Yes."

"It says, 'Quiet time'?"

"It doesn't say 'quiet time,' but it doesn't take two hours and forty-five minutes to just write those several pages," Devlin said. "Obviously, as I testified to, he was reflecting, he was pensive, and he was super upset."

Devlin, who'd started with the claim that he'd written down what Walter said verbatim, now said that Walter must have been sobbing, even if the statement didn't say so, because otherwise the statement wouldn't have taken close to three hours to write out.

Apparently, it wasn't Judge Stout's job to ask the prosecutor why her star detective was now telling a fundamentally different version of Walter's confession than he'd told at the suppression hearing, when she ruled Walter's statement could be used at trial.

The tension between Greenberg and Devlin increased when Devlin testified that Walter had read over the entire statement when it was finished. Greenberg asked him to explain why, if Walter read all of it, he only fixed some mistakes (the date, for example), and not others.

"Well, he was reading the things that apply to himself and his statement," Devlin said.

"How do you know that?" Greenberg yelled.

"I am sure he did," Devlin retorted.

"This is a courtroom, not a place for shouting, so keep your voice down," Judge Stout told them.

"Are you saying, sir," Greenberg asked, "you were able to detect as he is reading through this statement and picking and choosing that which he wanted to read, that is what he did?"

Rubino objected and Stout sustained the objection, so Devlin never answered.

Greenberg had a few more questions—why Devlin and Worrell felt the need to ask Walter, a grown man, if he knew what *ejaculate* means if they really never noticed anything "off" about him; how long it took them to get a search warrant and go search 7244 Rutland Street that night; if they found anything in the house related to Barbara Jean (no, it was years later, after all); if Walter had been handcuffed that night (only when he was officially taken into custody).

Then Greenberg was done. He'd tried to expose the serious problems with Devlin's version of events but hadn't made much progress; Devlin was good on the stand, though David Miller, the alternate juror, did think Devlin tried a little too hard to convince the jury how Walter's statement happened. Miller wasn't sure Devlin was *lying* but felt certain he was shading his version of the truth.[3]

On redirect, Rubino did touch-ups on possible issues in Devlin's testimony, starting with why the interrogation hadn't been recorded. Devlin explained that he'd never seen a confession audiotaped or videotaped.

"I don't make policies," he said. "I obey policies. . . . It is the policy of the Philadelphia Police Department, they don't do that. I follow the policy of the company I work for."

Rubino then had him explain one last time that he and his partner had not noticed that Walter was slow, "off," tired—nothing.

"Thank you, nothing further," Rubino said.

"I have no questions, Judge," Greenberg said.

Greenberg's sentence had a deflated quality to it, as if maybe after years of fighting on Walter's behalf against the monolith of the DA's office his frustrations finally began sapping his will. Rubino was smoothing the possibilities and impossibilities of her case into a damning story, and every time Greenberg tried to disrupt that story by establishing that something was actually impossible or at least highly unlikely, he faced experienced witnesses who knew what Rubino needed them to say and wouldn't be moved from it.

Greenberg kept fighting with the stubbornness of a boxer in the tenth round who can't make every punch but stays on his feet and keeps swinging. He just needed the jury to see reasonable doubt in the fact that Walter looked nothing like the man with the box and that his alleged "confessions" conflicted with each other and with the evidence.

———————

Rubino's next task was to explain Joseph Casey's 2:30 AM trip to the homicide office on the night of Walter's interrogation. She began by putting on the stand William Kushto, the charging DA who'd signed off on charges against Walter, to explain the six-hour rule and its importance to being fair to suspects. Kushto said Walter's statement was faxed to him at 12:04 AM on Monday, April 6; he reviewed it, signed it, and faxed it back to homicide so they would have documentation.[4]

Greenberg asked few questions, none about the 3:38 AM time stamp on the faxed statement; he didn't raise the possibility that the statement faxed at 12:04 AM was a placeholder designed to show, no matter how long Walter's statement took, that the statement was finished in less than six hours.

Casey was Rubino's next witness. He said he got the call about Walter's statement at 1:30 or 1:45 that morning and got to the Roundhouse at about 2:30 AM.[5]

"I wanted to review the confession," he said, "to see if there were additional legal matters or things that should be done."

Casey testified that when he arrived at the homicide offices, he saw Walter in the interview room having a cup of coffee and reading the newspaper. He saw Devlin or Worrell go in and talk to Walter a couple of times and heard Walter call "Paul!" once, and Detective Worrell went in and asked, "What do you want, Walter?"

Casey's little tableau of the homicide offices offers an image of just how completely Marty Devlin's version of the Reid Technique had worked on Walter: there it was, 3:00 AM, and Walter, a suspect either in the middle of a long interrogation or having just confessed to a murder, was on a first-name basis with the detectives.

Casey said he reviewed Walter's statement, approved the detectives' application for a search warrant for 7244 Rutland Street, and went home around 7:00 AM

It was Greenberg's turn for cross-examination, and there were plenty of questions to ask: How often did Casey get out of bed to go to the Roundhouse at 2:30 AM? Why did he need to review Walter's statement if the overnight DA had already signed off on it two and a half hours earlier? What kind of "additional legal matters" had he been working on? Had the six-hour rule ever come up in discussions that night? Had any additional materials about the interrogation or even the final version of the statement been faxed to the charging DA *after* Casey had a chance to review it, which would allow the 3:38 AM time stamp to fit nicely into Casey's timeline of the night? If not, what was the explanation for the 3:38 AM time stamp?

Greenberg, however, didn't ask any of them.

"Mr. Casey, were you inside the Police Administration Building on April the 5th, 1992, between 3:45 PM and 11:45 PM?" Greenberg asked.

Casey said he wasn't.

That was it.

Greenberg's point, that Casey couldn't know how the interrogation went because he wasn't there, was fine as far as it went. But instead of arguing that the confession took a lot longer than the detectives said it did, he'd just implicitly accepted the detectives' timeline.

Thomas James had found Devlin to be a very effective witness, and the details in Walter's statement to be damning. The defense had tried to get Devlin to change his story about how the confession had happened, but Devlin had been too strong, James remembered, and all Greenberg had done with his pushing was to annoy the jury and Judge Stout.

James's journal gives a glimpse of just how badly the case was going for Walter: he didn't write down a single issue Greenberg had raised about the statement, accepted the pull-down bar as the murder weapon without mentioning how unsure the medical experts had been, and highlighted that the fact that Barbara Jean hadn't been wearing shoes was in the statement as if it were something only the killer would know, though in fact police had known that even before her body was found.

More ominously for Walter, James had a hard time sleeping that night. The images of the murder from the confession got to him.

24

MR. BANACHOWSKI

THE NEXT MORNING, with the jury out of the room, Judge Stout ruled, at Judi Rubino's request and over strenuous objections by Mark Greenberg, that Jay Wolchansky could testify against Walter under a false name in order to preserve his safety in jail.

When the jury was brought back into the courtroom there was a witness on the stand already, a prisoner; Thomas James thought he looked like a loser and assumed correctly that the morning delay had been caused by the lawyers' arguments about him.

This was Jay Wolchansky, burglar, forger, drunk, and paranoid schizophrenic protégé of John Hall—the man to whom, the Commonwealth would argue, Walter had told the *full* story of Barbara Jean's murder. On the stand, Wolchansky spelled out a false name—Jason B-a-n-a-c-h-o-w-s-k-i—and swore to tell the truth.

Walter couldn't believe it. What was this guy doing? This guy he'd known from jail, not well, had made up a story about him and now was sitting there on the stand, not looking at him, trying to get him executed.

Rubino led Wolchansky through a description of himself as a good man who'd hit hard times, his lengthy criminal record the result of drug and alcohol problems caused by a difficult divorce. He said he'd never committed a violent crime and felt that if not for his troubles with alcohol and drugs he would've been the productive citizen he'd always wanted to be. He was through committing crimes, he said, and was coming forward to take his punishment and, at great risk to himself, tell the truth about the horrible child killer he'd met in prison.

To emphasize that Wolchansky was willing to take his punishment, Rubino repeated three times that he'd pled guilty to his latest round of attempted burglaries. He'd actually pled "no contest," but "guilty" sounded better for Rubino's image of a man who was taking responsibility. "No contest" sounded more like a man cutting a deal.[1] Rubino understood that in the battle for the jurors' perceptions, every bit counted.

Wolchansky explained to the jury that he'd come forward not out of any desire for personal gain but because Walter's crime was disgusting. He said he had a daughter roughly Barbara Jean's age, so Walter's bragging about getting away with murder made him particularly sick. He swore he never got any favors from prosecutors in exchange for his information about Walter.

Rubino reiterated that Walter had lied to Devlin and Worrell to protect himself but had told "Mr. Banachowski" the truth, which he would now tell the jury. She led him through the story he claimed Walter had told him, of Walter killing Barbara Jean to pin the crime on John Fahy so he could marry Sharon.

As Wolchansky described this version of the crime and revulsion built in the courtroom, Rubino slipped in an important question: Had anyone introduced Wolchansky to Walter Ogrod?

"Yeah," Wolchansky said. "John Hall."

That was all she needed; it wouldn't have been good for the jury to hear about Hall from the defense lawyer first, but there was no need to linger on his involvement in the case.

She went back to Walter.

"How many times did [Walter] talk about [the murder] with you?"

"Dozens," Wolchansky said; they talked a couple of hours a day, out on the block. He didn't take notes but wrote down everything he could remember when he got back to his cell so he could report it.

"And can you tell us why you were going to do that, Mr. Bana-chowski?"

"Because I have a daughter of my own, and the whole thing disgusted me."

Rubino wanted to make the point that Wolchansky's daughter would've been roughly the same age as Barbara Jean. But Wol-chansky was visibly shaking,[2] too nervous to follow his lines, the same problem he'd had testifying against David Dickson.

"How old is your daughter?" Rubino asked.

"Fifteen."

"And what year was she born?"

"'81."

"And how old would your daughter have been in '88?"

"Ten."

"Well if she were born in '81, I could guess she would be about six or seven?" Rubino corrected him.

"Yeah," Wolchansky agreed.

"In fact, is your daughter in the courtroom today?" Rubino asked.

"Correct."

Rubino had seated Wolchansky's daughter, Heather, in the front row, and Wolchansky pointed her out; there she was, living proof of Wolchansky's determination to take responsibility for his crimes and change his life.[3]

She had him tell the story of the murder, then asked him regarding Walter, "How did he talk about these things?"

"I don't understand," Wolchansky said, missing his cue.

"What was his demeanor while he was telling you these things?"

"He was trying to fit in. There was only a few of us on the block that accepted Walter."

At the defense table, Walter stopped taking notes on a legal pad—his usual activity during testimony—and just stared at Wol-chansky. He couldn't believe this was happening, Wolchansky lying his ass off with his daughter sitting in the front row waving to her daddy so he'd look good to the jury.

"After [Walter] told you all of these things, what did you do with the information he had given you?" Rubino asked.

"I wrote a letter to Joe Casey, Assistant District Attorney, and then I wrote a second letter to Lynne Abraham."

"Did you ever ask the District Attorney's office to do anything for you in connection with your cases?" Rubino asked.

"No."

"Did they ever do anything for you connected with your cases?"

"No."

"Up and until today, has anybody lessened your sentences because of your cooperation in this case?"

"No."

Rubino went back to Walter's supposed attitude when he discussed the murder. Wolchansky, in his nervousness, hadn't made several of his points, and Rubino needed to make sure he did.

"He wasn't embarrassed to tell you [about the murder]?" Rubino asked.

"At first he was. He didn't know if he could trust me."

"And then how did he become?"

"Flamboyant."

"Did he say anything about what he intended to do after his trial?"

"He planned on suing the city for false arrest. . . . He said that his lawyer would get him off because all they had on him was a signed confession."

"And how did his lawyer tell him he was going to get off?"

"[By] saying that he was tired and stressed out when he went to the Police Administration Building."

Actually, Wolchansky said, Walter said he'd been *excited* to get to the Roundhouse, thinking the detectives were finally going to get John Fahy, but then had gotten scared.

"He thought his mother had said something to the police," Wolchansky said.

"And what made him think his mother might have said that to the authorities?" Rubino asked.

"After they started questioning him, he thought that was the only person who knew anything," Wolchansky said.

"Thank you, Mr. Banachowski," Rubino said. "I have nothing further."

Wolchansky, despite his nerves, had done well: the *Philadelphia Inquirer* described his testimony as "riveting."[4]

For his cross-examination, Mark Greenberg had decided to take Wolchansky through his second snitch letter line by line, demonstrating that the structure and syntax of the letter itself proved the story in it was made up.[5]

The first sign that this might not be a good strategy had come a few days earlier when he'd tried to explain it to Stout and Rubino in chambers.

"How can you tell that [it was made up] from the structure of the letter?" Rubino had asked.

Greenberg pointed out Wolchansky's use of parentheses in the passage about Walter forcing Barbara Jean to perform oral sex.

"What does the parentheses have to do with it?" Judge Stout asked.

"Because the parentheses, I'm going to argue to the jury, Judge, reflects an individual who is not recounting what was told to him by Walter Ogrod but is rather coming up, bald-faced, with a story he concocted with himself as well as with other people."

"What are you talking about?" Rubino asked.

An argument that confused Judge Stout and Judi Rubino was likely to confuse a jury, but Greenberg persevered. It must have seemed to him that if he just pushed hard enough on each line of the letter, on the things in it that made no sense, Wolchansky would make a mistake and the letter would be exposed as fraudulent.

Greenberg's main weapon for this assault would be sarcasm, which he employed from his first question.

"So, you're telling this information [about the murder] to Joe Casey, to Lynne Abraham, because you're performing a public service, right?" he asked.

"I meant to do the right thing," Wolchansky said.

"Right. You're performing a public service because a man has confessed to you in jail about killing a four-year-old child who was just like your daughter in 1988, correct?"

"Correct."

"And your daughter, she's a pretty girl, sitting right there . . . is that correct?"

"That's right, correct."

Greenberg, trying to mock Wolchansky, had instead pointed out his daughter again. He asked about Wolchansky's criminal record, the eighteen convictions for burglary and forgery, and Wolchansky said it had all started because of a drug addiction.

Greenberg picked up Wolchansky's January 1995 letter to Joseph Casey about Walter.

"Would you read along with me?" he asked. "And I'm going to mention punctuation, because you used some punctuation in these letters, is that correct?"

Greenberg began reading the letter to the jury.

"'Mr. Casey,'" the letter started, "'I'm the father of a young daughter, and little Barbara Jean would have been about the same age if she had continued to live. I want to do what is right but I have difficulty communicating with you or anyone at the District Attorney's office. . . . I also have personal safety concerns about doing this, since I'm here in Philadelphia prisons with this person, his friends, and others who will put me in harm's way. But . . . he can't be allowed to go free and get away with the horrible and disgusting things he says he did to that poor little girl. He acts like it is all a game, and he laughs at killing that little girl.'"[6]

During her direct examination Rubino had tried to get Wolchansky to repeat the part about Walter laughing about the killing. He'd missed his line, but Greenberg had just read it for her.

Greenberg pointed out that this first letter had no information about the actual murder and asked if Wolchansky had had his notes from his conversations with Walter when he wrote it.

"Some," Wolchansky said.

"All right, and you basically put down everything in the notes in the letter?"

"No, I just sent the letter for them to contact me, and I was going to explain to them."

"All right. So, basically you put nothing from the notes that you had taken from these conversations with Mr. Ogrod in the letter, is that right?"

"Right. In the first letter."

"What you're suggesting is that you put it in the second letter?"

"Correct."

Greenberg turned to Wolchansky's second letter and read aloud: "'Dear District Attorney Abraham, I am writing in regard to Mr. Walter Ogrod and his admitted murder of Barbara Jean Horn to me. He has told me the full story of this murder and of the events that led up to this murder. Mr. Ogrod goes on with this long-planned story of why he murdered the little girl, to set up the girl's stepfather to be arrested for her murder. He also told me how he was going to get this little girl two times before the day he did, in fact, get her, and murder her. He had all this planned out for some time, and he had a place picked out,' quote, 'on the other side of Castor Avenue on Friendship Street.' Period, end quote."

"Right," Wolchansky said.

Greenberg asked him about his use of quotation marks. "You're telling Ms. Abraham what Walter is saying, is that correct? You're not using your words, you're using his words, is that right?"

"Some of them."

"Some of them? Well, when you put the quotation marks around, 'on the other side of Castor Avenue on Friendship Street,' were those your words or his?"

"They were Walter's words."

"They were Walter's words. All right. So, does that mean that where the quotation marks were not located in the other parts of the letter, they were not his words or they were your words?"

"They were a combination of both."

"OK, so you're mixing and matching his words and your words . . . is that true?"

"Yes."

Greenberg had gotten Wolchansky to admit to using a lot of his own words in what was supposed to be Walter's story, but at the cost of the jury hearing more horrible things about Walter.

"So he's telling you a story where he plans all this in advance," Greenberg said, "putting the electrical cord in the basement so he can strangle her so he can set up John Fahy in order to win the love of Sharon Fahy. . . . So he's telling you he did this master plan with all these tools in advance?"

"Right," Wolchansky said.

"OK. 'When he went for the cord, it was missing,'" Greenberg read. "'He became enraged that someone took it.' Now . . . you used the word 'enraged' a number of times?"

"Right."

"All right. Did he use that word with you, 'enraged,' 'he became enraged,' or is that a word that you used?"

"He used it."

"He used that. So Walter Ogrod, in describing how he became angry and mad, used the words, 'I became enraged,' right?"

"Right."

Greenberg's point—that "I became enraged" doesn't sound anything like Walter—couldn't matter to the jury, who'd never heard him speak.

"'He then took Barbara Jean out his back door and down a driveway/alley,'" Greenberg read. "That's what you have there, right?" he asked.

"Right," Wolchansky said.

"Now, when he told you about taking her down the driveway, slash, alley, did he say 'Driveway, slash, alley,' or—"

"No," Wolchansky interrupted. "I'm—I wasn't sure on that point, if it was driveway or alley. He said he took her out the back."

"What does that mean, that you didn't write it down in your notes and get it accurately here or you weren't sure what it was?"

"I wasn't sure what he said," Wolchansky said.

"You weren't sure what he said, so you just put something in there that you thought he might have said?" Greenberg asked.

"Right," Wolchansky said.

Wolchansky admitting that Walter's confession was full of things he thought Walter only "might have said" was the kind of victory Greenberg hoped for. But to jurors trying to keep track of the back-and-forth, what Wolchansky was saying sounded reasonable.

Greenberg read about Walter crossing St. Vincent Street going south and continuing for another block.

"Now, by the way, he's telling you that he's carrying the body out in trash bags, right?"

"Right."

"There's no television box?"

"Not at this point."

Greenberg's point—that this part of the snitch story is impossible—was important, but the jurors were caught in the middle of claim and counterclaim, and Greenberg didn't highlight it.

He kept reading:

"'A dog started to bark. [Walter] became scared and left her body near the bushes, still in the trash bags. He then went home the same way and looked out of his window to see if anyone noticed the girl missing. Everything looked fine to him. He also became scared now and thought he might have left fingerprints on the trash bags, and says he went back to the bushes where he left the body, this time with a TV box he found on his street. When he went back he left the TV box near the curb at St. Vincent and Loretto Streets, got the body in the trash bags, and dumped her body, naked, into the TV box. He said she was lying on her side in a fetal position. He then went down to Tyson Avenue, to Castor and Magee, and dumped his gloves and the trash bags into a Dumpster.'

"So Mr. Ogrod is telling you that the trash bags he used to carry the child out initially, he ditched them in some Dumpster at Castor and Magee along with the gloves that he had stashed in the basement where he preplanned this murder, right?" Greenberg asked.

"Right," said Wolchansky.

"Ok," Greenberg said. He did not press Wolchansky about how long that walk would've taken, or how, in the middle of rush hour on busy Castor Avenue, Walter could've done it without anyone else seeing him.

Instead, he kept reading: "'He says he then went home by the rear of his house. He says he looked out the front window, again things looked OK, he became excited and masturbated and showered. He said he was mad because he didn't put the electrical cord around her neck to make it look like,' quote, 'John Fahy,' end quote, 'did the killing, and also didn't put her in the alley as he planned because things went wrong,' parentheses, 'didn't have the cord in the basement because someone took it, and because he was scared by the neighbors and a barking dog on Friendship Street,' end parentheses. Is that how it reads?"

"Right."

"OK. Now, the name John Fahy is there in quotations, is that correct?"

"Correct."

"All right. Now let's continue. 'He says if he only put the cord on Barbara Jean's neck, then the police would have gotten John Fahy.' And in that sentence, John Fahy is not in parentheses, is that correct?"

"Correct."

"And I guess that's because you've already used parentheses before, so you did not have to repeat it, right?"

"With the parentheses, I was just emphasizing what he said," Wolchansky said.

"When I say—I should have said quotation marks, the first John Fahy was in quotation marks, the second is not in quotation marks?"

"Right."

Greenberg was trying to point out areas of the snitch story that made no sense, but there was no way for jurors to know that from a name being in quotes once but not the next time. Saying "parentheses" when he meant "quotation marks" only added confusion.

"'He confessed to save himself,'" Greenberg read. "'He says the reason he recants his statement is because his attorney told him the statement is all that the police have, and if we get rid of this, they have nothing.'"

Greenberg had just repeated Wolchansky's claim that he, Greenberg, was the one who told Walter to recant his statement. The idea stuck with the jury; Thomas James felt that the witness had just exposed Greenberg's defense strategy by revealing the real reason Walter had recanted.[7]

Greenberg read more of Wolchansky's damaging claims about Walter to the jury: he "'admits not having sex with adult women, but enjoys sex with young virgins because they have a sexuality at a young age, and because they are untouched by anyone. . . . He says he masturbates here two or three times a day, thinking of young virgins or the nurses and guards. He says that he became aroused by thoughts of young virgin girls or full-figured women.' Is that what he said?"

"Right," Wolchansky answered.

"And that's the word he used?"

"Right."

"Full-figured?"

Greenberg had read those accusations about his client aloud to the jury just to argue that *full-figured* wasn't a term Walter would've used.

Greenberg's strategy for proving Wolchansky's letter was a lie might have worked if he'd been able to compare it with John Hall's original letter about Walter, since Wolchansky's story was Hall's story, his motives for snitching were Hall's motives, and even the format of his letter was Hall's format—the page crammed with handwriting, key details added in parentheses or written in the margin, just like Hall's. As it was, Greenberg had just read Wolchansky's entire letter to the jury.

Greenberg turned to Wolchansky's interview in March 1995 with Detective Gross and read that out loud, too—Gross asking Wolchansky if he wrote the letters, if anyone helped or advised him in writing them (no), when he'd first heard of the Barbara Jean Horn case, was the letter truthful (yes), was there anything he wanted to change (no), did anyone in law enforcement promise or offer him anything to write the letters (no), no one influenced what he wrote (right).

"Now, John Hall you know from prison, right?" Greenberg asked Wolchansky.

"I met him at the same time I met Ogrod."

"All right. Let me ask you a question. Is his lawyer, John Hall's lawyer, Marc Frumer?"

"Correct."

"Who is your lawyer?"

"Marc Frumer."

"You have the same lawyer?"

"We had the same lawyer."

"You had the same lawyer," Greenberg repeated, but he didn't follow up on why this mattered, on how well Wolchansky knew Hall.

"Let's continue," he said.

He read the rest of Wolchansky's interview with Gross to the jury, confirmed the date it happened, and moved on to the deal Wolchansky signed two days later. Rubino used objections to scoff at the notion that Wolchansky's interview with Gross and his deal two days later were connected, but Wolchansky admitted he got eleven and a half to twenty-three months in jail and three years probation instead of the thirty years he might have gotten.

"So, in fact, you got a bargain, right?" Greenberg asked him.

"Right," Wolchansky said.

Greenberg's next line of questions was crucial: he was entitled to know if Wolchansky had any psychological problems that might have affected his ability to understand or remember what Walter had told him.

"Mr. Banachowski," Greenberg asked, using the alias, "back when Mr. Ogrod is confessing to you, did you have mental problems?"

"No."

Greenberg pointed out that he'd written, "I am currently receiving mental health treatment, but I know what is going on today" on his plea agreement.

"So in point of fact you did have mental problems when Mr. Ogrod is confessing to you, right?" Greenberg asked.

"No, that was drug and alcohol-related."

"Well, sir, what's written there is 'mental health treatment,' right?"

"I was going to the clinic for alcohol treatment."

"There's a difference between alcohol treatment and mental health treatment?" Greenberg asked.

Rubino objected, stopping Wolchansky from answering. She had the records showing he was paranoid schizophrenic and depressive and that throughout his time in jail with Walter had been filing requests to have his medication increased.

Judge Stout upheld the objection.

"That's all I have," Greenberg said. "Thank you, sir."

On redirect examination Rubino had Wolchansky explain that the deal outlined on his plea deal arrangement wasn't actually a deal because it didn't protect him from the "backtime" he'd have to do for violating his prior parole. He testified that the judge who'd approved his deal hadn't even been told he'd informed against Walter—in other words, that Marc Frumer, the lawyer Hall had gotten for him specifically to cut a deal for his Dickson and Ogrod stories, had never even told the judge that Wolchansky had cooperated with prosecutors.

"Did anybody ask you back then if you would testify against Mr. Ogrod?" Rubino asked.

"No."

Then Wolchansky, under Rubino's guidance, went even further: he told the jury he'd never even told Frumer, his own lawyer, that he'd cooperated with authorities.

"Did you ever discuss with your attorney that you had talked to a homicide detective and that he should bring that to the judge's attention?" she asked.

"No," Wolchansky said.

Rubino was pushing her story as far as she could, seeing if she'd get called on it.

Greenberg used a final rebuttal question to mock Wolchansky once more.

"You're done being a criminal now?" he asked.

"Correct," Wolchansky said.

"Good. That's all I have."

For her last question, Rubino turned Greenberg's sarcasm around.

"And why are you done being a criminal now?" she asked.

"I have my daughter to take care of and my mother is getting old and I want to take care of her, too, and I'm going to stop using alcohol and go to treatment again," Wolchansky said.

With that, the prosecution rested.

———————

When I eventually found Jay Wolchansky, he wouldn't talk. Later I found his daughter Heather. The first time I talked to her, she told me what a wonderful father he'd been, always keeping in touch when he was in jail; she described the elaborate calendars and decorations made from cigarette cartons that he sent her for Christmas or her birthday.

We talked about the Ogrod case. I told her I wasn't suggesting her father thought Walter Ogrod was innocent and didn't care. Hall probably told him Ogrod was guilty anyway and it didn't matter how he got convicted, so why shouldn't they use the story to help themselves?

No, Heather told me at first. That wasn't possible—her father wasn't like that.

She was hanging on to what she could of her father, I thought. Fair enough. He'd had a difficult life and some of his hardest times had come during her childhood, so she reflected a lot of his damage and had difficulties of her own.

I was surprised when she called back the next evening. She'd been thinking about it, she said, and she was sure her father would never have lied on purpose but the more she thought about it the more she thought I was right, Hall had made up the story and given it to her father. That made sense to her. She said there were boxes of papers in what had been his room at his mother's house; he'd been back living with her in the little row house across the street from the Eastern State Penitentiary when he died. Yes, she'd show them to me if I came down.

I went to Philadelphia and sat with her; she didn't say much, and her mother, Rose, Jay's ex-wife, lurked angrily through the threadbare apartment. Heather took me over to Jay's mother's house and up to his room; there were boxes, but none of them had legal papers in them. Heather said she'd thought they'd been in there—maybe he'd thrown them away before he died.

I eventually got Jay's medical records from his sister. Jail intake evaluations and psychiatric notes offer a look at his schizophrenia and addiction issues. But he can't ever tell us in his own words what he knew about Hall and the stories Hall made up.

Marc Frumer knows a lot of the story and may even have correspondence and paperwork from Wolchansky and Hall that makes all this clear. When I got him on the phone, he was friendly at first. I told him I was working on the Walter Ogrod case and he cheerfully said I had the "wrong Marc," that Mark Greenberg worked that case.

I'd talked to Greenberg, I said. But hadn't he, Frumer, been John Hall's lawyer?

Yes, he said, oh, yes, he had been, but he hadn't had any involvement in the Ogrod case.

But hadn't he been Jay Wolchansky's lawyer, too? I asked.

There was a pause before he said, "You've done your homework." Then he told me if I wanted to interview him I would have to write a formal letter requesting an interview.

Couldn't he just tell me now if he would talk to me or not?

I would have to write the letter, he said. He confirmed that both Hall and Wolchansky had gotten deals in exchange for their Ogrod information but said I should take any other questions I had to the DA's office. He hung up and hasn't returned a call or answered a letter of mine since.

After the prosecution rested, Judge Stout called a lunch break. After lunch, in chambers, Greenberg told Rubino and Stout he'd have only five witnesses, three of whom were in the hallway waiting to testify. The others were out of town. Stout could let the jury know the defense would be done that afternoon, and closing arguments would happen on Monday.

Rubino was incredulous.

"You're not putting Walter on?" she asked.

"No," Judge Stout said, also surprised.

"We'll have to colloquy him," Stout said. That meant they would question him on the record, in court, to satisfy the judge that he was lucid, understood what his lawyer wanted to do, and agreed with the decision.

"Are you going to put on any character [witnesses]?" Rubino asked.

"No, I told you," Greenberg said.

"None of the stuff you had on before?" Rubino asked, referring to the first trial.

"No," Greenberg said.

"All of this has to be on the record so that there is no ineffective assistance [of counsel]," Rubino said, doubting her good fortune and wanting to ensure that Walter couldn't claim on appeal that Greenberg didn't know what he was doing. It's one of the odd things about claims of ineffective assistance of counsel: no matter how bad a lawyer's decision is, it can't be considered ineffective assistance of counsel if the lawyer thought it was strategic.

"I have no problem with all that," Greenberg said.

"You had all these character witnesses named," Rubino went on, still in disbelief. "Let's do a colloquy with Walter about character [witnesses], too."

It's true that every character witness Greenberg could have put on had a downside: people saying good things about Walter would give Rubino a chance to rebut them with people who would say bad things about him. But without character witnesses the jury wouldn't hear from the people in Walter's life who'd watched him get manipulated his whole life, who knew you could get him to do anything or give you anything—his car, his money, his house. They wouldn't hear from his bosses that he'd been an honest, hard worker or from his friends with children that they'd trusted Walter to babysit, that he'd never shown any inappropriate interest in children.

Likewise, there was a risk if Walter testified: Rubino would have a chance to cross-examine him, and how Walter would do under cross-examination by a lawyer as smart, tough, and aggressive as Rubino was a fair question. But the jury was being told he'd confessed to the murder twice; how could they doubt it if they never heard his voice, watched his facial expressions, and listened to him try to explain his emotions? How could they doubt the detectives who said they never noticed Walter's speech impediment or that he was "off"?

The jury would never hear from Walter or from an expert witness who could explain that false confessions did happen and that Walter was, on the night of his interrogation, essentially a walking risk factor for giving one. In fact, Greenberg would never even mention maybe the most important fact about Walter's interrogation: that he hadn't slept in two days by the time it ended.

A reporter was puzzled by the omission.

"At the earlier trial," the *Philadelphia Inquirer* noted, "the defense said the defendant was exhausted [when he confessed], had been sleepless for 48 hours and that, under the circumstances, police were able to put words in his mouth. Greenberg did not make the same argument at this trial."[8]

Without any context for the interrogation or testimony from people who liked him, Rubino's vivid, sinister portrait of Walter went unquestioned, the jurors left to decide if the reasonable doubts his lawyer insisted on were enough for an acquittal.

Greenberg's three witnesses, all detectives, were called to put focus on Ross Felice: the detective who'd noticed his behavior the night of the murder; one who'd taken David Schectman to the gym to identify him; and one (who turned out to be unavailable so Greenberg read out his testimony from the first trial) who'd taken Michael Massi's statement a couple of days after the murder that the composite sketch was a "good likeness" of the man with the box.

With that, the defense rested. Thomas James and the rest of the jury were shocked. That night, James felt protective of Wolchansky, whom he considered a "hero" for doing a selfless act. He was even annoyed at Heather, Wolchansky's daughter, for the apparent shame she felt about her father. He believed that Wolchansky was finally taking responsibility for his crimes without seeking a deal for his information, and that he was snitching because he felt terrible for the Fahys. During Wolchansky's testimony he'd watched Walter's reactions, and he wasn't sure if everything Wolchansky said was true but was sure Walter recognized what Wolchansky was saying. He also didn't think Walter looked angry enough for someone who really thought he was being lied about like that.[9]

In his journal, James wrote out Wolchansky's story about Walter carrying the body in a garbage bag and only ever carrying an empty box without mentioning any of the ways it contradicted the facts of the case. He didn't mention any of the issues Greenberg had tried to raise about the grammar or syntax of the letter; he was just surprised Greenberg read something so damning aloud.

David Miller, for his part, didn't believe anything Wolchansky said and thought Rubino was using him to prop up her case. The whole story was too pat: *Oh look, how convenient, they got a snitch.* Wolchansky was too shifty and willing to please on the stand and, Miller thought, lied about not getting a deal.

As for the Devlin/Worrell statement, Miller wanted to scrutinize how it was phrased. He hadn't trusted Devlin entirely, but it was hard to keep everything straight; the jury couldn't take notes and would hear something one day, something else the next. It all went so quickly.

———————

Walter's colloquy came next, a bizarre courtroom moment in which meaning has been subjugated to words, when all the rules created to ensure fairness are silent in the face of a proceeding that defies common sense. A man whose entire defense hinged on the fact that he was not a fully functioning adult, mentally, that he was incredibly malleable, especially under stress, and especially when he wanted to please authority figures, stood in front of a judge who believed he was guilty and stated under questioning from his own lawyer that he understood his complicated legal situation well enough to make the informed decision to put on almost no defense. The lawyers said the words and he gave the answers, Greenberg going over every aspect of the trial so that Walter could say over and over that he approved every strategy, undermining his defense and damaging any chance he might have on appeal.

Yes, Walter agreed when asked, every juror had been selected with his approval; yes, he'd taken notes during the trial; yes, he knew what was going on in connection with the evidence presented against him and the evidence presented on his behalf; no, he was not dissatisfied with Greenberg's performance in any way, not now or at the first trial; yes, they had specifically discussed whether he'd testify.

"We discussed the pros and cons about [testifying], is that correct?" Greenberg asked.

"Yes," Walter said.

"And you would agree, sir, that, at that time, you agreed with my analysis that it was not necessary for you to testify based upon the presentation of the Commonwealth's case?"

"Yes."

"All right. Now, sir, let me ask you this question: Did I force you in any way not to testify?"

"No, you did not."

Greenberg said he had witnesses on telephone notice who would come testify if Walter wanted them to.

"Sir, would you agree that at this stage you do not want to present character testimony, is that right?"

"That is so," Walter said.

"Have I threatened you or forced you or coerced you to do anything in this trial, Mr. Ogrod?"

"You have done nothing. You have left me my own choice. This is my choice."

"Judge, I think that does it," Greenberg said.

You have done nothing. . . . This is my choice.

It was a fitting epitaph for his defense, Walter saying what Greenberg wanted him to say and what Rubino and Stout wanted to hear.

Judge Stout accepted the colloquy.

25

VERDICT

ON MONDAY, MARK GREENBERG rose to give his closing argument.

"When Walter Ogrod appeared in front of you a week ago today and in a loud, clear voice said that he was not guilty, he had two strikes against him," he said. "The first strike was the horrible nature of the crime . . . and the second strike against him was a courageous and dignified family that hated and loathed him because they felt he took their child away from them."

The jury's job was to consider the evidence impartially, he said; the prosecution was required to present evidence, and innuendo was not evidence.

He said there were four reasons Walter was not guilty: he did not fit the description of the man seen carrying the box; the two statements allegedly taken from him were so diametrically opposed that they could not be believed; the evidence showed that another individual was positively identified as the man carrying the box; and, finally, the physical evidence showed Walter's innocence.

The three eyewitnesses, Greenberg said (limited to discussing only the ones who'd given evidence at the trial), fell all over each other to convince the jury that they didn't get a good look at the man with the box. But what were the odds of three people looking at the same man from three different perspectives at the same time coming up with the same description if it wasn't accurate? All three described a shorter, thinner man than Walter, and a T-shirt wouldn't have hidden Walter's extra weight. As for the man's age, between twenty-five and thirty, Greenberg argued that even now, at age thirty-one and having spent four years in jail, Walter looked a lot younger than he was; in 1988, he'd been twenty-three and looked like a teenager. He reminded the jury that many people in the neighborhood had known Walter by sight if not by name, so if it had been him carrying that box around the neighborhood at rush hour, someone would've recognized him.

"Are we talking about a stranger? If anything, Walter Ogrod was notorious in that neighborhood," Greenberg said.

He moved on to Walter's supposed confessions.

"I want to make perfectly plain here, ladies and gentlemen, that both confessions are bogus," he said. "It's not as if the police confession is right and the Banachowski confession is false or the Banachowski confession is true and the police confession is false. . . . The evidence here, members of the jury, is that both confessions are bogus."

On the Devlin/Worrell statement, Greenberg asked why Walter would sit in the waiting area for two hours on the day of his interrogation if he was just an informational witness and free to go. And if Walter signed his rights waiver when the detectives said he did, why didn't they note the time or mention it in the written statement?

"I'm not saying that this is a technicality here, that you should acquit Walter Ogrod because the police violated his rights," Greenberg said. "No. I'm telling you that common sense says that if, in an abundance of caution, this man was going to be given his rights, that detectives would've had him sign it. That's not what happened here."

The Devlin/Worrell statement, Greenberg said, flowed on the page as if Devlin never lifted his pen from paper, though it was supposed to have been a labored and difficult process.

"No, ladies and gentlemen of the jury, that is not Walter Ogrod's confession. It's bogus. A 'labored' confession?" he asked, mocking the term Devlin had used. "You saw the mistakes that were made, three spelling errors. . . . Do you mean to say, members of the jury, that for those two hours and forty-five minutes the only mistake that's going to be made, the only cross-out that's going to be made are three single words that are misspelled?"

Greenberg was challenging the Devlin/Worrell statement, but since he hadn't brought up Walter's lack of sleep during the trial he couldn't bring it up now.[1] The jury never heard an explanation for why a man would falsely confess to something so terrible.

Greenberg moved on to the snitch story: wasn't it a strange coincidence that for two and a half years in jail Walter never told anyone he'd committed the murder—until right after the superior court ruling that he could be tried again, at which point he told two snitches?

"By the way, where is John Hall?" he asked. "I can't believe Ms. Rubino is saving him for a more important case."

"Objection," Rubino said.

Judge Stout sustained the objection and the jury never knew anything about Hall's involvement. Or that Rubino was, in fact, holding him for the Ernest murder trial in a few months.

"What does common sense say happened in this case?" Greenberg said. "Isn't it coincidental . . . that two days after Jason Banachowski is interviewed by Detective Michael Gross and reaffirms his statements about Mr. Ogrod killing this child . . . two days later, *two days later*, he enters into a plea agreement with the District Attorney's office. . . . Members of the jury, in fact there was a deal. There was a deal between Jason Banachowski and the Commonwealth of Pennsylvania, and he got the benefit of that deal."

Greenberg argued that the detectives and the snitch had given diametrically opposed versions of the killing, and yet by calling them Rubino was vouching for the credibility of both. Which was true, Greenberg asked, Walter the "incredibly manipulative, craven, pre-planning, premeditated individual" in the snitch statement, or Walter the guilt-ridden wreck who broke down to Detective Devlin? The creep who stalked Barbara Jean and lured to his house to sexually assault her or the impulse killer who grabbed her when she came over to play with Charlie Green? As for carrying the body and box around the neighborhood, Greenberg said, the snitch statement couldn't be true, so he supposed they were left to believe the detectives' statement, which was also full of inaccuracies but in which Walter at least dragged and carried the box down St. Vincent Street.

"Members of the jury," Greenberg said, "what the prosecutor is asking you to believe is Chinese menu justice: A little bit from column A, a little bit from column B; mix them all together; mix and match them.

"And what proof beyond a reasonable doubt? Are you telling me that as members of the jury of his peers . . . we can pick and choose what version we want to believe? No. The internal inconsistencies of this case, members of the jury, with respect to the two bogus statements, establish conclusively that neither of them is true."

Greenberg held up a picture of Ross Felice alongside the police sketch.

"This photograph . . . and this sketch, I submit to you, are so similar as to be almost exact," Greenberg said.

He described again the incident at the gym when Ross Felice ran from David Schectman. It wasn't his job to prosecute anyone, Greenberg said, but to present "compelling evidence to show that Walter Ogrod is not the individual who committed this atrocious crime," and the identifications of Ross Felice were compelling evidence.

Greenberg allowed that Walter probably did tell Wolchansky all about his case, about suing "the living daylights" out of everybody when he finally went free. But, he said, that didn't mean Walter had admitted to the crime.

Greenberg closed with "the one piece of evidence that shows, beyond any doubt, that Walter Ogrod is innocent"—the pull-down bar from the weight set. He outlined the medical examiner's descriptions of Barbara Jean's wounds—no fractures to her head or her shoulder blade, not a broken bone on her—and asked, "Do you really believe, members of the jury, that if Walter Ogrod, in a fit of rage, took this pull-down bar and beat that delicate four-year-old child in the head, what do you think her head would look like? . . . A cracked egg, as horrible as that might sound, as horrible as that might be to envision.

"Imagine what that poor child's skull would be like if she was hit with this object," he went on. "No, ladies and gentlemen of the jury, that child may have been beaten to death, but she was not beaten to death by that pull-down bar, she was beaten to death with something maybe lighter, maybe a stick, maybe a pole, maybe a handle of a cleaning instrument, broom, mop, something like that, but not that pull-down bar.

"This is conclusive evidence that the man who sits at that table right now not only is *presumed* to be innocent but *is* innocent.

"Thank you."

It was 11:40 AM; Greenberg's closing had taken fifty minutes. He'd left the jury with a vivid, disgusting image of the murder but without making the clearest argument against the pull-down bar as murder weapon: that the original doctor who performed the autopsy had said the weapon was flat.

Thomas James thought it was a good closing. He watched reporters, especially the one from Channel 6 news, "scribbling frantically" in their notebooks.

Greenberg's defense of Walter had highlighted the differences between the two statements and argued strongly that a case built on two irreconcilable versions of a crime had a reasonable doubt built in, that both statements were bogus. But Greenberg's case at the second trial left Walter a blank, hiding behind a lawyer. Walter's lack of facial expression—part fear, part self-control, part inability to understand and convey emotion—contributed to this; not only did Thomas James note at one point that Walter didn't seem angry enough about what was happening, but the subject of Walter's emotionless, remorseless, blank face came up in newspaper stories about the trial.

Juries are instructed that a defendant deciding not to testify shouldn't be held against him, but this jury never heard any information about how false confessions could and did happen and never heard Walter say he did not murder Barbara Jean. They never had a chance to get a sense of this man who'd supposedly admitted to a murder he hadn't done, which can only have added to their sense that Walter had something to hide: most of us believe that if we were falsely accused of killing a little girl, nothing could prevent us from taking the stand and telling everyone we didn't do it.

Judi Rubino began her closing by reassuring the jury that they shouldn't worry about the contradictions and gaps in the case against Walter, because even clear-cut murder cases can have details that never quite make sense. The jury, she said, had to determine "what manner of person killed Barbara Jean Horn."[2]

In other words, this case was about feel, and she set about making the jury feel comfortable that Walter was that "manner of person," sometimes pushing and sometimes flouting the rules of what she was allowed to say, daring Mark Greenberg to stop her.

First, she needed to go over the evidence again, beginning with the eyewitness testimony.

"It's often been said," she told the jury, "that identification testimony is the weakest type of evidence and the most unreliable."[3] If the eyewitnesses had said Walter was the man with the box, she said, the defense would be arguing that identification testimony was unreliable.

None of the witnesses really saw the man, Rubino argued, because he was bent over carrying something heavy. Also, Walter might look different all these years later, she said; maybe after four years of getting three squares a day, he'd put on weight. The police sketch was wrong and had "nothing to do" with the witnesses, who "never identified anybody else as being the person who did the killing."[4]

Rubino finished her muddling of the eyewitness testimony by telling the jury again that the sketch looked as much like Walter as it did like Ross Felice.

"Walter," she said, "fit the description . . . as well as anybody did."[5]

She'd succeeded in turning one of the biggest weaknesses in her case into a strength, twisting the eyewitnesses until it seemed Walter had essentially been identified as the man with the box. Even as she did so, she reminded the jury that David Schectman said the man had nothing unusual about his voice—which would've helped Walter if the jury had heard his speech impediment.[6]

Rubino next had to make the two conflicting stories she had into one narrative of the crime. To do this, she would move between the them, blending them as she went so that the jury, unable to take notes or ask questions, would lose track of which detail came from which story and hear it all as one narrative.

She started with the snitch description of Walter's excitement to get downtown to talk to detectives because he thought they were finally going after John Fahy; gone was the horrible guilt Devlin and Worrell said had compelled Walter to the Roundhouse (and with it the entire basis for their version of events). Though even Worrell said Walter tried to leave the Roundhouse twice that afternoon, Rubino told the jury Walter was so excited to be interviewed he waited the two hours for the detectives without even trying to leave.[7] And she now argued that Walter's hysterical crying during the interrogation had been fake, a ploy to cover his shock at finding out his mother had turned him in and give him time to come up with a story.[8]

Judge Stout, who hadn't changed her mind about allowing Walter's statement even when Devlin admitted it wasn't verbatim, now listened as Rubino changed Walter from a guilt-ridden wreck to a world-class manipulator able to deceive two of the best homicide detectives in the city.

Rubino told the jury, "The judge will tell you that you can believe all, part, or none of any witnesses' testimony, and you can believe all, part, or none of the defendant's statements. And when you put the two statements together . . . you will see that the two stories, the two versions he gave, are consistent in the most important details."[9]

In other words, the jury should mix and match, accepting the pieces of whichever version made sense to them. It was indeed Greenberg's pick-and-choose, buffet-style justice.

Rubino also tried to reinforce Wolchansky's credibility. She asked how he would've known any details of the Henry Fahy case—the case that was supposedly Walter's inspiration for his plan to murder Barbara Jean—if he hadn't heard them from Walter.

"[Wolchansky] didn't live in that neighborhood; there was nothing in any newspapers about any of this stuff," she said of the Henry Fahy case.[10] But the Henry Fahy case had gotten a lot of news coverage and had been through the courts for more than a decade; there were plenty of sources for information about it. Rubino inadvertently acknowledged this when she argued that Walter had "stud[ied] up on Henry Fahy's case" at the library.[11]

Furthermore, Rubino's claim about Walter allegedly researching the Henry Fahy case violated an important rule: lawyers are not supposed to mention things in closing arguments that they did not bring up and support with evidence during the trial. But Greenberg did not object.

Rubino went on to the murder weapon: How could "Mr. Banachowski" possibly have known there was a weight set in Walter's basement, she asked, or that the child had been hit on the head with something that matched the pull-down bar?

In fact, all of that information could've (and did) come from Hall, from the newspaper coverage of Walter's arrest or first trial, or from court documents about the case. Or from Walter himself describing the crime to explain why he was innocent.

Rubino told the jury again that Wolchansky hadn't snitched to gain anything for himself, repeating that he hadn't even told his own lawyer about it. Rubino had the right to argue that Wolchansky's motives were pure, as long as she didn't have evidence to the contrary. But it's hard to imagine she actually believed Wolchansky never told *his own lawyer* about his informing against Walter.

As Rubino's closing argument reached its climax, she layered additional innuendo on her portrait of Walter as the "manner of person" who would kill a child. Mark Greenberg rarely objected. Rubino said that Walter had moved out of his house in the fall of 1989 because he was worried the investigation was catching up with him, though it had come up in the first trial that Walter's aunt actually owned the house and had evicted everyone.[12] She told the jury that Walter's mother thought he was guilty, a bit of actual hearsay from a dead woman that came from Hall's story, which Rubino embellished with a description of Walter's thought process when the detectives told him they had a witness.

"He said to himself, 'Well, that must be my mother,'" Rubino told the jury, though the detectives' bluff about a witness had been specific, that a neighbor had seen Walter let Barbara Jean in his house.

Each little distortion or overstatement of the evidence added to Rubino's case. But her next distortion, also based on hearsay, wasn't little.

"Well," she said to the jury, referring to Walter, "if you never told your mother [that you were the killer], why would you tell [Wolchansky] that you did? And if your mother suspected you, why was that? Was it because you're that kind of person? Did [Walter's mother] know he was a pervert? Did she know he had never dated? Did she know he liked going to sex shops and porn shops and have [*sic*] child pornography around?"

Greenberg finally objected. Rubino hadn't brought up any evidence to support any of these claims during the trial—because there wasn't any—so it was against the rules for her to bring them up now.

Stout sustained Greenberg's objection, but that didn't stop Rubino.

"Did [Walter's mother] know that he liked only young girls, like four years old?" she asked rhetorically.[13]

Greenberg and Stout said nothing.

Later, in chambers, Rubino admitted to Judge Stout that the child pornography claim had never been mentioned during the trial. It had come, she said, from Alice Green telling detectives that her boyfriend had told her Walter once said he knew where to get child pornography.[14]

Convictions have been overturned because prosecutors mention far less inflammatory things than child pornography in their closing arguments without having put on evidence of the claim during the trial.[15] But Judge Stout, who had told Rubino before trial that she couldn't use the issue of child pornography, let it go.

When it came to the murder itself, Rubino told the jury that whichever of Walter's statements they believed, the crime was premeditated. If they believed the detectives, all that was needed for premeditation was enough time to pick a weapon, grab it, and use it. If they believed the snitch, the premeditation was clear.[16]

"Nobody saw Barbara Jean go with anybody" that day, Rubino said.[17] This also wasn't accurate: there was the neighbor down the block who'd seen her being led down the street at three o'clock on the afternoon of the murder.[18]

If Walter were innocent, Rubino asked, why didn't he help John Fahy search for Barbara Jean or tell him she'd come by earlier in the day? This was the story from the Devlin/Worrell statement that actually put Walter in his living room, talking to John Fahy, possibly at the very moment the man with the TV box was walking down St. Vincent Street.

Rubino told the jury that Barbara Jean would've been comfortable going with Walter because she knew him, and reminded them of the pull-down bar in his basement that "could have" been the murder weapon.[19] Then she brought up more hearsay from a deceased witness, telling the jury that Sarge Green had suspected Walter of having something to do with killing Barbara Jean. Green, who'd died before the first trial, had, at least initially, told his daughter he didn't think Walter could be the murderer.[20] And he never told anyone he suspected Walter—not on the day of the murder, not four months later when he was arrested for assaulting Walter, and not in 1992 when he was interviewed by Devlin and Worrell.

She told the jury again, "Walter Ogrod fit the description of the person carrying the box as well as anybody else did."[21]

Then Rubino added more innuendo: Everyone on the block had helped search for Barbara Jean except Walter (actually, the Greens hadn't, either). Was that because he was trying to stay out of the limelight so nobody would remember him? Why had he moved out of the house in '89—wasn't it because he didn't want to be around while the investigation was going on?

"The defendant said he was beaten up by Chuck [Green] because Chuck suspected he did it," she said. "There has been no denial of that. The defendant admitted to his mother that he killed Barbara Jean and threatened his own mother; there has been no denial of that."[22]

Greenberg objected. Since if Walter had testified he would have denied the stories, both of which originated with Hall and came into the trial through Wolchansky, Greenberg argued that by mentioning them Rubino was essentially telling the jury that Walter was admitting guilt by not testifying.

Judge Stout sustained Greenberg's objection but, again, Rubino didn't stop.

"The defendant," she said, "when confronted by inmates in the jail who say to him things like, 'Baby in the box,' doesn't say to them, 'I didn't do it.' What does he say? 'Whack 'em and sack 'em.' Well, isn't that just what he did to Barbara Jean? He whacked her and threw her in a bag. He sacked her, that's a great line, 'whack 'em and sack 'em.'"

Greenberg didn't object. Later, in chambers, he asked to go on the record and said he was making a "tactical decision" not to ask for a mistrial based on what Rubino had said in front of the jury because he knew Judge Stout would explain to the jury that defendants were not required to testify—as if the judge's explanation could undo the damage Rubino's barrage of damning hearsay had done. And Greenberg's emphasis on the record that his decision was "tactical" would make it harder for Walter's appeal lawyers, if it came to that.

It's hard to imagine the difficulty of Greenberg's task—one lawyer up against the power of the state wielded by a prosecutor determined to win at all costs. But it's hard to understand why he didn't object more to what Rubino was doing, and why he made such a point of enshrining his silence as a trial tactic.

———

Rubino reached her grand finale.

"When you go in that jury room," she said, "close your eyes for a minute. Put yourself back inside that basement on July 12 of

'88, imagine just for a minute that you're Barbara Jean, imagine the fright and the fear that that child must have felt. Imagine the horror she went through, and then when you look, think to yourself, what face appears to you? I submit to you that the face you will see is the face of Walter Ogrod, the man who sits right there, and no other."[23]

The prosecution of Walter Ogrod had come full circle, from Devlin telling him to "imagine in your mind what happened next" to Rubino asking the jury to imagine being Barbara Jean and seeing Walter's face as he attacked her.

"There has been no contradiction to any of the testimony dealing with Walter's version of what happened," Rubino said. "And when you put the two statements together, what he was telling Mr. Banachowski over a couple of months' period and what he told the detectives over a two-hour period, you will see that the two stories, the two versions, are consistent in the most important details, in that he hit Barbara Jean, tried to force her to put his penis in her mouth, tried to molest her, and that she screamed and that he then hit her with the bar from his weight set; that is consistent throughout.

"Not for the family and friends of Barbara Jean Horn," Rubino said, "not for retribution, but for justice, we ask you, ladies and gentlemen, to find the defendant, Walter Ogrod, guilty of murder in the first degree, rape, and involuntary deviate sexual intercourse.

"Let Barbara Jean finally rest in peace, knowing that her killer has been convicted."

After lunch Judge Stout gave the jury their charge, explaining the laws involved and the standard of proof necessary for a conviction. Thomas James noticed a woman and two men sitting in the gallery behind Walter; with a shock, he realized one of them looked like a thinner, bespectacled version of Walter and was probably his brother. (This despite the fact that the brothers were both adopted.)

The man noticed James staring and whispered to the woman, whom James later saw looking at him.

When the jury began deliberating, David Miller, the alternate juror, wasn't needed, so he was released from jury duty and went back to his office a block from the courtroom. He wasn't sure how he would've voted; he had some doubts about Walter's guilt, all hinging on the statement to the detectives, and wanted to listen to more of the testimony about it read back. Maybe it was fanciful to think he could've picked something up in the statement that proved Walter hadn't given it, but he would've tried. He called a court officer and asked for a ten-minute heads-up before the verdict was read so he could come back to hear it.[24]

In the jury room, a preliminary vote came out ten to two for conviction. Thomas James voted guilty on the sexual assault charge, not guilty on rape, and guilty on first-degree murder.

The foreman suggested they all listen to the reasoning of the "not guilty" voters, which revolved around problems believing Walter's confession to the detectives. The "guilty" voters went through the doubters' concerns about the confession step-by-step, and when they voted again they had unanimous "guilty" verdicts on the sexual assault and on first-degree murder. It had taken less than an hour and a half. They couldn't settle on the rape charge because they weren't clear on the definition of rape.

Thomas James argued that other than the jailhouse snitch, there was no proof Walter had attempted to rape the little girl— the medical examiner had reported no damage or tearing despite the snitch's story that Walter tried to enter her but she was too small. The jury sent a note to Judge Stout, asking for clarification about whether or not the intent to rape was enough to convict a defendant of rape. She responded that it was late and she would answer the next morning. Court was adjourned for the day.

It took the jurors a while that evening to come down from the intensity of the experience of deciding a man's fate; one member seemed in shock, ashen-faced and quiet. They had a good dinner, drank some beer, and back at the airport Hilton some of them started packing. Two jurors did a guard's nails, and they all went to bed at around 10:00 PM. Thomas James didn't sleep well; he was too keyed up for what would happen the next day.

At 10:30 the next morning Judge Stout clarified for the jury what constituted rape under Pennsylvania law. They went back to the jury room and acquitted Walter of that charge in five minutes, finalized their verdicts, and sent a message to Judge Stout that they were finished. A guard rehearsed them for what would happen in court, and they returned to the courtroom at 10:50.

When the jury walked in, John Fahy knew from the way they looked right at him and Sharon that they'd found Walter guilty. He thought one of the jurors even nodded at him slightly; he wasn't sure. He squeezed Sharon's hand.

"They got him," he whispered. "I know they got him."[25]

"Ladies and gentlemen of the jury, have you agreed upon a verdict?" the court crier asked.

Walter stood and faced the jury. He thought the verdict could go either way.

Thomas James had never been more conscious of his role in what was happening than at that moment. He looked mostly at Mark Greenberg.

On the first count, rape, how did the jury find?

"Not guilty," the foreman said.

A gasp of dismay went up in the courtroom. Walter looked shocked and leaned on the table for support; Thomas James thought he could see hope growing in him.

They're going to find me not guilty on everything, Walter thought.

On the next count, attempted involuntary deviate sexual intercourse?

"Guilty."

The courtroom was silent. Thomas James saw Walter withdraw, standing up straight, blanking his face out.

On the last charge, murder?

"Guilty of murder in the first degree."[26]

What the hell? Walter thought. He felt lower than he ever had in his life. *Were they listening?* he wondered about the jury.[27]

John Fahy slumped with relief.[28] A sob burst out of someone in his family and someone else said "Yes!"

"It's over," John thought. "It's finally over. They finally got him."

For Sharon, it was like somebody took bricks right off her back. She tried not to cry as her family wept around her.

Greenberg had the jury polled; each member stood and agreed with the verdict. Judge Stout thanked them for their service and released them until the penalty hearing the next day, when they would decide whether Walter was sentenced to death or life without parole.

No one on the jury made a sound until they got back to the jury room. Thomas James felt it was hard to hold his composure but couldn't break down the way he needed to. One juror wept quietly; another had tears running down her cheeks. They all talked about it, trying to put in perspective what they'd done. James told them that they were just instruments in the process, instruments of justice. They all seemed to find solace in that.

Outside court, John Fahy addressed reporters.

"He's an animal," he said. "He's got no remorse for what he's done at all. If he had any remorse, he wouldn't have put us through two trials. The guy is evil, and I'm just glad we don't have to deal with him anymore. I'm relieved that this nightmare is finally over. I don't care what happens to Walter Ogrod from here on out, as long as he is never able to harm another child and do this to another family ever again."

Sharon also said she didn't care how the penalty phase ended.

"Nothing will bring Barbara Jean back," she said. But the conviction was a big relief. "Now we can remember Barbara Jean with all the good times we had, and not have to think about this part of it. I know she is looking down on us, and she's with us all the time."

A reporter asked Mark Greenberg for Walter's reaction.

"Mr. Ogrod is obviously disappointed," he said, trying to sound level. "It's obvious that no matter what the jury says [about his punishment], he feels his life is over, regardless."

There was, he said, something fundamentally unfair about a man coming within a vote of being acquitted only to be tried again, three years later, with a change of jury and a change of prosecutor, and possibly get the death penalty. It was a perfect example why the death penalty was an arbitrary sentence.

Rubino wasn't having it.

"If one jury is stupid, it doesn't mean the next one has to be," she told a reporter. "This was an intentional killing during attempted deviate sexual intercourse, and the type of killing it was absolutely calls for the death penalty."[29]

She told another reporter that the snitch story buttressed the statement to Devlin and Worrell "because it was so detailed, even more detailed than the statement to police. It was a different jury, and the evidence was put in a different way."[30]

For once, Judi Rubino could be accused of understatement.

———————

The jurors went back to the hotel. Tropical Storm Josephine rolled in, filling the sky with heavy rain. Thomas James was too upset to eat. He felt he couldn't be alone, so he went to the TV room and watched *Mission Impossible* with other jurors. When the movie ended, the other jurors left. James sat for a moment. A promo for the evening news came on. Their verdict in the Ogrod case was the lead story. He watched in silence.

By dinnertime the mood had changed. In need of release, the jurors laughed and joked, bonding over their shared experience.

One juror said a guard had told her they were the closest and nicest jury she'd ever had.

David Miller hadn't gotten a call from the court officer, so he didn't hear the verdict in person. He was annoyed, felt he was owed the courtesy of a phone call. He wasn't all that surprised Walter was found guilty, because of the alleged confession to detectives, but the lack of evidence bothered him: no fingerprints, no strong eyewitness testimony, and the prosecutor wasn't sure what the murder weapon was; even as she'd waved around the pull-down bar she'd told the jury the murder weapon was "something like this." Miller wasn't bothered that Walter didn't testify—the case against him wasn't that strong, and if none of it were true what could he have said to disprove it?

One thing did surprise Miller: how quickly the jury had decided. An hour and a half just didn't seem long enough to consider the case properly.

That night a reporter for the *Philadelphia Daily News* spoke to Charles Graham, the foreman from Walter's first trial.

"I really don't think he did it," Graham said. "If I thought for one second that he did it, I would have voted guilty. I feel terrible for the family. Somebody killed that little girl. But I don't think it was him."

Walter, Graham said, didn't match the description given by eyewitnesses and was a big, stupid guy. It had been easy for detectives to pressure him into confessing.

"If you would listen to him talk," Graham said, "his words don't sound like that of the confession."

When asked about the second jury's interpretation of the facts, Graham said, "It's all in the presentation. That's the jury system. . . . It's based on people. People aren't perfect. People are flawed. It's a shame."[31]

26

PENALTY

CAPITAL MURDER TRIALS HAVE TWO PHASES—in the guilt phase, jurors decide whether the defendant committed the crime and, if he did, in the penalty phase they decide whether he deserves life in prison or death. To guide the decision, states provide lists of aggravating or mitigating circumstances. As Judge Stout explained when the jury convened for Walter's penalty phase, "aggravating circumstances are things about the killing and the killer which make a first-degree murder more terrible and deserving of the death penalty, while mitigating circumstances are those things which make the case less terrible and less deserving."[1]

Mark Greenberg wanted the jury to consider the following official mitigating circumstances: Walter had no significant history of prior criminal convictions; he was under the influence of extreme mental or emotional disturbance at the time of the killing; he was emotionally disturbed at the time of the killing; he'd suffered from child abuse that affected his emotional and psychological development but had attempted to better himself throughout his life by seeing a psychiatrist to deal with his emotional problems, by attempting to join the army, and by working at various jobs to support himself.

Much of Greenberg's argument against executing Walter might've helped Walter's claim of innocence during the guilt

phase: information about his background and the documentation in his medical records of how slow, immature, and easily
manipulated he'd been his whole life might have helped the jury
understand why he'd signed a false confession and been tricked
by a sophisticated snitch. Now, however, this testimony sounded
more like excuses for something for which there is no excuse—
killing a little girl.

Walter's onetime psychiatrist, Dr. Ganime, testified, describing the psychological and neurological tests he'd done on Walter
and his conclusions about Walter's limited intellectual capacity
and developmental disabilities. He discussed Walter's relationship
with his mother as well as some of the efforts Walter had made
to be independent: joining the army, working in the landscaping
company, his other jobs.

"Basically, what you're testifying to is that as Mr. Ogrod aged,"
Greenberg said, "basically his emotional condition was consistent
with when you first saw him back in 1976. Would that be accurate
to say?"

"Pretty much, yeah," Dr. Ganime said.

On cross-examination, Rubino highlighted that Dr. Ganime
had never thought Walter suffered from a major mental illness and
quoted Dr. Ganime's 1982 letter to the army, which said Walter
would "make a fine soldier." She highlighted that Walter saw Dr.
Ganime only four times in 1986 and not at all in 1987 or early
1988, but he did go to see him on September 30, 1988—implying
that Walter's desire to check in with his longtime therapist was
brought on by the murder he'd committed.

She probed, trying to get Ganime to say that Walter hated
women because of his mother and had some interest in young
girls. Ganime said that Walter had never said anything about hat-
ing women, had tried to date women his own age, and had never
expressed any interest in children.

Greenberg next called Father John Bonavitacola, who'd become
close to Walter over the years. Father John could have testified
during the guilt phase that Walter seemed exhausted the morning after the confession and said he hadn't slept since Saturday

morning, that his confession had been coerced. Instead, his job at the penalty hearing was to explain that in prison the worst crime you could be charged with was a crime that involved a child and to explain what happens in prison to such people, apparently in an effort to get the jury to think life in prison was bad enough. Rubino shut down this line of questioning with an objection.

Greenberg moved on, asking Father John to describe how Walter treated other people. Father John said he treated them well.

Walter then took the stand to save his own life again, though this time the alternative, life without parole, wasn't much better. He wore the wrinkled gray suit and white sneakers; he'd been up since 4:30 AM in order to be prepped and delivered to court on time, and was on antistress medication. His voice barely rose above a mumble.[2]

"What was the relationship between you and your mother—can you describe that for the jury?" Greenberg asked.

"Weird," Walter answered.

"What way?"

"Well, she kept on trying to say that I was, like, nuts, and trying to yank me out of schools. That's one of the reasons I ended up in special schools—I kept getting yanked in and out, couldn't keep up with anything. She would be, like, filing these suits on my father, stuff like that, yanking me downtown with her when my brother was in school. I didn't know what was going on. Come back, try to catch up. It was hard and all. And she would be, like, taking me from person to person, like, doctors, saying that I was not too well in the head, that, she said, I needed to go to a home or something, and I was wondering, 'What's going on? Why is [sic] my parents taking me from one parent, now all of a sudden saying I need to be put away' or something."

"How did that affect you, Walter?"

"Well, not seeing my father for a while and then being denied a lot of visits and all, then I didn't do too well. And then having my mom thinking, you know, like, it was something wrong, and that maybe I was the one that wasn't with it, it's like, 'What did I do to deserve this, why am I being treated like baggage?' or something like that. And being young at the time, I just did not know what was going on. It was hard to understand anything."

His voice dropped so low Judge Stout interrupted to ask if the jury could hear him.

Greenberg asked Walter to describe the 1976 Nazareth Hospital incident.

"All I know is we were supposed to see my grandmother that night," he remembered, "and then the next thing I know, we drive up into the emergency thing, and just saying I need to be admitted and I didn't know what was going on, put you in the emergency—you're a little kid, you're like, 'What's happening?' and just put me in a room like where there was, like, these emergency tables, everything else in there, like you're just wondering what's going to happen to you next. And I'm trying to find out."

"Now," Greenberg asked, "did you ever sustain any physical abuse or psychological abuse from your mother before you were admitted to the Nazareth Hospital?"

"Yeah. She kept on saying I, like, was nuts like my father, that she is, like, you know—throw me around the house, threw a couple of things every now and then and all, she did the same thing to my brother and all.

"It wasn't too good seeing that and all. She was saying that, 'Maybe I should get rid of you and [have you] put away.' She would be taking me from one guy to another, I don't know what's happening with all these doctors asking questions and all, taking me to these hospitals, throwing me in there, I don't know what's going on."

Walter described his relationship with his father.

"Like, around the early '80s, sometime in '82, I would have to drive him around. He was able to get me a learner's permit early under state law. I passed the test. I'd drive him to the hospital when he needed care. He went for, like, dialysis. . . . When his eyes started going, I had to write out checks for him, sign legal documents, explain everything for him. I would have to draw his insulin for him, couple of needles a day, inject it . . . once in a while if he needed it."

Greenberg tried to get him to explain the emotions he'd had about his father's illness and death.

"How did [your father's death] affect you?"

"Seeing him the last two years going to the hospitals for two months at a time, staying in there, coming back, you know, he couldn't see. Just see him wasting away, almost like an AIDS patient."

Walter sobbed.[3]

He described some of the jobs he'd held over the years, and, with pride, how difficult it had been to pass the tractor-trailer license test in 1988.

"Walter, can you tell us what it's like in prison, now that you've been there for four years—over four years?"

"You've gone to hell, basically, is what it is, and—"

"How do the other prisoners treat you, Walter?"

"The majority of them—like, you're the lowest thing on earth, some of them are treating you all right and all because they don't judge others and I did—the guards and all, they treat me like any other prisoner and all, not special."

Father John, he explained, "was like my rock and all. He was always by me and all, he was like my father was before he died, he was always there. . . . He was there when my mother died, when they came and told me about that."

Walter's testimony was an effort to put a human face on Rubino's skillfully drawn monster, but to the jury, already convinced he'd beaten a little girl to death, it sounded like a sob story.

———————

Rubino now got her chance to cross-examine Walter. She asked him about his attempt to join the army and the fights he'd gotten into during basic training; she asked him about his medications and the many prison fights he'd been in.

"When you've been teased, have you teased back or given remarks back?"

"Yes. Yes, I have."

"Was one of the things you said back 'Whackem and Sackem'?"

"No, that was Jason Bona—what's the last name, it can't—Banachowski."

"You never said that?" Rubino asked.

"No."

"What kind of things would you say back?"

"I've been yelled at and things from guys who been arrested for smacking their own children around and I have been—one guy who shot his own brother in cold blood and he's, you know, [teasing me]. I wouldn't back down and all. . . . I was brought up to fight one-on-one, but nobody seems to know how to do that in jail, no matter who fights, you know. . . . It's more like when it's two other people fighting, one guy usually gets jumped by three or four or something like that."

Rubino asked about his neighbors on Rutland Street, whether he dated, how the Greens came to live in his house. She tried to suggest that Walter had moved from Rutland Street to get away from the murder investigation, but he explained that his aunt had thrown them out because there had supposedly been a buyer for the house. She asked about his work history and any mental issues he might have once had, then finished.

Walter had held his own.

———

Walter Ogrod, Judi Rubino explained as she began her closing argument for a death sentence, despite having opportunities from the age of eleven to see different counselors, never told any of them he had sexual fantasies about children.

She was using the fact that he'd never said anything about having sexual interest in children as evidence of what a monster he was.

"He was going to a special school. He was living with a concerned parent who cared about him," she said. "He had a brother

who loved him and who was concerned with him. And he graduated from high school. He even went into the service but had
the same problem in the service that he's finding in prison: he
can't get along with people, he fights when he can't get along. He
didn't like the service because he didn't like the rigors of basic
training. . . . So he washed out."[4]

She closed with her assessment of Walter's character.

"Now you have to consider the person and character of that
man that did those things," she said. "You saw him on the witness
stand, and remember that he's on medication for depression, but
he's been on that same medication for four years, and that that
affects how he seems on the witness stand, but you saw him.

"Did you hear one word of 'I'm sorry for what I did?' Did you
hear one word of—to the parents—'I'm sorry about Barbara Jean'?
All you heard was what Walter Ogrod is interested in: himself.

"He is self-centered. He only cares about what is good for him,
how he's treated in prison . . . his welfare, whether or not he was
under stress, whether or not he suffered anxiety. Nothing at all
about what this family has gone through or what that child went
through. . . . Well, if he doesn't like life in prison . . . well, we
can take care of that and he won't have to do it."

They could give him the death penalty, she meant.

"We submit to you . . . that if there is anybody living on this
earth who deserves to die for the kind of crime he committed,
it's Walter Ogrod, a child molester, a child killer," she went on,
blending the two snitch stories again. "It's bad enough [if] you
use a gun, if you use a knife, but to take an instrument and to
inflict blows on her head and to attempt to molest her and then
to dump her in a box and take her out for the trash, and say you
have nothing but junk in the box, and then to go back home, and
you've had such a high from what you did that you went home
and you masturbated, you took a shower? He didn't feel one bit
of regret for what he had just done.

"We submit to you, ladies and gentlemen, that this man
deserves the ultimate penalty. Not because we don't like him but
because of the kind of person he is, just the kind of person his

mom, that *nut*, according to Dr. Ganime," Rubino said, sarcastically, "saw in him so many years ago when he was eleven, when she tried to have him hospitalized because she thought he might kill her. Well, he did kill. It wasn't the mother, but he did kill, and he killed not just Barbara Jean, but her entire family and community.

"We ask you, ladies and gentlemen, to find that the aggravating circumstance that he tortured this child," Rubino said. "[The] killing and with the kind of sexual assault he made on her is deserving of the death penalty.

"Thank you, ladies and gentlemen."

Mark Greenberg couldn't argue in his closing that Walter hadn't done it or that any small doubt a juror might have about the case, even if it hadn't been enough for acquittal, should be enough to spare his life. Those arguments were over. Greenberg had to somehow argue that the sum of the difficulties in Walter's life and his efforts to improve himself outweighed the horror of the murder he'd committed by enough that he should be allowed to live. This was a difficult argument to make to a death-qualified jury because anyone who believed in the death penalty was likely to agree with Rubino that if ever a crime called for it, Barbara Jean's murder did.

"Ladies and gentlemen," Greenberg started, "it's difficult to come to a jury after the jury has found your client guilty of first-degree murder because, basically, what the jury has done is . . . ruled against what I had to say, what I attempted to prove, which makes me disappointed in the verdict. . . .

"And even though the case went against me, I'm not here to say that you were wrong, I'm here to say that under the facts of this case, the mitigating factors, the facts of Walter Ogrod's life from the time he was adopted by his mother and the things that he has attempted to do within the limitations of his emotional abilities, his mental abilities, and psychological abilities, outweigh the . . . brutal nature of this crime. . . .

"Walter Ogrod. Can you imagine what it must have been like, members of the jury, to be rejected not only by your birth mother but to be rejected by an adopted [*sic*] mother also? . . .

"Yes, I know that from age eleven on Walter Ogrod was raised by a concerned and loving father, but as Dr. Ganime said, how important is it in a child's development, emotional development, to be raised by a mother who loves and nurtures the child, and how must Mr. Ogrod feel and how much it played in his development, emotional and psychological, that he was rejected not only by a woman, a birth mother . . . but also rejected by an adopted [*sic*] mother."

On Greenberg went, through all of Walter's difficulties. He argued that Walter had tried hard to lead a productive life.

"This is a situation where a guy tries to better himself," Greenberg said. "And if, in fact, he's picked on, and if, in fact, he fights back, isn't that an example . . . of a guy who gives it a shot, makes an effort, tries to better himself and, for whatever reason, whether it be the organic brain problem that he had, whether it was because of his mother who rejected him, whether it was because he couldn't get along with his neighbors, at least he gave it a shot to help himself."

Greenberg tried to use the prosecution's case to help Walter.

"I think it's fair to say, ladies and gentlemen, by your verdict . . . with respect to the rape charge, that you . . . rejected the testimony of Jason Wolchansky, because in the statement of Wolchansky, he says Walter told him he raped the child."

Rubino missed (or didn't bother with) Greenberg's use of the snitch's real name.

"I can't read your minds," Greenberg continued, "but I submit to you that you rejected that testimony but you accepted the testimony of the detective, who described for you how Mr. Ogrod broke down and, in convulsive sobs, cried, and everything that he has bottled up in him for four years came out, and then explained to the detective what happened. . . .

"So when Ms. Rubino says he did not stand up on the stand and say 'I'm sorry,' that wasn't the reason why he was called to the stand. . . . If you believe the testimony of the detective, [Walter's] convulsive sobs, his head in his hands, his statement, 'give me some time.' 'Be patient with me,' doesn't that reflect somebody who is horribly sorry for what he did?"

Life in prison would be worse for Walter than being executed, Greenberg said, and a life sentence in Pennsylvania meant no parole: Walter would truly be in prison until he died.

"Imagine what he's going through, members of the jury, in prison, with the fear that somewhere between now, when he's thirty-one years old, and whenever he dies in jail, that he will be living in constant fear that someone is going to kill him. . . . Yes, he is going to suffer and he should suffer. . . . As I stand here before you right now, I can't think of a more humble experience than to plead for a man's life, but I also can't think of a more noble thing to do than to save a man's life, and you have a chance, ladies and gentlemen, to examine all the evidence in the case, both aggravating factors and the mitigating factors, and you can say, 'Yes, this is a horrible crime,' as you will say because it's a horrible crime . . . it's an evil act. There's no doubt about it, but I submit to you, under the facts of this case, under the facts of Walter Ogrod's life, it wasn't committed by an evil man.

"I submit to you that there is a difference. I submit to you that there is a man who has tried to better himself. He has gotten jobs, he has tried to do things in life, so I submit to you, ladies and gentlemen of the jury, that under all the facts of this case, I would ask you to return a verdict of life imprisonment. Thank you."

Greenberg had tried his own buffet approach, hoping the jurors would pick up on one mitigating factor or at least agree that the death penalty was too easy on a murderer such as they'd found Walter to be. For the lawyer of a convicted child killer who needed the jury to find one reason to spare his life, it was the best he could do.

Judge Stout explained the law to the jurors and at 3:03 PM they left the courtroom to deliberate.

In the jury room, the initial vote was nine for execution, two for life—the same two who'd originally voted "not guilty" during the guilt deliberations—and one, Thomas James, undecided. After some discussion, the vote changed to ten for execution, one against, and James still undecided. There was debate, and those in favor of the death penalty grew frustrated, unable to understand how anyone could be against the death penalty in this case.

James asked to be left alone; it was hard for him to think with so many people arguing at him. He understood that Walter's crime matched the criteria for a death sentence but could not stop thinking what a terrible thing it was to hold someone's life in your hands. He decided to take a step back, be logical, consider how the case had gotten to this point. He was satisfied Walter was guilty. He looked at the DA's charge, why Walter should get death, and at Walter's actions that led him there; he thought about people having free will, that every single step of the way Walter made choices—when Barbara Jean came to his door he could've said Charlie Green wasn't home and closed the door; he could have let Barbara Jean go as soon as she screamed. He'd made some very definite choices, choices he knew would have consequences.

James voted for the death penalty.

The remaining juror who opposed the death penalty seemed to oppose it for anyone, which frustrated the other jurors, who wondered what he was doing there if he wasn't able to impose the sentence.

The foreman asked Thomas James to explain to the holdout why he'd decided for death. James spoke of individual choice and the burden of imposing death; it was an emotional conversation, and James started crying. After they talked a bit, the last juror changed his mind.

It had taken the jury an hour and thirty-two minutes to decide Walter's punishment.

They took their places in a strangely empty courtroom at 4:35. Barbara Jean's family was there. The foreman stood up.

"Have you found at least one aggravating circumstance?" the court crier asked.

"Yes, we have," the foreman said.

"Have you found any mitigating circumstances?"

"No, we haven't."

"What is your sentence, life in prison or death?"

"Death."

Thomas James watched Walter, whose face remained expressionless.[5]

Greenberg asked for the jurors to be polled, so they stood up one by one and stated their agreement with the verdict. Sharon Fahy smiled and nodded as each one spoke.[6]

Judge Stout dismissed the jury, thanking them for their service.

In a back room, jurors cried and stared into space. The court crier told them that normally the judge and the DA would come back to speak with them and thank them for their work but that Judge Stout thought they were too fragile at the time and just wanted everybody to go home and be with their families. They were taken back to their hotel to get their clothes and then home, which was jarring in itself—finding yourself, after three weeks, suddenly on your doorstep two hours after sending a man to death row, with your bags at your side and no support.[7]

————————

Sharon Fahy told a reporter she wanted to thank the jury "for a job that needed to be done."[8] She went on, "He got what he deserved. I think the jury made a good decision."

At her side, John agreed. "He's going to pay the price for killing our daughter. I'm satisfied. Justice was done."[9]

27

INNOCENCE

STATE SUPREME COURTS AUTOMATICALLY review death penalty convictions. If the court denies that automatic appeal, the conviction is considered final, which means the next round of appeals, the post-conviction appeals, can begin. This round isn't about the defendant's guilt or innocence but only about whether he or she got a fair trial. This is why convictions are so hard to overturn: the defendant is now presumed guilty and can only get a new trial by convincing the appeals judge that his trial was somehow unfair.

There are two main ways for this to happen. The first is for a defendant to claim ineffective assistance of counsel (IAC)—that your lawyer was so bad his work denied you a fair trial. The problem here, as mentioned before, is that nothing a lawyer did as a conscious strategy can be considered "ineffective," and Greenberg had made a point of enshrining many of his questionable moves as rational strategic decisions.

The other most common violation that can get a defendant a new trial is called a *Brady* violation, which refers to a case in which the Supreme Court ruled that the state must turn over to a defendant any information that might help his case. What information exactly this applies to is left up to prosecutors, and if they withhold something crucial it can take years for a defendant to even find out about it—if he ever does.

Then, even if a defendant does prove that one or both of these violations occurred, a judge has to find that the bad lawyer or the withheld evidence could have made the jury vote differently—another very high bar to get over, since prosecutors will always argue that the bad lawyering or the withheld evidence wouldn't have changed the outcome of the trial. And unless the DA has withheld something truly shocking—a videotape of someone else committing the murder, say—it's all too easy and common for judges to agree with them.

As Lara Bazelon explained on *Slate* in 2015, "the Supreme Court has repeatedly declined to hold that the federal Constitution allows for so-called freestanding claims of innocence, that is, the right to be let out of prison simply because you didn't do it, without any other 'technical' violation to back up your argument." Actual innocence claims, the court ruled, were too "disruptive and unfair to the state, which needed to have things settled once and for all."

In 2009, Justice Antonin Scalia summed it up starkly: the Supreme Court has "*never* held that the Constitution forbids the execution of a convicted defendant who has had a full and fair trial but is later able to convince a . . . court that he is 'actually innocent.'"

In other words, innocence by itself is not a legal basis to overturn a conviction.[1]

A couple of examples of possible *Brady* material from Walter's case: Was Mark Greenberg entitled to know about Devlin and Worrell's interrogations of the Fahys in February 1992? Would the jury knowing about them have likely changed their verdict? What about the fact that Jay Wolchansky was schizophrenic and having trouble with his medication at the time he supposedly was talking to Walter? Greenberg deserved to know that—he even asked about it and was lied to. Would it have been enough to change the jury's verdict?

And that's how these appeals go: defendants raising these violations, prosecutors blindly dismissing them, an occasional judge agreeing there was a violation but saying it wouldn't have mattered. The cases plod through the courts for years and years; the lucky defendants find a judge who is either willing to say that a particular action by a defense lawyer or a particular *Brady* violation by a prosecutor is enough for a new trial or is willing to look at how the whole case fits together and order the state to allow DNA testing of all the evidence.

When I first contacted Mark Greenberg a few years after Walter's conviction, he said he'd talk to me, though I could tell he didn't much want to. He gave me all the information about the case he could; he told me to get over my idea that trials are about seeking justice. He understood that for appeals purposes, Walter had to claim he'd been ineffective, but it was clear he didn't like it. While I recognized he'd fought harder and longer for Walter than anyone else and had come within a second of getting him acquitted, I thought he'd been steamrolled by Judi Rubino and seemed at times to have given up objecting to some of the outrageous things she said. Also, his decision to not put Walter on the stand at the second trial was, according to every lawyer I've spoken with, a mistake.

"It's a bad case. A bad, bad case," he said, shaking his head as our interview ended.

I thought of him when I read this description of what it's like to lose a case when your client is innocent from David Feige, a public defender in the Bronx:

"If you lose, the case haunts you, so that in the middle of the night and until sunrise you wonder what you did wrong, what you forgot, what you could have said or done—how such a thing could have happened. It is a searing, guilty pain that can last for years, if not forever."[2]

Over the years, Greenberg always did what he could to help Walter; he took my calls to briefly answer questions or try to point me in the right direction. Once, in the summer of 2003, he called me from his car.

"Lightning might just have struck," he said. Raymond Sheehan, one of the men David Schectman had positively identified in 1988 as the man carrying the TV box, had been a suspect in Barbara Jean's murder because he was a suspect in the 1987 murder, not far from Rutland Street, of his young neighbor, Heather Coffin. Now, all these years later, DNA testing had finally connected Sheehan to the Coffin murder and he'd admitted to killing her.

Greenberg wrote to officials in the DA's office to make sure they were aware of Sheehan's connection to Barbara Jean's case. To this day they've done nothing to follow up. On the contrary, they've been fighting DNA testing in Walter's case on the grounds that it wouldn't provide any useful information—though, of course, if the DNA from Barbara Jean's fingernail scrapings matched Sheehan, Felice, Ward—or Walter, for that matter—the case would be solved.

I went to Philadelphia to watch Sheehan plead guilty to Heather's murder. I expected something dramatic; certainly the solving of the case had been. But the event was mundane: Sheehan walked into court, a short and by then very fat man in an oversized, dirty T-shirt, quietly admitted to raping and killing a child, and was led away to spend the rest of his life in prison. Through his lawyer, he denied having anything to do with Barbara Jean's murder.

———————

I met Judi Rubino in the fall of 2003 at the courthouse in Philadelphia; she had a case going, so I got there an hour early to watch her work. She came in, a distinctive figure, wide and solid in a bright red jacket, hobbling slightly. She had silver-blonde hair, and when she sat at the prosecution table, she put on big, round, 1970s-style eyeglasses. A defense lawyer talked with her for a while, arguing while she arranged her papers. She told him, "There's been a preliminary hearing; there's nothing I can do," and the lawyer said, "The description was of a guy 6', 190 pounds and my guy is 5', 110 pounds."

The defense lawyer was getting frustrated, as was the young defendant sitting in front of me. I thought of the parallel with

Walter's case—a defendant who looked nothing like the person described by eyewitnesses.

When the hearing was over, Rubino got up to leave the courtroom and I introduced myself. She said, "Come with me."

We sat in a small conference room just outside court with three other people, one a uniformed police officer and two I took for detectives. They were looking over crime scene photos, one of a car that looked like it had been in an accident, and barely glanced at me. The room was so small my chair was in the doorway.

Rubino was friendly. "So how'd you get on this one?" she asked, meaning Walter's case.

"Completely at random," I answered. She glanced at me and kept working, occasionally asking me a question.

When she finished her meeting we moved to a bench outside the courtroom. She was pleasant, which wasn't surprising, and modest, which was, given what I knew of her courtroom demeanor. She smiled and maybe even reddened a bit when I mentioned her legendary status in Philadelphia legal circles, and when I asked about her background, she said, referring to her accomplished siblings, that she was the "dummy" in her family. I asked how long she'd been an ADA (thirty-three years, thirty-one in homicide) and if she'd really never lost a case. She smiled and said of course not, everyone lost some; she'd lost the Jogger case. I said I thought that was the first one she'd lost, and she shook her head.

Did she remember Barbara Jean's murder, Walter's arrest, the first trial?

"I do," she said, "because it was a big case. I was [working] in the [DA's homicide] office when it happened. I think I was in the courtroom [the day of the mistrial]. I can't remember for sure because I visualize it so easily. It was a big case. We may have all gone over."

———

At one point Rubino referred to Alfred Szewczak, the holdout juror from the first trial, as having "backbone." I thought about backbone, specifically about the one I'd wished to insert in the back of many of the ADAs in New York who'd overseen the release of my father's murderer.

We want prosecutors to be tough on murderers, we want murderers punished, and most people don't mind if police or prosecutors push the rules to do it. But what, then, is too far?

I asked Rubino if they'd offered Walter life in prison in exchange for a guilty plea, something Walter had told me he'd rejected but Mark Greenberg didn't remember.

"We would've offered life for a guilty plea," she said. "It's more or less the policy of the office that if they'll plead for life we'll do it unless it's the killing of a police officer or fireman in the line of duty."

Walter, then, had decided that risking death was better than pleading guilty to something he didn't do. To this day he feels the same way; he doesn't want a deal, he wants to be exonerated and freed. Sometimes when a DA realizes there's a real possibility there's going to be an exoneration, he or she will offer the inmate a hellish bargain: plead some version of guilty to the murder, get sentenced to time served, go home. This way the DAs never admit they got it wrong and the inmate is never officially exonerated— but he gets to go home.

This is what happened at the end of the very famous West Memphis Three case—three young men convicted on the basis of a false confession given by one of them, who was intellectually disabled, an outlandish story about satanic rituals without any other evidence to back it up. After almost twenty years, when DNA results undermined the case even more, the DA offered the three young men *Alford* pleas, the ultimate in half measures: the defendant acknowledges the prosecutor has enough evidence to convict him but maintains his innocence; the judge sentences him to time served, and he goes home.

Two of the West Memphis Three defendants wanted to take the deal; the third, Jason Baldwin, didn't. But Jason's friend and codefendant, Damien Echols, was on death row and could be executed, so Baldwin took the deal.

To that point in our conversation, nothing I'd asked Rubino seemed to give her much pause. But when I asked about John Hall and Jay Wolchansky, she seemed like someone jumping from rock to rock in a fast-moving river.

"We didn't use John Hall," she said, referring to the Ogrod case.

"Right. And why not?" I asked.

"He just had a lot of baggage."

But she'd tried to use him in the Kimberly Ernest case.

"Well, I'm not sure what year that happened," she said. "I—I'm not sure whether the jogger [Ernest] case had even occurred yet."

I reminded her that the Jogger trial was in March 1997, five months after Walter's, and that Hall told a defense investigator in August 1996 that he wasn't being used in the Ogrod case because she was going to use him in the Ernest case.

"Yeah, but then I didn't use him in the Jogger case," Rubino said. "So I wasn't going to use him. I just didn't want to use John Hall, period, if I didn't have to. And I didn't use him in either case [Ogrod or Ernest]. John Hall had been involved in too many cases, and I just didn't want to use John Hall. I didn't use John Hall against his stepson, either, on the Jogger case."

Was she saying she'd decided not to use Hall on the Jogger case before it became public that he'd had evidence fabricated?

"No," she said, "I didn't want to use him, but I probably would have used him just because of the relationship [with the defendant, his stepson], but then when I looked into things further, there was no way I was putting him on the stand."

So she may not have wanted to use Hall if she didn't have to, but she was going to until it became public knowledge that he'd had evidence created to frame his stepson. I believed Rubino hadn't been thrilled to use Hall; they probably brought Wolchansky in because they both knew his credibility wasn't good and having a second source would be helpful.

I asked Rubino if the differences between the snitch story and Walter's statement to Devlin and Worrell had concerned her.

"I don't remember now what the differences were," she said. "But I don't think that defendants necessarily tell it all when they're

talking to cellmates . . . they try to make it look good for themselves, they want to tell something to get it off their chests, but
they don't necessarily want to tell all the details. And Wolchansky
may not have remembered all the details precisely. I think that . . .
probably the statement [to detectives] was more accurate, but the
substance [of Wolchansky's letter] was that he had done it."

This surprised me, since it was the opposite of the story she'd
told at Walter's retrial.

"What if I could prove that Hall had made up the Wolchansky
story?" I asked.

"Well, he could've helped [Wolchansky] write it; I don't believe
that he fabricated the story," she said. "John Hall's going to admit
that he made that up? I don't know how you would document it,
and I wouldn't believe anything John Hall said, period."

This amounted to two surprising concessions: first, that Hall
might have helped Wolchansky with the Ogrod story, since Wolchansky had testified that no one helped him with it, and second,
that John Hall was a chronic liar.

"Has Jay Wolchansky said that [Hall made up the Ogrod
story]?" she asked. "Unless Jay says that he committed perjury on
the stand, then I don't know what proof there could be. If Jay
wants to say he committed perjury, that's something different."

"So John Hall's involvement in this case is peripheral?" I asked.

"Absolutely," she said. "He wasn't a witness. He wasn't used as
a witness. And he got nothing for it. And as far as I'm concerned,
neither did Jay."

"My understanding is that John did get a—"

"He didn't get anything from me," she said. "I don't know
what he could've gotten from anybody else. He didn't get anything
from us on any of the cases. I mean, Bucks County may have done
stuff for him, but they kept locking him up. And we caught him
in lies, and we did nothing with him."

This was more like the courtroom Rubino, subtly overstating
her case. She hadn't been the one to catch Hall's lie in the Jogger case, and even after it came out she had still wanted to use
him. As for any deals Hall may have gotten, she was being very

specific: Hall hadn't gotten anything from her or her office but could have received help from other agencies. And it was true that the four Philadelphia homicide detectives who showed up at Hall's hearing before Judge Biehn in the spring of 1996 to testify about Hall's cooperation in the Ogrod case and several others were not from the DA's office. But there had also been the letter from the former head of the DA's homicide office.

"OK," I said. "But, again, it's [Hall's] relationship with Jay [Wolchansky] that I find worrisome."

"I don't know what their relationship was," Rubino said. "I don't know when either spoke [to authorities about Ogrod]. You're telling me [that Hall making up the Ogrod story and giving it to Wolchansky is] documented. I don't know what documentation you have, and unless you have something from Jay saying none of that was told to him by Walter and that he made it all up and he's willing to testify to the fact that he committed perjury, that's something else. And that doesn't eliminate the statement. That doesn't make Walter innocent."

I agreed that proving the snitches lied didn't prove Walter innocent. But it would prove that his trial had been unfair.

"I mean, it might get [Walter] a new trial if it were [proven]— and then you'd have to believe that [Wolchansky] did commit perjury," Rubino said. "I mean, we have people recanting all the time."

In other words, she wouldn't believe any of this unless Wolchansky told her he'd committed perjury, and even then she wouldn't believe him, because people recant all the time. Recanting a bogus story apparently requires a level of proof that passing off the story initially did not.

I thought of what Rubino had said to Greenberg in one of their arguments in Judge Stout's chambers: *Once we get a conviction, I will worry about error.*

I asked Rubino about Marc Frumer, the former ADA, with whom, I'd been told, she was friendly.

"Nice little guy," she said. "I don't know him real well."

"Did you know at the time of the Ogrod trial that he and his father had both done work for Walter and his brother? That he represented Ogrod's brother?" I asked.

"No," she said. "No. Why would I? Frumer had actually no connection to me and the Ogrod case."

"He was Wolchansky's lawyer," I said.

"I didn't even remember that," she said. "I don't even remember dealing with him on this one."

"Dealing with [Frumer] on this one at all?"

"Right."

I started to ask her about some of Hall's other snitch cases.

"I don't even know what they are," she said.

But she'd already said that she'd known about the Dickson case and that Hall had "too much baggage" to use him against Walter. So she'd known at least that some of her own colleagues had found Hall stories to be false.

I told her about Hall's 1996 claim that he'd spoken to Walter at Joseph Casey's suggestion.

"I don't believe that either," Rubino said. "He might've done it on his own because he wanted something. Because John always has an axe to grind. But I don't think Joe Casey sent him in to talk to Walter Ogrod. Because that's not something we do. We do not send inmates in, because then their testimony's worthless."

She said she'd never heard that Hall read a Bucks County inmate his Miranda rights in the fall of 1994 before taking his confession or of the August 1994 proffer of cooperation between Hall and Joseph Casey on the Martorano case.

"I just didn't want to use John," she said again. "He had been using drugs, he was involved in too much—phony scripts and, I mean, he just had too many credibility problems to suit me."

Wolchansky, she said, she believed.

"Jay's situation was totally different than John's," she said. She believed his letter; she talked to his daughter, talked to him, and found him credible in a way she didn't find Hall.

"[It was] my own evaluation of his credibility," she said. "I think he had been a witness in another case, but it didn't involve me, and I didn't know him from before," she said, dismissing his botched testimony at Dickson's first trial. "He was concerned about this case because of his daughter. And she came to the courtroom and she was just a sweetheart."

She insisted that as far as she knew, Wolchansky got nothing for testifying against Walter, that any deal he got on his open cases was part of "whatever arrangement there was on that case itself."[3]

"I mean, we didn't do anything to get him a better sentence," she said. "If that [Wolchansky's 1995 plea deal] was not kept open, then it wasn't part of this case. Anytime there's testimony that's a quid pro quo for a deal, we don't sentence them until after they've testified."

This sounded good but didn't address the many ways the state can help a snitch. And the fact remains that Hall, Wolchansky, and their lawyer all believed they'd gotten deals.

For a moment during our back-and-forth Rubino seemed mildly annoyed, touching her forehead as if she felt a headache coming on.

"I thought you were just writing a book, not trying to get the guy a new trial," she said.

I asked what the difference was. I'd set out to tell a story, found out the story was of an innocent man on death row, and thought he at least deserved a new trial, one without John Hall all over it.

Rubino was convincing but had contradicted herself or her previous positions on important issues several times. Could she be unaware of these contradictions? And if she did understand them, how could she be so certain of Walter's guilt?

I'd talked about this with Mark Greenberg.

"Forget the requirement that the prosecutor seek justice and not just convictions," he'd said. "I mean, that's the goal, but from [Rubino's] standpoint, she is invested with the belief that this guy is guilty."

How could he be sure Rubino really believed that? I'd asked him.

"Because she told me," he said. "She said to me, repeatedly, 'You know he's guilty. How can you fight so hard for a guy like that?' She kept saying that to me."[4]

That sounded to me like Rubino gaming him during the trial, trying to get in his head. But Greenberg believed her.

Sometimes I look at old newspaper clippings of Walter Ogrod in handcuffs being led down the hallway and read the old head-lines—he *confessed*. It's easy to see what John and Sharon Fahy see: a face for the hate, a man who killed their little girl, a psychopath.

But if you look at the picture and think he's innocent, does he look evil or scared, a psychopath or a bewildered and terrified young man with ASD who knows he didn't kill anyone but also knows everyone around him thinks he did and wants him dead?

Walter was arrested and tried based on a confession, but a jury didn't believe it. So the Commonwealth of Pennsylvania took him back to trial using a story made up by one known liar and told by another, a story presented to the jury as the true facts of the case even though if it were true the original basis for Walter's confes-sion and arrest was false. Despite the many impossible details in it, Walter was convicted. And now Rubino had just told me that any problems there might be with the snitches fabricating that story didn't really matter because, after all, Walter's original statement to police was the truth.

And that wasn't just Judi Rubino's argument to me: it's the position the Commonwealth of Pennsylvania has taken in defend-ing Walter's conviction against the six hundred–plus page appeal brief, overwhelming in its detail of the many problems with his case, put together by his private lawyers working with lawyers in the Philadelphia federal defender's office and filed in 2011. The DA's response denies that any of the problems with this case were problems but also argues that even if any of them were actual problems, none of them mattered enough that Walter deserves a new trial now because the Devlin/Worrell statement would have been enough to convict him anyway.

Only it wasn't.

28

A LITTLE SCARED

AFTER PHYLLIS HALL AND I talked extensively about John Hall's snitch-ings, she wrote to him to ask if he ever worried the truth about his Ogrod fabrication would come out. No, he wrote back, he'd only *created* the Ogrod story; Jay Wolchansky was the one who committed perjury by telling it to the jury.

"Even if I had testified and the allegation was that it was per-jury," he wrote, "this would also be irrelevant as the trial occurred in 1996 and the statute of limitations is five years. Obviously out-side the limit, even for Jay. If he wants to come forward and say he lied, he can, without legal liability. In fact he did lie because Ogrod did not speak to him. Ogrod hated Jay. He only liked me. I'm the one he spoke to."[1]

In another letter he addressed the Ogrod snitch again.

"I have <u>no</u> [perjury] liability," he wrote. "In consideration of the fact that I gave my statement on Ogrod in January 1995, they only had until January 1997 to prosecute me. . . . But Jay Wolchan-ski [*sic*] testified. He would be viable for a perjury prosecution.

"As for Dickson and Ogrod," Hall wrote, "I gave him [Jay] both of those cases. Jay testified first [against Dickson] and there was a hung jury. He got a retrial (sneaker case) and they passed over Jay and came to me. I nailed [Dickson] with a life sentence. Jay and I <u>both</u> gave statements in <u>both</u> cases. They used Jay for

Ogrod because of my involvement in the Jogger case. Ogrod got death.

"If you are going to become involved in this sort of thing you can't be troubled about it long after you get the desired result," he wrote. "They'll crucify you if you start to recant testimony in cases of that magnitude."[2] They would give him ten to twenty years or more if he reversed a death sentence.[3]

"I have <u>no</u> liability with Ogrod," he reiterated. "I didn't testify. Jay did. But I didn't just give it to him. I used it first. . . . Everybody made out."

Later, he verged on introspection again.

"All these cases are crap," he wrote of his snitchings. "They are all based on hearsay with no physical evidence of anything in any of the cases. Just words."[4]

Hall got out of jail for the last time in the fall of 2006. Phyllis picked him up on a street corner, he just said "Hi baby," and got in the car. He wanted to get a hoagie. He had fake scripts for Percocet and they ate some and hung out like old times. Phyllis took him to see his mother, who was furious he was high again. A couple weeks later, he took a lot of painkillers and two forties of beer to a creek under a bridge near one of the jails he'd spent so much time in, sat down, took too many painkillers, and died. Phyllis believes he committed suicide, but the overdose could have been an accident.[5]

Hall had written his own best epitaph years before, in a nasty postcard to his stepson Herb: "There is no use in snitching. It is only another dead end."[6]

Strangely, Jay Wolchansky died a couple of weeks later, apparently also from a combination of alcohol and too many pills, though it's unclear if he overdosed or if his much-abused body just finally gave out.

Kimberly Ernest's murder remains unsolved.

———————

Lynne Abraham's ambition for higher office never left her, but she retired as district attorney in 2010. She ran for mayor in 2015, losing in the Democratic primary.

———————

Toward the end of my interview with John and Sharon Fahy, Sharon had said, "The only thing I'm waiting for and that I think about is when we can go see him get put to death. We want to be there for Barbara Jean. We feel somebody should be there for her."

"I hope he looks right at me before he dies," John said, "just so he knows, 'I'm fucking glad you're dead.' That's the real reason to be there, you know?"

But they didn't expect Walter's execution to help them much.

"On a daily basis, I very rarely think of Ogrod anymore," John said. "Him being killed is not gonna make it any easier. If it comes, it comes, if it don't, it don't. If they decide to change the law and they're gonna put him in prison for life, I don't care. Whatever happens to him happens to him. I know eventually he's going to die in prison. The only thing that really matters is that he never gets the opportunity to hurt a kid again, then that's OK."

"I hope the day comes that I can see him actually take his last breath," Sharon said. "I really do. That's what he did to Barbara Jean. I hope he's miserable, that every day of his life is just horrible where he's at. It's not like I need this day to come—I hope it comes, I hope I'm here when it happens, I hope I can see it. But I don't dwell on that. The only thing that could hurt me is if he gets out for any reason. Then I think I will actually go crazy. I don't think someone else did it. It makes sense to me. That house makes sense to me. That's how it could've actually happened."

We talked for a while about what I thought were the problems with the case against Walter. I told them I had real concerns about his conviction, and they said they knew some people didn't think Walter was guilty. They said they would support DNA testing if any DNA were available to test (at that time, it was unclear if any DNA material from the case had survived and could be tested) and had no desire to see someone punished just because it's supposed to make them feel better.

———————————

In June 2004, almost two years after I met the Fahys, I published an article about the case in the *Philadelphia City Paper*. John called, furious, and accused me of lying to them, of coming to their house under false pretenses. He vented for a while, then I reminded him that I'd been honest about my concerns about the case and offered to send him a transcript of our interview if he wanted it.

He paused for a minute, then said, *I just want this over*, his voice allowing more pain. I knew the tone; it had been mine at the end of many frustrating conversations with DAs about my father's killer.

In the years following my meeting with the Fahys, when I learned something important about the case or when something was going to happen, like my article coming out or Walter getting new lawyers or Walter's postconviction appeal finally being filed, I wrote to them, offering to meet and go over any questions they had. In the summer of 2016, as this book was being completed, Sharon and John agreed to meet with me to go over my concerns about their daughter's case. We had a good, long conversation, I answered any question they had about my views of the case, and they gave me the pictures of themselves with Barbara Jean that appear in this book. They still believe Walter is guilty.

———————————

In one of my first letters from Walter he explained that he'd spoken with the lawyer handling his appeal, J. Scott O'Keefe, a couple of times in five years, including only once in person, for a few minutes before a court hearing. I tried to interview O'Keefe a few times but never could get him to talk. He did (at Walter's request) let me come to his office and read Walter's file. He is now a common pleas court judge in Philadelphia.[7]

After my article about Walter's case ran in 2004, Bingham McCutchen, a large (now defunct) law firm based in Boston took his case pro bono, replacing O'Keefe. In the ensuing years the firm put enormous resources into reinvestigating the case, bringing in some of the foremost experts in the country on forensics, false confessions, and snitch testimony. Working with lawyers in the Federal Community Defender Office in Philadelphia, they filed a long, comprehensive postconviction relief application in 2011, making it clear that Walter deserves a new trial untainted by a John Hall story.

The Ogrod team persuaded the judge on the case, Shelley Robins-New, to allow the possible DNA material from Ross Felice's apartment and Wesley Ward's house that had been located in storage to be tested. The DA eventually went along with these tests but would not agree to test the scrapings from under Barbara Jean's fingernails, which they maintain are irrelevant. Judge Robins-New deferred to the DAs on this point. Then, in September 2016, when the DNA results finally came back but offered no new information, Judge Robins-New denied Walter's request for more discovery—in other words, there would be no DNA test for the fingernail scrapings, and Walter's appeal was going to be denied, too. As with many judges, Robins-New came from the DA's office; then just Shelley Robins, she'd in fact been a homicide prosecutor, working in the same office as Judi Rubino and Joseph Casey until 1995. It's not uncommon for appeals to end up in front of former DAs who, as judges, can be slow to rule that their former colleagues did anything worth throwing out a conviction over. In Walter's case, this means his second trial happened before a judge, Juanita Kidd Stout, who'd said she thought he was guilty, and his latest appeal has been denied by a judge who used to work with Judi Rubino and may well have been in the courtroom on the day of his mistrial, cheering for a conviction. Since judges in Philadelphia are pretty much left to their own judgment as to when they have a conflict of interest in a case, Judge Robins-New isn't required to announce how she decided she had no conflict in this case.

After her ruling I called Judge Robins-New to ask her the following questions: When she was in the DA's office, what was her professional relationship with Judi Rubino? What was her professional relationship with Joseph Casey? Did she ever consult with either of them about the Walter Ogrod case? Was she in the courtroom at the moment of the mistrial in 1993? Had she ever worked on a case involving John Hall or Jay Wolchansky, and if/when she'd had her cases reviewed to check.

I spoke to a clerk in her office, who said he understood the questions and would pass them on to the judge. I haven't heard back.

Walter awaits his next court date in a twelve-by-seven cell painted "some kind of green," with a bed, a shelf, a cabinet, and a stainless steel toilet/sink combo. He has a small TV. He reads science fiction books. He has a window with two aluminum strips in it that still gives him a nice view of the hills. He gets up at 6:00 AM for morning count, breakfast is put through his door at 6:30, and he has to return his tray at 7:00. Lunch comes at 10:15, trays back by 10:30, and dinner at 4:00 PM. He's allowed an hour a day of yard time, Monday through Friday, which means he can go outside into what look like big dog kennels, one inmate to each, but sometimes they'll put an inmate in the next kennel over, and they can play checkers through the fence.

He talks to a counselor once a week, a psychologist once every three months. He works; the best job he had was clearing snow because it got him outside. When I visited him, he had a cleaning job, which got him out of his cell and earned him a little money to put toward typewriter ribbons, paper, and basic cable TV. He goes to the law library and types out endless letters to newspapers, bar associations, lawyers' groups—anyone who might have information about the snitches, the lawyers, or detectives involved in his case.

"I feel a little scared," he said about the possibility of being executed. "It's something you got to realize and all, but you try not to think about it or you'll go crazy. I'm hoping—I'm hoping. I'm doing whatever I can."

———————

A few hundred miles away, Barbara Jean's fingernails are in a storage facility in Philadelphia. DNA from those fingernails could answer the many questions about this case by matching any of the three suspects at the time of the murder or someone in the DNA database. Casual touch does not produce skin cells under fingernails; if Barbara Jean patted a friend on the shoulder or hugged someone an hour before she died, that person's skin won't be under her fingernails. But if she fought her attacker, his skin cells could be.

And yet the DA fights to keep that DNA from being tested, the judge rules for them, the DNA sits in its storage container, and Walter sits in his cell, his life, the chunks of time between court hearings, dissolving. He'll turn fifty-two in 2017, his twenty-fifth year in prison.

ACKNOWLEDGMENTS

I AM DEEPLY GRATEFUL TO everyone who helped me with this book. Thanks to Nick Yarris for giving my letter to Walter Ogrod and to David Cymerman for sharing his research with me. Thanks to Mike Farrell for his advice and support. I relied for key information on the work of four writers: Will Bunch (who also provided much-needed advice); Howard Altman (who was also the editor at the *Philadelphia City Paper* who agreed to publish my article on the case); Tina Rosenberg; and Arthur Magida, in whose book *The Rabbi and the Hit Man* Detective Devlin also plays an important role. Thank you to Emily Kaplan and Jon Selkowitz for their help with research (and, in Emily's case, some key interviews) and to Hilary Chart for her support, as well as to Joe Thornton for his advice. The Fund for Investigative Journalism supported my work with a crucial grant, Dan and Helen Stevenson provided endless lodging and advice (while Elias joined me for important games of Madden 2k2), and Brian Hickey at the *City Paper* oversaw publication of the article itself. Thanks to Amanda Baker for help with some of the images.

Thank you to the many lawyers and journalists and experts who took time to discuss an aspect of the case or of my writing about it: Jim Trainum, Rachel Chmiel, Angie Elleman, Jeff Walsh, Peter Neufeld, Jon Amsterdam, Walter Robinson, Doug Lowenstein, and David Gessner. Scott Stossel and Robert Kutner gave me early encouragement at the *American Prospect*. Thanks to Thomas Beller, Christopher Schultz, and John Adcock for their reading and advice, to Lisa Davis for being my first beta reader, and to Adam O'Connor Rodriguez for his terrific edit of the manuscript. And thank you to my editor at Chicago Review Press, Lisa Reardon, for her belief in the book and her help and guidance in seeing it through to completion, and to Devon Freeny for his guidance as well.

Special thanks to Bari Pearlman, whose support at the beginning kept me going and whose reemergence later has ensured that this case gets the kind of public attention it needs. Thanks also to Carrie Nelson for all her help.

Thank you to the people who were willing to be interviewed, most especially to John and Sharon Fahy. There would be no book without their willingness to tell me their story. And to Phyllis Hall, whose courage in coming forward with what she knew is what really brought this story to the surface.

Most special thanks and love to Don Cutler, who, as my agent, took this book under his wing for many years, providing a level of attention and care that I could not have hoped for, and who, as my pastor, performed the ceremony at my wedding. And to Alice Perry, who gave me my first good pen.

Finally, thanks to my family: my brother Frank for much good advice over the years; my sister, Kate, for more than I can explain but in this particular case for reading every draft of everything and obsessing over every angle for many, many years; Mom and Nick for their endless support always. And Bridget, Stella, and Henry, for love and family and putting up with all that this book entailed (and with me talking about all of it) for so many years.

NOTES

All quoted material that appears in the text of this book comes directly from written or published sources as specified below or, in the case of reconstructed conversations, from the accounts given to the author by a participant in the conversation.

AUTHOR'S NOTE

1. Approximately 65 percent of homicides are solved. Thomas Hargrove, "Breakdown of Homicide Clearance Rates," Scripps Howard, accessed March 9, 2015, http://projects.scrippsnews.com/story/state-state-breakdown-homicide-clearance-rates/ (site discontinued).

I. BARBARA JEAN

1. Michael Boyette and Randi Boyette, *Let It Burn: MOVE, the Philadelphia Police Department, and the Confrontation that Changed a City* (Chicago: Contemporary Books, 1989).

2. John and Sharon Fahy, interview with author, September 2002.

3. Ibid.

4. Patrick Sweeney, Philadelphia PD investigation interview record, July 12, 1988.

5. Margaret Kruce, Philadelphia PD investigation interview record, July 12, 1988; Margaret Kruce, interview with author, n.d.

6. Linda Green, Philadelphia PD investigation interview record, April 7, 1992.

7. My description of the Fahy family's actions on July 12, 1988, is taken from my September 7, 2002, interview with John and Sharon, from their testimony at both Ogrod trials, and from the investigation interview records of their interviews with police on the following dates: John, July 12, 1988, 6:30 PM, July 12, 1988, 9:00 PM, July 18, 1988, April 3, 1989, and March 1, 1990; Sharon, July 12, 1988 and July 18, 1988. Occasionally, these sources conflict, and in such instances I have tried to reconcile the different versions. Where this has proved impossible I have given precedence to the version told closest to the events described, e.g., to the interview with police the night of the murder over trial testimony five years later.

8. Bill Miller and Roger Terry, "Painful Reminders of a Child's Murder." *Philadelphia Inquirer,* August 21, 1988.

9. John is adamant now that he did not cross the street and knock on the door of 7244 but that Linda came out on the steps and he talked to her from across the street. On the day of the murder, however, he told police he "went across the street and talked to the little boy, Charlie's, mom," and Linda, her daughter, Alice, and Walter Ogrod all told police that John knocked on their door that afternoon. John Fahy, Philadelphia PD investigation interview record, July 12, 1988, 6:30 PM: "Then I went across the street to Charlie's. I spoke to his mother. She said she had not seen her." Ogrod suppression hearing, 1:80; John Fahy, Philadelphia PD investigation interview record, July 12, 1988, 9:00 PM: "Next, I went across the street and talked to this little boy Charlie's mom. . . . I asked if she had seen Barbara. She said she saw her around two PM." Ogrod suppression hearing, 1:81. Kathleen Ritterson, who lived down the block, remembered John telling her that afternoon that he had just been to Charlie's house. At Ogrod's second trial, in 1996, John said he couldn't remember whether he knocked on the door or just talked to Linda from across the street (Ogrod second trial transcript, 11:155), but it seems most likely that he did cross Rutland Street and knock on the door of 7244 Rutland Street that afternoon. This would mean John knocked on the door and talked to Linda and Walter at the time Walter was supposedly killing Barbara Jean in the basement.

10. Kathleen Ritterson, interview with author, fall 2002.

11. Sharon Fahy, testimony, Ogrod second trial transcript, 12:6.

12. Joan Zablocky, testimony, Ogrod second trial transcript, 12:139–141.

13. John Torrante, Philadelphia PD investigation interview record, July 15, 1991.

14. Police Officer Erman Hendricks, Philadelphia PD investigation interview record, July 12, 1988.

15. Sharon Fahy, Philadelphia PD investigation interview record, July 12, 1988.

16. At the time of the murder, Detective Maureen Kelly was not yet married and was still Maureen Royds. For purposes of clarity I will refer to her as Detective Kelly throughout.

17. Postmortem report, case #3336-88, July 13, 1988; summary of Dr. Hoyer's report, July 13, 1988; Dr. Hoyer, interview by Mark Greenberg, September 27, 1993.

18. Lieutenant Maureen Kelly, testimony, Ogrod second trial transcript, 11:76.

19. John Fahy, interview with author.

2. JOHN AND SHARON

1. John and Sharon Fahy, interview with author.

2. Ibid.

3. Ibid.

4. Ibid.

5. Ibid.

6. Miller and Terry, "Painful Reminders of a Child's Murder."

7. John and Sharon Fahy, interview with author.

8. Ibid.

9. Walter Ogrod, interview with author, July 2002.

10. Many people described the Greens, both to the author and to Walter's defense team. See affidavits of Hal Vahey, Dawn Vahey, Greg Ogrod, Heidi Guhl, Melanie Ostash, and Tara Doherty, all contained in the appendix of the Ogrod post conviction relief application (PCRA).

3. INVESTIGATION

1. Kelly, testimony, Ogrod second trial transcript, 11:77.

2. John Fahy, Philadelphia PD investigation interview record, July 12, 1988.

3. In Massi's original statement to police on the night of July 12 he put the time closer to 4:00 PM, but given the testimony of the other people who saw the man carrying the TV box—and given that one of them, David Schectman, was consulting his watch frequently—it seems likely that the actual time was right around 5:00 PM.

4. Peter Vargas, affidavit, Ogrod PCRA, 1:177. When shown a photograph of Walter Ogrod in 2005, Mr. Vargas said that wasn't the man he'd seen with the box on July 12, 1988.

5. Margaret Kruce, interview with author, n.d.

6. Detectives Walsh and Duffy, note in Philadelphia Police Daily Complaint Summary, July 14, 1988.

4. AFTERMATH

1. Sharon Fahy, interview with author.

2. Philadelphia Police Neighborhood Survey, n.d., detective's signature looks like "Schultz" #978.

3. Jack McGuire and Gloria Campisi, "Child's Slaying Has NE in Panic," *Philadelphia Daily News*, July 13, 1988.

4. Paul Baker, Joe O'Dowd, and Kathy Brennan with Jack McGuire, "Police Intensify Hunt for NE Girl's Slayer," *Philadelphia Daily News*, July 14, 1988.

5. Daniel Rubin and Robert J. Terry, "In Victim's Neighborhood, It's a Time of Special Care," *Philadelphia Inquirer*, July 15, 1988.

6. Ibid.

7. Henry Goldman and Robert W. Fowler with Thomas J. Gibbons Jr., "Dead Child Found Naked in a Carton," *Philadelphia Inquirer*, July 13, 1988.

8. John and Sharon Fahy, interview with author.

9. Gabriel Escobar, "Hundreds Mourn for Barbara Jean," *Philadelphia Daily News*, July 16, 1988.

10. Mark McDonald, "'You Wonder If It's Him': Fear Haunts Neighbors in Wake of Killing," *Philadelphia Daily News*, July 20, 1988.

11. Hal Ward, Philadelphia PD investigation interview record, July 20, 1988.

12. Kathy Brennan and Marilyn Martinez, "Suspect Questioned in Girl's Death," *Philadelphia Daily News*, July 22, 1988.

13. Ibid.

14. ADA Joseph Casey, Ogrod first trial transcript, 1:248.

15. Jonathan Jones, Philadelphia PD investigation interview record, August 31, 1988.

16. Regarding Chris Cochan ID, see Ogrod second trial transcript, 11:75; for David Schectman ID, see Ogrod first trial transcript, 1:248, among other places.

17. Philadelphia Criminalistics Lab report, September 8, 1988; FBI fingerprint report, September 8, 1988.

18. Sharon Fahy, interview with author.

19. Ibid.

20. Ibid.

21. Ibid.

22. Ibid.

23. Miller and Terry, "Painful Reminders of a Child's Murder."

24. Ibid.

25. Bill Miller, "Man Held in Calls to Slain Girl's Home," *Philadelphia Inquirer*, September 17, 1988.

26. For the description of the calls, see Sharon Fahy, Philadelphia PD investigation interview record, September 10, 1988; for the precise number of calls that morning, see Miller, "Man Held in Calls."

27. Dave Racher, "Man Jailed for Obscene Calls to Murder Victim's Mom," *Philadelphia Daily News*, April 13, 1989.

28. John Fahy, interview with author.

29. Racher, "Man Jailed for Obscene Calls."

30. Bill Miller, "Residents Air Pain over a Killing in Oxford Circle," *Philadelphia Inquirer*, September 11, 1988.

31. Richard V. Sabatini and Bill Price, "When Death Is by a Stranger's Hand," *Philadelphia Inquirer*, October 20, 1988.

32. Bill Miller, "A Broader Plea for Help in Murder Case," *Philadelphia Inquirer*, November 6, 1988.

33. Philadelphia PD, incident report, November 17, 1989.

34. John Fahy, interview with author.

35. Detective Michael Fahy, Philadelphia PD investigation interview record, June 9, 1989. (Detective Fahy is of no relation to Barbara Jean's family.)

36. Ibid.

37. Ibid.

38. John Fahy, interview with author.

39. Ibid.

40. Jack McGuire, "Police Link Suspect to Girl Found in Box," *Philadelphia Daily News*, January 12, 1990.

41. Edward Moran, "'There Is Always Someone Who Knows,'" *Philadelphia Daily News*, June 14, 1990.

42. John Fahy, interview with author.

5. DETECTIVE PERFECT

1. Arthur J. Magida, *The Rabbi and the Hit Man* (New York: HarperCollins, 2003), 178–80. "One of the smartest detectives on the force" from Larry Nodiff, interview with Emily Kaplan, November 2002; "short and cocky" from John and Sharon Fahy, interview with author. For description of Devlin's dressing habits, see Howard Altman, "The Wacker Squad," *Philadelphia City Paper*, May 20–27, 1994.

2. While Magida quotes Devlin's *conviction* rate ("And Marty Devlin's conviction rate, the percentage of his arrests that resulted in a conviction, was one of the best on the force—95 percent"), homicide detectives usually track their *clearance* rate—the percentage of their cases that lead to an arrest (or some other conclusion, e.g., if the suspect dies). Several experienced attorneys and former law enforcement officials who read this manuscript raised the concern that they've never heard of a detective's "conviction rate," so I'm using *clearance* instead of *conviction*.

3. Nodiff, interview with Kaplan, November 2002.

4. Magida, *Rabbi and the Hit Man*.

5. Frank Lewis, "A Profoundly Disturbing Case," *Philadelphia City Paper*, June 22–29, 2000.

6. Joseph A. Slobodzian and Tommy Rowan, "25 Years Later, Freed By DNA Evidence," *Philadelphia Inquirer,* August 25, 2016.

7. Magida, *Rabbi and the Hit Man.* "Tall, soft-spoken, and solid" from John and Sharon Fahy, interview with author. For description of his dress, see Altman, "Wacker Squad"; and Paul Worrell, testimony, Ogrod first trial transcript, 2:303.

8. Magida, *Rabbi and the Hit Man.*

9. Paul Solotaroff, "Why Is This Man Still in Jail?," *Rolling Stone,* March 12, 2015.

10. Ibid.

11. Altman, "Wacker Squad."

12. Ibid.

13. Both detectives describe this thought process in their trial testimony. For "unreliable," see Worrell, testimony, first trial, 1:221; for Devlin's thought process, see Marty Devlin, testimony, Ogrod second trial transcript, 13:29.

14. Sharon Fahy, interview with author.

6. WALT

1. Worrell, testimony, first trial, 2:224.

2. Ibid.

3. John and Marie Terpeluk, interview with author.

4. Michael Smalley, affidavit, Ogrod PCRA, 1:168–69.

5. John Fahy, interview with author.

6. Penalty hearing, Ogrod second trial transcript, 17:51–52.

7. William Daka, affidavit, Ogrod PCRA, 2:73.

8. John and Marie Terpeluk, interview with author.

9. Many of Walter's friends describe him in these terms; see affidavits of Hal Vahey, Greg Ogrod, William Daka, Alonzo Balthrope, etc., in Ogrod PCRA.

10. Dr. Dattilio, Ogrod PCRA, 6:59.

11. Nazareth Hospital intake notes, April 12, 1976.

12. Penalty hearing, Ogrod second trial transcript, 17:53.

13. Dr. Peter Ganime, affidavit, Ogrod PCRA, 1:171.

14. Dr. Peter Ganime, penalty hearing testimony, Ogrod second trial transcript, 17:15.

15. Ibid., 17:19–21.

16. Alonzo Balthrope, affidavit, Ogrod PCRA, 1:20.

17. Walter expressed this understanding to the author many times.

18. As John Elder Robison wrote in his My Life with Aspergers column for *Psychology Today*, "We're described as arrogant, aloof, uncaring, and inconsiderate. I contend that we are none of those things. I believe we are simply blind, emotionally." John Elder Robison, "Are Aspergians Really Rude and Inconsiderate?," *Psychology Today*, November 10, 2008, www.psychologytoday.com /blog/my-life-aspergers/200811/are-aspergians-really-rude-and-inconsiderate.

19. Walter Ogrod, penalty hearing testimony, Ogrod second trial transcript, 17:55–56.

20. Ganime, affidavit, Ogrod PCRA, 1:171.

21. Ibid.

22. Walter Ogrod army records, Ogrod PCRA, 7:52.

23. Ibid.

24. Ogrod, penalty hearing testimony, 17:73.

25. Ibid., 17:59.

7. GREG AND MAUREEN

1. Quotations are taken from multiple affidavits, including those of John Shinn, Greg Ogrod, Heidi Guhl, John Trasser, Hal Vahey, Alonzo Balthrope, and Kim Ward (see Ogrod PCRA, vol. 1).

2. Greg Ogrod, affidavit, Ogrod PCRA, 1:75.

3. Heidi Guhl, affidavit, Ogrod PCRA, 1:84–86.

4. Steven Mulvey, affidavit, April 27, 2011, Ogrod PCRA, 2:67–68.

5. Melanie Ostash, affidavit, Ogrod PCRA, 1:165–66.

6. Anna Newsham, affidavit, Ogrod PCRA, 1:22. Several other neighbors and associates of Walter's described the Greens the same way, as did the Fahys and Walter himself.

7. Green mentioned this to many people. See Hal Vahey, affidavit, Ogrod PCRA, 1:79–82; also John and Sharon Fahy, interview with author; Walter Ogrod, interview with author; Greg Ogrod, interview with author.

8. Ostash, affidavit, Ogrod PCRA.

9. Jane Zacher, affidavit, Ogrod PCRA, appendix, 1:93.

10. John Trasser, affidavit, Ogrod PCRA, appendix, 1:132.

11. Vahey, affidavit, Ogrod PCRA.

12. Stacy Meigs, affidavit, Ogrod PCRA, appendix, 2:58.

13. Walter Ogrod, interview with author, June 2002.

8. INTERROGATION

1. Father John Bonavitacola, interview with author, July 2001.

2. In the early years of my contact with Walter I'd become convinced he fit the description of a person with Asperger's, a diagnosis that didn't exist when he was a child and that, in 2013, was folded into the term *ASD*. In 2011, after a battery of tests, Walter was diagnosed with Personality Disorder Not Otherwise Specified with Avoidant, Inadequate, Dependent, and Obsessive Tendencies (a diagnosis that is also part of ASD). See report of Dr. Neil Blumberg (who summarizes other doctors' reports as well), Ogrod PCRA, 6:79.

3. Devlin/Worrell Activity Sheet, March 30, 1992. Worrell also described this at the first trial.

4. Philadelphia Police interview record, Alice Green, April 7, 1992.

5. Jim Trainum, report, Ogrod PCRA, appendix, 6:32.

6. Worrell, testimony, first trial, 3:310.

7. Howard Serotta, suppression hearing testimony, Ogrod suppression hearing, 2:112–24. Serotta, Walter's landlord in 1992, testified that when Devlin and Worrell came to his door on April 1, 1992, they asked (among other things) if Walter owned a weight set. If so, the detectives knew about the existence of the pull-down bar before they ever talked to Walter, which would mean it was not a detail "only the killer would know," as they claimed, and that they were considering Walter a suspect as early as April 1, which would mean Walter's interrogation did violate the six-hour rule. On cross-examination Serotta said it was possible the question about the weight set came during a phone conversation with a different detective after Walter's arrest, but at the end of the suppression hearing, Judge Stout listed twenty-seven "Findings of Fact." Number five read: "Five, two detectives contacted Mr. Howard Serotta, owner of Crystal Chandelier, two or three days before the defendant was questioned and asked Mr. Serotta questions about [Ogrod], where he lived and worked. They also inquired about his dog and whether or not he had any weightlifting equipment." On September 23, 1993, ADA Casey asked Judge Stout to reconsider this finding of fact. "I could strike that," she said. "That is not really important anyhow." (Ogrod Suppression hearing, 4:12–13.) It was actually very important.

8. Worrell, testimony, first trial, 2:228.

9. Magida, *Rabbi and the Hit Man*. It is possible that this description of how to pressure a suspect comes from Devlin himself. Magida doesn't identify this detective by name, but Devlin was one of his sources.

10. Michael Matza, "After Verdicts, Questions on Not Taping Confessions," *Philadelphia Inquirer*, March 16, 1997.

11. Walter says he arrived at about one thirty and waited outside the homicide offices for a couple of hours, which means he was taken into Interview Room D at about three thirty. His name appears on the Roundhouse log sheet as having arrived at 3:45 PM, but in Worrell's handwriting; if Walter is right about the time, Worrell went downstairs and signed him in when they took him into the interview room.

12. Magida, *Rabbi and the Hit Man*, 26–27.

13. Dr. I. Bruce Frumkin, affidavit, Ogrod PCRA, 6:57.

14. Dr. Frank M. Dattilio, affidavit, Ogrod PCRA, 6:59.

15. "Journal *SLEEP*: Sleep Deprivation Affects Moral Judgment," American Academy of Sleep Medicine, March 1, 2007, www.aasmnet.org/articles.aspx?id=293.

16. This description of the Reid Technique is taken from Trainum, report, Ogrod PCRA, 6:32.

17. David Simon, *Homicide: A Year on the Killing Streets* (Boston: Houghton Mifflin, 1991), 34–35.

18. Ibid.

19. Ibid., 15.

20. Magida, *Rabbi and the Hit Man*. I suspect the detective quoted, in a chapter about Marty Devlin, is Devlin himself.

21. Ibid.

22. Trainum, report, Ogrod PCRA.

23. Robert Mayer, *The Dreams of Ada* (New York: Broadway Books, 2006; orig. publ. 1987), p. 417. My summary of the case is distilled from earlier chapters.

24. "False Confessions," Innocence Project, accessed September 3, 2106, www.innocenceproject.org/causes/false-confessions-admissions/.

25. Walter Ogrod, statement to detectives, April 5, 1992.

26. Joseph Casey, testimony, Ogrod second trial transcript, 13:139ff.

27. Peter Blust, suppression hearing testimony, September 8, 1993, Ogrod first trial transcript, 1:130–31; Peter Blust, interview with author, summer 2004.

9. LOOSE ENDS

1. Bonavitacola, interview with author.

2. Hahnemann University Hospital notes, April 7, 1992.

3. Alice Green, interview with author, March 2016; Alice Green, Philadelphia PD investigation interview record, April 7, 1992.

4. Devlin and Worrell field notes, April 1, 1992.

5. Linda Green, interview with Detective Worrell, April 7, 1992.

6. Hal Vahey, affidavit, Ogrod PCRA 1:80.

7. Howard Serotta, suppression hearing testimony, September 8, 1993, Ogrod first trial transcript, 1:112–25.

8. Dawn Vahey, affidavit, Ogrod PCRA, 1:159.

9. Robert Fritz, affidavit, Ogrod PCRA, appendix, 2:33.

10. Trainum, report, Ogrod PCRA, 6:45.

11. Peter Blust, suppression hearing testimony, September 8, 1993, Ogrod first trial transcript, 1:125–59.

12. In an interview with the author, Brignola denied that any of this took place. But it is clear from Casey's cross-examination of Blust at the suppression hearing that Casey had, in fact, heard of Blust's and Brignola's meeting directly from Brignola, and Blust confirmed that Brignola told Casey.

13. Tina Rosenberg, "The Deadliest DA," *New York Times Magazine,* July 16, 1995.

14. Michael Kroll, "Justice on the Cheap: The Philadelphia Story," Death Penalty Information Center, May 1992, www.deathpenaltyinfo.org/node/744.

15. Clark Fuss, affidavit, Ogrod PCRA, appendix, 1:30–32.

16. Rosenberg, "The Deadliest DA."

10. "OFF"

1. Interviews with Walter's family and friends; Dr. Ganime notes and school notes.

2. Greg Ogrod, interview with author, summer 2001. Other descriptions of him come from affidavits of his friends and family; see Ogrod PCRA, appendix.

3. Jill Porter, "A Long-Ago Mother Fights to Save Her Son," *Philadelphia Inquirer,* October 9, 1992.

4. Later, Walter's defense attorneys would hire experts who diagnosed Walter with a form of ASD similar to Asperger's, which no longer exists as a diagnosis. See reports of Doctors Tepper, Frumkin, Dattilio, etc., Ogrod PCRA, appendix.

11. RELIVING IT ALL OVER AGAIN

1. John Fahy, e-mail to author, August 26, 2002.

2. Nick Reding, *Methland: The Death and Life of an American Small Town* (New York: Bloomsbury, 2010), 51–52.

3. Alice Green, interview with author, February/March 2016.

12. FINDINGS OF FACT

1. Stout info from Robert Thomas Jr., "JK Stout, Pioneering Judge in Pennsylvania, Is Dead at 79," *New York Times,* August 24, 1998.

2. Marty Devlin, testimony, Ogrod second trial transcript, 13:80.

3. Marty Devlin, suppression hearing testimony, September 7, 1993, Ogrod first trial transcript, 1:104–105.

4. Ibid., 52.

5. Ibid., 98.

6. Ibid.

7. Howard Serotta, suppression hearing testimony, September 8, 1993, Ogrod first trial transcript, 1:112–25.

8. Judge Juanita Kidd Stout, finding of fact, suppression hearing, 4:1–22.

13. LIKE TV STUFF

1. Dianna Marder, "A Taut Opening to Trial in Girl's Rape, Slaying," *Philadelphia Inquirer,* October 22, 1993.

2. John and Sharon Fahy, interview with author.

3. Joseph Casey, opening statement, Ogrod first trial transcript, 1:17–38. Later, at Walter's second trial, prosecutor Judi Rubino would also go with the "one witness created the sketch" idea, only she'd say it was Mrs. Schectman, not her husband.

4. This description of the Fahys during the testimony and in the hallway afterward is from Marder, "Taut Opening to Trial"; description of Walter is from Kathy Brennan, "DA Says 4-Year-Old Was Killed for Refusing Sex," *Philadelphia Daily News,* October 22, 1993.

5. Cellmark labs, letter to Mark Greenberg, November 8, 1995.

6. Michael Massi, testimony, Ogrod first trial transcript, 1:167.

7. Kathy Brennan, "I Told Her to Go Outside," *Philadelphia Inquirer,* October 23, 1993.

8. Worrell, testimony, first trial, 2:395.

9. Worrell's first trial testimony covers pages 2:323–98.

10. Ogrod second trial transcript, 10:87–88.

11. Dr. Haresh Mirchandani (medical examiner), testimony, Ogrod first trial transcript, 3:449–50.

12. Dr. P. J. Hoyer, autopsy notes, case 3336, July 13, 1988.

13. Alice Green, interview with author.

14. Dianna Marder, "Weightlifting Bar Called Consistent with Slain Girl's Wounds," *Philadelphia Inquirer*, October 26, 1993.

15. Officer Bob Patrick testimony, Ogrod first trial transcript, 4:583.

14. REASONABLE DOUBT

1. Joseph Walsh testimony, Ogrod first trial transcript, 5:695.

2. Dianna Marder, "Witness Admits He Didn't See Suspect He Described," *Philadelphia Inquirer*, October 29, 1993.

3. David Schectman, testimony, Ogrod first trial transcript, 6:770–71.

4. "Eyewitness Misidentification," Innocence Project, accessed March 2, 2015, www.innocenceproject.org/causes-wrongful-conviction/eyewitness -misidentification.

5. Schectman, testimony, first trial, 6:770–71.

6. Marder, "Taut Opening to Trial."

7. Ibid.

8. Walter Ogrod, testimony, Ogrod first trial transcript, 7:799.

9. The showmanship and cynicism of these questions became clear later, when, in his closing, Casey told the jury he was not suggesting that Walter had planned the attack after seeing Barbara Jean out the window and that it would be dishonest to do so.

15. "LOOK AT THE DEVIL"

1. Mark Greenberg, closing argument, Ogrod first trial transcript, 8:1015.

2. See Casey's cross-examination of Walter Ogrod, Ogrod first trial transcript, 7:832–949.

3. Jane Mayer, "The Black Sites," *New Yorker*, August 13, 2007.

4. Joseph Casey, closing argument, Ogrod first trial transcript, 8:1042–86.

5. Charles Graham, affidavit, Ogrod PCRA, appendix, 1:26–28.

6. Judi Rubino, interview with author, fall 2003.

7. My narration of the mistrial and John's leap at Walter draws on the court transcript, my interviews with John and Sharon and with Walter, the newspaper coverage (particularly Kathy Brennan and Dave Davies, "Victim's Kin Explodes," *Philadelphia Daily News*, November 5, 1993), and TV news clips taken in the hallway outside the melee.

8. Brennan and Davies, "Victim's Kin Explodes."

9. John Fahy, interview with author.

10. Charles Graham, letter to *Daily News*, November 6, 1993, Ogrod PCRA, appendix, 5:174.

16. THE MONSIGNOR

1. Falls Township Police Department, incident report, April 5, 1994.

2. Philadelphia Police Department, investigation report, June 28, 1994.

3. John Hall, letter to Phyllis Hall, July 21, 1994, postmarked July 23, 1994.

4. John Hall, letter to Phyllis Hall, October 20, 2003.

5. Will Bunch, "The Snitch: Career Thief a Master at Dropping the Dime," *Philadelphia Daily News*, February 27, 1997.

6. John Hall papers, author's collection.

7. John Hall, affidavit, August 19, 1994, author's collection.

8. Philadelphia Police Department, interview with John Hall, August 3, 1994. "Gene's Pharmacy" discussed in John Hall, letter to Marc Frumer, December 28 or 29, 1994, their first correspondence re: Walter Ogrod. Several of the pharmacies Hall used were near Walter's old neighborhood, and when the two men met, Walter used one of them to describe to Hall where his house was. Hall's imperfect knowledge of the neighborhood could explain why his snitch story about Walter gets so much wrong—close, but wrong.

9. John Hall papers, notes titled "Genesis."

10. John Hall criminal record, available in author's collection and many other places; see Ogrod PCRA, appendix.

11. Phyllis Hall, interview with author.

12. Ibid.

13. John Hall, letter to Phyllis Hall, July 28, 1994, p. 7.

14. John Hall, letter to Phyllis Hall, October 1, 2003.

15. Phyllis Hall, interview with author.

16. David Keightly, letter to C. Theodore Fritsch, January 2, 1990.

17. Ibid.

18. Jim Austin, "Killer Suspect Is Accused of Offering Hit Money," *Times Herald* (Montgomery County), July 15, 1989.

19. David Keightly, letter to John Hall, January 23, 1990.

20. David Keightly, letter to Lynne Abraham, August 1991.

21. C. Theodore Fritsch, letter to Lynne Abraham, August 15, 1991.

22. Tom Bell, "Witness for the Prosecution," *Burlington County Times*, April 10, 1991.

23. Fritsch to Abraham, August 15, 1991.

24. Howard Barman, letter to Stuart Phillips (Hall attorney), August 27, 1991.

25. Sergeant Thomas Mills, letter to Lynne Abraham, date illegible, attached to Hall's petition to reconsider sentence, Spring 1995.

26. Bruce Castor, letter to Dean Arthur, May 24, 1993.

27. Bruce Castor, letter to John Hall, December 14, 1995.

28. Bunch, "The Snitch."

29. John Hall, letter to Phyllis Hall, June 24, 1996. The letter was written over the course of a few days, so it's not clear on exactly which day he wrote the passage; it was clearly written as the Kimberly Ernest murder case was ongoing.

30. John Hall, letter to Phyllis Hall, October 21, 2003.

31. John Hall, letter to Phyllis Hall, July 28, 1994.

32. "The Causes of Wrongful Conviction," Innocence Project, accessed April 15, 2016, www.innocenceproject.org/causes-wrongful-conviction (page discontinued).

33. Robert Bloom, "Jailhouse Informants," *Criminal Justice Magazine*, Spring 2003; Steve Mills and Ken Armstrong, "Part Three: The Jailhouse Informant," *Chicago Tribune*, November 16, 1999.

34. Bloom, "Jailhouse Informants."

35. Jordan Smith, "Anatomy of a Snitch Scandal," *Intercept*, May 14, 2016.

36. Ibid.

37. Alexandra Natapoff, quoted in ibid.

38. Radley Balko, "End the Use of Jailhouse Informants," *Washington Post*, May 8, 2015.

39. John Hall, letter to Phyllis Hall, July 21, 1994, postmarked July 23, 1994.

40. John Hall, letter to Phyllis Hall, July 20, 1994.

41. John Hall, letter to Phyllis Hall, July 21, 1994, postmarked July 23, 1994.

42. Ibid.

43. Ibid.

44. John Hall, letter to Phyllis Hall, July 29, 1994.

45. Ibid.

46. Joseph Casey, letter to Marc Frumer, August 1, 1994, signed by John Hall and Marc Frumer August 2, 1994, Ogrod PCRA, appendix, 5:59–60.

47. John Hall, affidavit, October 9, 1994, Ogrod PCRA, appendix, 5:93.

48. John Hall, statement to detectives, August 3, 1994.

49. John Hall, statements to detectives, August 4 and August 15, 1994.

50. John Hall, letter to Phyllis Hall, September 27, 1994.

51. John Hall, letter to Phyllis Hall, July 24, 1994.

52. Ibid.

53. John Hall, letter to Phyllis Hall, September 1, 1994.

54. Elmer Smith, "An Undercover Rat? Or Just a Rat?," *Philadelphia Daily News*, March 5, 1997.

55. John Hall, "Verification for Affidavit," November 6, 1994, Ogrod PCRA, 1:47.

56. Marc Frumer, letter to Joseph Casey, October 12, 1994.

57. John Hall, letter to Phyllis Hall, September 27–28, 1994.

17. "THE DEADLIEST DA"

1. David Dickson, affidavit, June 16, 2011, Ogrod PCRA, 1:34; David Dickson, interview with author, December 8, 2007.

2. Dickson, affidavit, Ogrod PCRA, 1:34; Dickson, interview with author.

3. Rosenberg, "Deadliest DA."

4. Associated Press, "Gubernatorial Candidates Fight over Pardons Board," *Bucks County Intelligencer*, October 6, 1994.

5. Summary of election from Rosenberg, "Deadliest DA"; final percentages from Our Campaigns, accessed September 6, 2016, www.ourcampaigns.com/RaceDetail.html?RaceID=187872.

6. Rosenberg, "Deadliest DA."

7. Ibid.

8. Ibid.

9. Ibid.

10. Ibid.

11. Ibid.

12. Ibid.

13. The McMahon tape is available on YouTube: www.youtube.com/watch?v=rv9SJPa_dF8.

14. "Former Philadelphia Prosecutor Accused of Racial Bias," *New York Times*, April 3, 1997, www.nytimes.com/1997/04/03/us/former-philadelphia-prosecutor-accused-of-racial-bias.html.

18. A BIG, GOOFY GUY

1. Shaffer (defense investigator), letter to Mark Greenberg, August 28, 1996, Ogrod PCRA, 5:197.

2. John Hall, letter to Phyllis Hall, October 27, 2003.

3. Barry Tarlow, "Silence May Not Be Golden: Jailhouse Informers and the Right to Counsel," *Champion* (magazine of the National Association of Criminal Defense Lawyers), September/October 2005.

4. Dickson, affidavit, Ogrod PCRA, 1:34

5. John Hall, letter to Phyllis Hall, October 27, 2003.

6. I found two of them mixed in with his papers years later.

7. John Hall, letter to Phyllis Hall, October 27, 2003.

8. John Hall, letter to Frumer, December 28 or 29, 1994.

9. Ibid.

10. Per John and Sharon Fahy, interview with author, Walter had once asked John Fahy if he was related to Henry Fahy, a question John thought was strange.

11. John and Sharon Fahy, interview with author.

12. John Hall, "composite summary" to Marc Frumer, December 29, 1994, author's collection.

13. Ibid.

14. Ibid.

15. Calculated on Google Maps, August 4, 2014; from where the box on St. Vincent Street was left to Castor and Magee is a thirteen-minute walk each way.

16. Hall, "composite summary."

17. John Hall, statement to detectives, January 6, 1995.

18. John Hall, letter to Phyllis Hall, October 27, 2003.

19. Phyllis Hall, phone conversation with author, September 2003.

20. Walter Ogrod, letter to "Sandy," February 28, 1995, found in John Hall's papers.

21. Walter Ogrod, interview with author, July 2003.

19. THE MONSIGNOR'S APPRENTICE

1. Jay Wolchansky Court of Common Pleas presentence investigation, July 12, 1989, Ogrod PCRA, 7:207.

2. Ibid.

3. Jay Wolchansky criminal records, Ogrod PCRA, 5:13–17.

4. Jay Wolchansky prison health progress notes and sick call requests, Ogrod PCRA, 7:215.

5. Dickson, interview with author.

6. Dickson affidavit, Ogrod PCRA (for "puppy"); Dickson, interview with author.

7. Jay Wolchansky prison health progress notes, December 26, 1994, Ogrod PCRA, 7:229.

8. John Hall, affidavit, August 10, 2005, Ogrod PCRA, 1:96.

9. Ibid.

10. Jay Wolchansky, letter to Joseph Casey, January 23, 1995.

11. John Hall, affidavit, August 10, 2005, Ogrod PCRA, 1:96; John Hall, letter to Phyllis Hall, October 14, 2003.

12. John Hall affidavit, Ogrod PCRA.

13. John Hall, Philadelphia PD investigation interview record, January 6, 1995.

14. Jay Wolchansky, letter to Lynne Abraham, March 20, 1995.

15. Jay Wolchansky, interview with Detective Michael Gross, March 20, 1995.

16. Jay Wolchansky plea agreement, Ogrod PCRA, 7:44.

17. John Hall, letter to Phyllis Hall, October 20, 2003.

18. Marc Frumer, interview with author, July 23, 2003.

19. Maria Gallagher, "Slain Student Eulogized," *Philadelphia Daily News*, December 6, 1984.

20. Linda Loyd, "Closing Statements Given in '84 Slaying," *Philadelphia Inquirer*, May 23, 1995.

21. Thomas Gibbons Jr., "Slain Drexel Student Found on Campus Steps," *Philadelphia Inquirer*, December 1, 1984; Linda Loyd, "Witness: Suspect Told of Killing Skill," *Philadelphia Inquirer*, July 1, 1993.

22. Linda Loyd, "Fellow Inmate Testifies Against Slaying Suspect with Fetish," *Philadelphia Inquirer*, May 16, 1995.

23. Linda Loyd, "Love Letter, Sneaker Fetish Linked at Murder Hearing," *Philadelphia Inquirer*, July 7, 1993.

24. Kathy Brennan, "Slay Suspect Fits Fetish Profile," *Philadelphia Daily News*, July 7, 1993.

25. Front page headline, *Philadelphia Daily News*, June 9, 1993.

26. Dwight Ott, "Retired, but Memories Stay for 35 Years," *Philadelphia Inquirer*, June 7, 2008.

27. Joseph R. Daughten, "He's 'Simply the Best,'" *Philadelphia Daily News*, March 6, 1995.

28. Loyd, "Closing Statements."

29. Dickson, interview with author; Walter Ogrod, interview with author, June 29, 2007.

30. Comm. v. Hall, hearing before Judge Kenneth Biehn, March 27, 1996.

31. Walter Ogrod, interview with author, June 29, 2007.

32. Don Russell, "Man with Fetish for Sneakers on Trial in Student's Slaying," *Philadelphia Daily News*, May 6, 1995.

33. Don Russell, "Ex-Drexel Prez Surfaces in Murder Trial," *Philadelphia Daily News*, May 11, 1995.

34. Don Russell, "Inmate: He Killed Her, Then Played with Her Feet," *Philadelphia Daily News*, May 16, 1995.

35. Ibid.

36. Loyd, "Fellow Inmate Testifies."

37. Russell, "Inmate: He Killed Her."

38. Loyd, "Closing Statements."

39. Don Russell, "Defense Lawyer: Foot Fetish Doesn't Make Him a Killer," *Philadelphia Daily News*, May 23, 1995.

40. Don Russell, "Jury: So What If He Likes Feet?" *Philadelphia Daily News*, May 31, 1995.

41. Rita Giordano and Linda Loyd, "Tipster Has History of Turning in People," *Philadelphia Inquirer*, November 30, 1995.

20. UP TO SOMETHING

1. Jeff Gammage, Thomas J. Gibbons Jr., and Linda Loyd, "Two Arrested in Jogger's Killing," *Philadelphia Inquirer*, November 30, 1995.

2. Ibid.

3. Ibid.

4. Ibid.

5. John Hall, letter to Phyllis Hall, October 5, 19[93?].

6. Ibid.

7. John Hall, letter to Phyllis Hall, December 21, 19[95].

8. John Hall, letter to Phyllis Hall, July 30, 1996.

9. John Hall, letter to Phyllis Hall, October 1, 2003.

10. Ibid.

11. Will Bunch, "Are These Really the Guys?," *Philadelphia Magazine*, December 1996.

12. Linda Loyd, "After Twists and Turns, Jogger Case Heads for Trial," *Philadelphia Inquirer*, January 5, 1997. Haak called police at Hall's suggestion, per Phyllis Hall, interview with author, September 14, 2003.

13. John Hall, letter to Phyllis Hall, December 21, 19[95] (the year is missing, but it's clear from context).

14. Larry King, Karen Miller, and Daniel Rubin, "Suspect Has a Long Trail of Trouble," *Philadelphia Inquirer*, December 1, 1995.

15. John Hall, letter to Phyllis Hall, December 21, 19[95].

16. Howard Goodman and Linda Loyd, "2nd Jury Convicts Ex-Guard in Drexel Slaying," *Philadelphia Inquirer*, December 3, 1995.

17. Commonwealth v. Dickson, supplemental post-sentence motions for new trial/ arrest of judgment, September 26, 1997.

18. Ibid.

19. Ibid.

20. Ibid.

21. King et al., "Suspect Has a Long Trail of Trouble."

22. Will Bunch, "Cops Try to Plug Holes in Jogger Murder," *Philadelphia Daily News*, July 15, 1996.

23. Judge John R. Padova, memorandum, Haak and Wise v. City of Philadelphia, US District Court for the Eastern District of Pennsylvania, February 11, 2002.

24. Loyd, "After Twists and Turns."

25. Bunch, "Cops Try to Plug Holes."

26. Bunch, "Are These Really the Guys?"

27. Commonwealth v. Dickson, supplemental post-sentence motions.

28. Ibid.

29. Goodman and Loyd, "2nd Jury Convicts Ex-Guard."

30. Commonwealth v. Hall, Bucks County Court of Common Pleas, before Judge Kenneth Biehn, March 27, 1996.

31. Commonwealth v. Dickson, supplemental post-sentence motions.

32. Russell Gold, "Despite Many Letters of Support, Jailhouse Informant Is Sentenced," *Philadelphia Inquirer*, March 28, 1996.

33. John Hall, letter to Phyllis Hall, date illegible, probably March 29, 1996.

34. Father John's thoughts are taken from Smith, "An Undercover Rat? Or Just a Rat?"; and Father John Bonavitacola, affidavit, Ogrod PCRA, 1:42.

35. Mark Greenberg, letter to Harry Seay, August 14, 1996, Ogrod PCRA, 5:183.

36. Shaffer, letter to Greenberg, 5:197.

37. Jay Wolchansky, letter to John Hall, August 8, 1996, Ogrod PCRA, 5:254.

38. Bunch, "Are These Really the Guys?"

39. Bunch, "Cops Try to Plug Holes."

40. Bunch, "Are These Really the Guys?"

41. Phyllis Hall, interview with author.

42. John Hall, petition for immunity from prosecution, received by DA's office August 10, 1996.

43. Bunch, "The Snitch." Phyllis Hall also provided details in her interviews with the author.

44. John Hall, letter to Phyllis Hall, July 21, 1996.

45. John Hall, letter to Phyllis Hall, n.d. (mid-1996 from context).

46. John Hall, letter to Phyllis Hall, December 23, 19[96].

47. Bunch, "The Snitch"; see also Howard Altman, "The Kimberly Conundrum," *Philadelphia City Paper*, January 7–14, 1999.

48. Loyd, "After Twists and Turns"; Matza, "After Verdicts, Questions."

49. John Hall, letter to Phyllis Hall, October 14, 2003.

21. A NEW VERSION OF EVENTS

1. Dave Racher, "2nd Trial In Killing of Girl, 4," *Philadelphia Daily News*, October 1, 1996.

2. Judi Rubino, interview with author.

3. Howard Altman, "Judi's Justice," *Philadelphia City Paper*, June 14–21, 2001.

4. Ibid.

5. Rubino, interview with author.

6. Ibid.

7. Ogrod second trial transcript, 10:86.

8. See ch. 13, n. 3; Casey, opening statement, Ogrod first trial.

9. Ogrod second trial transcript, 10:69.

10. Ibid., 10:82.

11. Ibid., 10:103.

12. Walter Ogrod, interview with author; Linda Green, interview with Detective Worrell.

13. Mark Greenberg, affidavit, Ogrod PCRA, 1:148.

14. Thomas James, interview with author, September 29, 2003.

15. David Miller, interview with author, n.d. (fall 2003).

16. Ogrod second trial transcript, 10:116.

17. Ibid., 10:126.

18. Ogrod second trial transcript, 10:127.

19. John and Sharon Fahy, interview with author.

20. Ibid.

21. Ogrod second trial trancript, 10:128–29.

22. BUILDING IN ERROR

1. Ogrod second trial transcript, 10:155ff. All quotes from the direct testimony and cross-examination are taken directly from the transcript.

2. Ogrod second trial transcript, 11:3–8.

3. See n. 1

4. Ogrod second trial transcript, 11:126.

5. Ogrod PCRA petition, 27.

6. Ogrod PCRA petition, 48–49.

7. Ogrod second trial transcript, 11:141–42.

8. Ibid., 11:155. This last version of the conversation, which even John Fahy said he couldn't be sure of and which conflicts with all his statements taken on the day of the crime as well as with Linda Green's, has become the official prosecution version of what happened.

9. Thomas James, interview with author, September 29, 2003.

10. Thomas James provided the author with a copy of his journal for review before our interview. While I do not quote the journal directly here, my conversation with James referred to it many times.

11. See ch. 12, n. 7.

12. Ogrod second trial transcript, 12:119. Fingerprint experts refer to the number of "points" in a print; different experts consider different numbers of "points" appropriate for making a fingerprint usable in a comparison. For this reason, two different fingerprint experts can have two different opinions on whether or not a print is usable.

13. Ogrod second trial transcript, 13:8.

14. Ibid., 13:9.

15. Ibid., 13:11–12.

23. MAYBE I CRY EVERY TIME

1. Linda Loyd, "Detective Breaks Down at Retrial," *Philadelphia Inquirer,* October 4, 1996.

2. James, interview with author.

3. Miller, interview with author.

4. William Kushto, testimony, Ogrod second trial, 13:138.

5. Joseph Casey, testimony, Ogrod second trial transcript, 13:139ff.

24. MR. BANACHOWSKI

1. Judi Rubino's examination of Jay Wolchansky, Ogrod second trial transcript, 14:3ff.

2. James, interview with author.

3. Heather Wolchansky, interview with author, October 4, 2007.

4. Linda Loyd, "Defendant Told of Killing 4-Year-Old, Inmate Says," *Philadelphia Inquirer,* October 5, 1996.

5. Ogrod second trial transcript, 10:48.

6. Wolchansky, letter to Casey, January 23, 1995.

7. James, interview with author.

8. Loyd, "Defendant Told of Killing."

9. James, interview with author.

25. VERDICT

1. Loyd, "Defendant Told of Killing."

2. Ogrod second trial transcript, 15:36.

3. Ibid., 15:37.

4. Ibid., 15:49.

5. Ogrod second trial transcript, 15:45, 64.

6. Ibid., 15:41.

7. Judi Rubino, closing argument, Ogrod second trial transcript, 15:48.

8. Ibid.

9. Ibid., 15:66.

10. Ibid., 15:51.

11. The case actually returned to the public eye in the summer of 1996, just before Walter's retrial, when Fahy volunteered to be executed, an idea he

later dropped. See Dave Racher, "Child Killer Wants to Die; Henry Fahy: 'It's Over,'" *Philadelphia Daily News*, August 9, 1996.

12. Ogrod second trial transcript, 15:60.

13. Ibid., 15:60–61.

14. Ogrod second trial transcript, 16:3.

15. See Andrew Cohen, "When Prosecutors Admit to Cheating," *Atlantic*, March 4, 2014, about a case in which federal prosecutors vacated charges against a convicted drug dealer because they had misled the jury during closing arguments about what luggage the defendant had had with him on a certain trip—an issue that had not been brought up during trial.

16. Ogrod second trial transcript, 15:67–68.

17. Ibid., 15:62.

18. Kruce, investigation interview record; Kruce, interview with author.

19. Ogrod second trial transcript, 15:68.

20. Alice Green, interview with author.

21. Ogrod second trial transcript, 15:64.

22. Ibid., 15:64–65.

23. Ibid., 15:66.

24. Miller, interview with author.

25. John Fahy, interview with author.

26. Ogrod second trial transcript, 16:3–5.

27. Walter Ogrod, interview with author, April 8, 2014.

28. Dave Racher, "Now We Can Remember," *Philadelphia Daily News*, October 9, 1996.

29. Ibid.

30. Linda Loyd, "Ogrod Is Convicted in Girl's Slaying," *Philadelphia Inquirer*, October 9, 1996.

31. Myung Oak Kim, "Foreman in First Trial Isn't Buying Verdict," *Philadelphia Daily News*, October 9, 1996.

26. PENALTY

1. Penalty hearing, Ogrod second trial transcript, 17:7.

2. Linda Loyd, "Jury Chooses Execution for Walter Ogrod," *Philadelphia Inquirer*, October 10, 1996.

3. Ibid.

4. Penalty hearing, Ogrod second trial transcript, 17:82–83.

5. Loyd, "Jury Chooses Execution."

6. Ibid.

7. Thomas James, interview with author, November 1, 2003.

8. Dave Racher, "Child Killer Gets Death," *Philadelphia Daily News*, October 10, 1996.

9. Loyd, "Jury Chooses Execution."

27. INNOCENCE

1. Lara Bazelon, "Scalia's Embarrassing Question," Slate.com, March 11, 2015, www.slate.com/articles/news_and_politics/jurisprudence/2015/03/innocence_is_not_cause_for_exoneration_scalia_s_embarrassing_question_is.html.

2. David Feige, *Indefensible* (New York: Little, Brown, 2006), 42.

3. Heather Wolchansky, interview with author.

4. Mark Greenberg, interview with author, August 1, 2002.

28. A LITTLE SCARED

1. John Hall, letter to Phyllis Hall, June 11, 2003.

2. John Hall, letter to Phyllis Hall, October 14, 2003.

3. John Hall, letter to Phyllis Hall, October 7, 2003.

4. John Hall, letter to Phyllis Hall, October 20, 2003.

5. Phyllis Hall, interview with author, October 13, 2006.

6. Will Bunch ended his 1997 article about Hall with this quote. I also have a copy of the postcard.

7. Jeff Gammage, "Once Again, Man Convicted in Deaths of 2 Sons," Philly.com, April 13, 2016, www.philly.com/philly/news/20160412_For_second_time_man_found_guilty_of_murder_in_arson_fire_that_killed_his_sons.html.